Questions of Modernity

Contradictions of Modernity

The modern era has been uniquely productive of theory. Some theory claimed uniformity despite human differences or unilinear progress in the face of catastrophic changes. Other theory was informed more deeply by the complexities of history and recognition of cultural specificity. This series publishes books that explore the problems of theorizing the modern in its manifold and sometimes contradictory forms and that examine the specific locations of theory within the modern.

Edited by Craig Calhoun
New York University

Questions of Modernity

Timothy Mitchell, Editor

Contradictions of Modernity, Volume 11

University of Minnesota Press
Minneapolis
London

Published by the University of Minnesota Press
111 Third Avenue South, Suite 290
Minneapolis, MN 55401-2520
http://www.upress.umn.edu

Printed in the United States of America on acid-free paper

Library of Congress Cataloging-in-Publication Data

Questions of modernity / Timothy Mitchell, editor.
   p.   cm.
— (Contradictions of modernity ; v. 11)
Includes index.
   ISBN 0-8166-3133-6 (hard : alk. paper) — ISBN 0-8166-3134-4 (pbk. : alk. paper)
   1. Developing countries—Social conditions.   2. Civilization, Modern.
I. Mitchell, Timothy, 1955–   II. Series
   HN980 .Q47 2000
   303.4'09172'4—dc21

                          00-009096

11 10 09 08 07 06 05 04 03 02 01 00   10 9 8 7 6 5 4 3 2 1

Contents

Preface

This book owes its writing to a conversation begun a decade ago, when Lila Abu-Lughod and I decided to bring together two groups of scholars working separately on new approaches to the making of modernity outside the West. We came from the disciplines of history, anthropology, and political science, and were often familiar with one another's work. But one group specialized on the societies of South Asia and the other on those of the Middle East, and the boundaries of area studies kept us apart. Although our paths might cross at conferences and professional meetings, we had no way to sustain a theoretical conversation. We decided to find a way to overcome these limits.

The pioneers of area studies, between the 1930s and 1960s, had hoped that the development of area studies would end another kind of professional isolation, that of scholars working in what had recently become the separate disciplines of the social sciences. They thought of areas such as the Middle East or South Asia as single regions and cultures, each providing a definable whole around which scholars from the different disciplines could integrate their knowledge and develop a comprehensive social theory. The study of non-Western regions would also expose ideas developed in the study of modern Europe and North America to a much larger testing ground, they thought, quickly revealing which concepts and theories were not of universal significance. In both these ways, area studies would cleanse the disciplines of their parochialism.

These hopes did not materialize, and it was area studies that came to seem parochial and isolated. After we had begun our own discussions, the Social Science Research Council and other bodies decided to abandon their long support of area studies. They turned to more general themes, whether the study of transnational processes affecting many different world regions, or forms of explanation that claimed to apply to any context. These approaches seemed to offer an alternative route to a less parochial social theory.

This was not our goal. Our concern was not to deparochialize Western history and social science, but rather—to echo an idea expressed by one of the contributors to this volume, Dipesh Chakrabarty— to rediscover the parochialism of the West. We were scholars for whom social theory was reached through the imaginative worlds of particular communities, places, and histories. We were aware, of course, that modern social theory claims to be a universal language and that the history of the West is always written as the world's history. We also knew that imperialism has given some truth to these claims, awarding the forms and categories of Western modernity a global significance. But we shared an interest in questioning this universalism. Our aim was not to uncover an infinite variety of modernities, but to explore some of the heterogeneity out of which this universalism is produced. The making of modernity is said to involve a splitting—of modern and non-modern, West and non-West, rational and non-rational. Since this splitting cannot be governed entirely by the categories that result from it, perhaps it could reveal things that trouble those categories, or happen differently, or exceed their grasp. To examine such questions was not the moment to abandon area studies, we felt, but to reformulate it.

Our efforts began after Lila Abu-Lughod had spent a year as a Mellon Fellow at the University of Pennsylvania, where she participated in the South Asia Seminar run by Carol Breckenridge, Arjun Appadurai, David Ludden, and others. The following year we began talking with Gyan Prakash at Princeton and with his help planned a workshop of South Asian and Middle Eastern studies scholars, which we held in Cairo in 1993, with support from the Social Science Research Council. The discussions were fruitful enough that we decided to continue to meet, calling our endeavor "Questions of Modernity" and bringing together a changing but overlapping group of scholars of the two regions for further workshops, held at the Hagop Kevorkian Center at New York University in 1996 and 1999. We were fortunate that in the same years NYU agreed to a major rebuilding of its area programs, beginning with Middle Eastern studies. Questions of Modernity provided us with the model for a less insular approach to area studies. We thought of the region of study not as a fixed geography and culture to be made available to history and social science but as a source of engagements and insights that offered an alternative imaginative terrain to the often self-enclosed disciplines of the North American academy.

We received the enthusiastic collaboration of NYU's new chair of Middle Eastern studies, Michael Gilsenan, and generous support from the dean for the humanities, Thomas Bender. In the same period Toby Volkman at the Ford Foundation launched a new program, "Crossing Borders: Revitalizing Area Studies," intended to counteract the move away from area studies among other organizations. The Foundation awarded the Hagop Kevorkian Center a major grant to support our new direction in area studies, including the most recent Questions of Modernity conference. In the interim we also organized a graduate student dissertation workshop with the University of Chicago, on the initiative of Lisa Wedeen and with the help of Dipesh Chakrabarty and Zachary Lockman and financial support from Chicago's Center for the Study of Politics, History and Culture.

This book is based on some of the essays from the second Questions of Modernity meeting. Besides the authors included here, many other participants contributed papers and ideas at that and other meetings. I especially want to thank Talal Asad, Khaled Fahmy, Deniz Kandiyoti, Zach Lockman, Uday Mehta, Aamir Mufti, Afsaneh Najmabadi, and Ted Swedenburg for their multiple contributions. Others who shared in this project and deserve our thanks include Soraya Altorki, Shahid Amin, Janaki Bakhle, Joel Beinin, Elliott Colla, Jenine Abboushi Dallal, Val Daniel, Huri Islamoglu, Ayesha Jalal, May Joseph, Jayati Lal, Huda Lutfi, Saba Mahmood, Gyan Pandey, Pramod Parajuli, Anupama Rao, Amina Rashid, Martina Rieker, Gayatri Chakravorty Spivak, and Mohammed Tavakoli-Targhi.

I also want to thank those at the Hagop Kevorkian Center at NYU who helped with our efforts, including the associate director, Shiva Balaghi, William Carrick, Alice Diaz-Bonhomme, Wilson Jacob, Kristine McNeil, and Ethel Brooks. I am also grateful for all the work of the editorial staff at the University of Minnesota Press, including

Carrie Mullen, Jennifer Moore, and Robin A. Moir, to the anonymous reviewers for the press, and to my colleague Craig Calhoun for supporting the book's publication.

My greatest debt is to the person with whom this project was first conceived, Lila Abu-Lughod, who has shared in its shaping and organizing at every stage.

Timothy Mitchell
Rough Park, Cornwall
May 1999

Introduction

Timothy Mitchell

The essays in this book approach the question of modernity by taking seriously the emergence of the modern outside the geography of the West. Each of the essays examines the realization of modernity beyond Europe, exploring the appearance of particular forms of politics, sensibility, temporality, and selfhood in locations ranging from nineteenth-century Bengal to contemporary Morocco. The purpose in bringing them together is not to offer a more global history of the modern. One of the characteristics of modernity has always been its autocentric picture of itself as the expression of a universal certainty, whether the certainty of human reason freed from particular traditions, or of technological power freed from the constraints of the natural world. So its history has always claimed to be a universal one, in fact the only universal history. For this reason, however, it has also depended on assigning a different and lesser significance to things deemed purely local, non-Western, and lacking a universal expression. The aim of this collection is to explore whether this dependence on such non-universal, non-Western elements might provide, in a paradoxical way, tools that can be borrowed to fashion a more complex, rigorous, and heterogenous understanding of how the modern comes about.

In the opening chapter, "The Stage of Modernity," I connect the European-centered cartography of modernity with the problem of its singular history. If the modern is inevitably associated with the rise and expansion of the West, what significance can we assign to an increasing awareness that its emergence was from the beginning a worldwide phenomenon and that the modern was not produced from within Europe alone? One long-standing and important answer to this problem has been to expand the narrative of modernization, or of capitalist development, by paying proper attention to its imperial dimension and acknowledging the impact and contribution of regions beyond Europe. Such approaches have offered a major correction to the limited geographical vision that still defines most writing on the modernity of the West, including two decades of writing about what is now called its postmodernity. However, expanding the history of modernity to portray it as a global phenomenon inevitably tends to homogenize other histories as aspects of the emergence of the West. The expanded vision acknowledges the significance of forces and contexts outside the European core. But their significance can be measured only in terms of their contribution to the singular history of the modern.

More recent approaches to this problem have talked instead in terms of "alternative modernities" or "multiple capitalisms." These ways of thinking stress the variety of local, regional, and global forces whose combination shapes the particular histories of capitalist modernity, producing different versions in different places. Such formulations provide a less Eurocentric way of acknowledging the importance and variation of non-European developments. An increasing number of studies of this sort, including those of several contributors to this volume, have begun to reveal the complex and multiple origins of what we too easily unify under the name of modernity. Yet the strength and consequent appeal of this work has also become its potential weakness. On the one hand, the language of alternative modernities can imply an almost infinite play of possibilities, with no rigorous sense of what, if anything, gives imperial modernity its phenomenal power of replication and expansion. On the other hand, the vocabulary of alternatives can still imply an underlying and fundamentally singular modernity, modified by local circumstances into a multiplicity of "cultural" forms. It is only in reference to this implied generic that such variations can be imagined and discussed.

My essay proposes that we talk neither of a singular modernity that defines all other histories in its terms, nor of the easy pluralism of alternative modernities. Instead, we should acknowledge the singularity and universalism of the project of modernity, a universalism of which imperialism is the most powerful expression and effective means; and, at the same time, attend to a necessary feature of this universalism that repeatedly makes its realization incomplete. Briefly, if the logic and movement of history—or of capitalism, to use an equivalent term—can be produced only by displacing and discounting what remains heterogenous to it, then the latter plays the paradoxical but unavoidable role of the "constitutive outside." Elements that appear incompatible with what is modern, Western, or capitalist are systematically subordinated and marginalized, placed in a position outside the unfolding of history. Yet in the very processes of their subordination and exclusion, it can be shown, such elements infiltrate and compromise that history. These elements cannot be referred back to any unifying historical logic or any underlying potential defining the nature of capitalist modernity, for it is only by their exclusion or subordination that such a logic or potential can be realized. Yet such elements continually redirect, divert, and mutate the modernity they help constitute.

To understand the force that this process of marginalization and mutation can acquire, my essay discusses a process whose importance to the constitution of capitalist modernity, I would argue, has still not been adequately recognized. As a shorthand, I call this process representation.[1] Representation does not refer here simply to the making of images or meanings but to forms of social practice that set up in the social architecture of the world what seems an absolute distinction between image (or meaning, or plan, or structure) and reality, and thus a distinctive apprehension of the real. This effect of the real has been generalized in modern social engineering and the management of nature, in organized schooling and entertainment, in the military, legal, and administrative disciplines of colonialism and nation-making, in all the mundane forms of invigilation and self-presentation that shape the lives of modern subjects, and, quite pervasively, in the organization of production and the market. In sphere after sphere of social life, an immediacy of the really real is promised by what appears in contrast to be the mere abstractions of structure, subjectivity, text, plan, or idea.

My argument, which I recapitulate here only in part, is that this constitution of the modern as the world-as-picture, in the expanded sense just outlined, is the source of modernity's enormous capacity for

replication and expansion, and at the same time the origin of its instability, the source of the liability that opens it up to rearticulation and
displacement. No representation can ever match its original, especially
when the original exists only as something promised by a multiplicity
of other imitations and repetitions. Every act of staging or representation is open to the possibility of misrepresentation. An image or simulation functions by its subtle difference from what it claims to simulate or portray, even if the difference is no more than the time-lag
between repetitions. Every performance of the modern is the producing of this difference, and each such difference represents the possibility of some shift, displacement, or contamination. If modernity is
defined by its claim to universality, this always remains an impossible
universal. Each staging of the modern must be arranged to produce
the global history of modernity, yet each requires those forms of difference that introduce the possibility of a discrepancy, that return to
undermine its unity and identity. Modernity then becomes the unsuitable yet unavoidable name for these discrepant histories.

The other essays in this book do not necessarily share the specific
direction of this argument. They have in common, however, a concern
with the forms of difference and discrepancy that indicate a more
complex genealogy of the modern. One of the most important explorations of these forms of difference has been the work of Partha
Chatterjee. His studies of the genealogy of nationalism in colonial
India reveal the rather different terms in which the modern versus the
non-modern was produced in the colonial context.[2] In the case of
India, he has shown, a Westernized colonial elite was able to turn
modernizing discourse against the civilizing prerogatives of a colonial
power, by constructing an Indian "tradition" that was not open to
colonization. This traditional culture was not the pure tradition posited by modernist discourses. It was a contramodernity produced by an
alternative indexing and defining of the categories of modern and traditional. A different deployment of the difference that produces the
categories of modernity gave rise to what appeared to the colonial
power as a confused and incomplete attempt to imitate European
modernity but which Chatterjee suggests we see in terms of the particular configurations of power that produced the colonial modern.

Chatterjee develops and refines these issues in his contribution to
this volume (see chapter 2). He takes up the theme of civil society, a
popular motif in recent discussions of the problem of democracy in

the non-West. In current debates about democratization, the weakness or absence of certain Western procedural forms and institutions in many non-Western political systems is ascribed to the failure to develop a civil society. The term refers to a set of intellectual habits and collective practices that inculcate the rules and attitudes required for building the larger institutions of representative democracy. Chatterjee argues that in colonial and postcolonial India there did emerge a Westernized, liberal sphere of rule-governed intellectual life, which one can describe as civil society. However, the shape of this sphere was given by its distinction not from an illiberal "traditional society," as colonial and other European discourses would suppose, but from another sphere for which he proposes we reintroduce the label "political society."

Composed of mass political parties, social movements, and non-party political formations, political society constitutes a zone of mediations between the state and the population, in which the rules and procedures of civil society are not necessarily followed. Indeed, part of the impetus shaping the emergence of political society was the desire of the liberal, nationalist elite to avoid being trapped within the narrow sphere of a Westernized civil society and to appeal in the nationalist struggle to a much broader population. This required a more fluid realm of maneuvers, resistances, and appropriations, including appropriations of "the traditional." Chatterjee proposes that we should understand the emergence of a political society distinct from the realm of civil society as revealing the attempt to create forms of modern community and democracy that cannot be thought by the social categories of the secularized Christian world.

The persistence of what appear as traditional social forms has been examined from another angle in the work of Dipesh Chakrabarty, who is particularly concerned with the way such forces have the ability to exceed the terms of modernity's representation of the non-modern. This excess often appears in the form of the traditional coexisting alongside the modern. Chakrabarty has examined one kind of apparent coexistence in a widely known essay on the emergence of modern domesticity in British-ruled Bengal.[3] During the colonial period, the development of the civil-political sphere (discussed in Partha Chatterjee's essay) required the definition of a contrasting non-public sphere of personal life and domestic relationships. Public debates of the period reveal two contradictory ways of interpreting the relationship between these two spheres. One set of narratives subordinates the domestic to the public, portraying civil-political life as the sphere in which personal happiness and moral improvement are to be found. But other accounts are critical of the work-discipline and political compulsions of the public sphere and celebrate the different temporality and ethics of the domestic world, whose rhythms are based on the cycles of Hindu rituals and the proper patterns of resting, working, the taking of meals, and meditation.

How does one make sense of these "non-modern" elements coexisting and reconfirmed in the face of capitalist modernity? A conventional account, Chakrabarty suggests, would treat the non-modern elements as no more than residuals, fragments of a past that cannot be relinquished only because Bengal's transition to modernity is incomplete, or has happened so rapidly that different phases have been telescoped together and therefore overlap rather than succeed one another. This is the inevitable analysis of modernizing approaches, which must gather all the different histories of colonialism into a singular narrative of the coming of modernity. They can deal with the non-modern only as the absence of modernity, only as forms that lack the discipline, rationality, and abstraction of the modern order of things—and therefore, since they are defined by what they are not, as essentially similar to non-modern forms everywhere else. It is not sufficient, Chakrabarty adds, to explain these forms as the "invention of tradition" or through the idea of the "modernity of tradition." These invocations of the restored, contrived, or resistant powers of a tradition accept the notion that there is a universal narrative of modernity, against which local variations can be measured. The alternative would be to acknowledge that modernity "is constituted by tensions that relate to each other asymptomatically," so that there cannot be "any one unitary history of its becoming."[4]

To explore the possibility of a heterogenous account of the birth of colonial modernity is the intention of Chakrabarty's contribution to this volume. His aim, recalling Foucault's famous essay on Nietzsche, is "to see 'birth' as genealogy and not a clear-cut point of origin, to make visible as Nietzsche said the otherness of the ape that always gets in the way of any attempt to trace human descent directly from God."[5] His essay explores the birth of the modern subject in colonial Bengal, through an analysis of the representation and self-representation of the Hindu widow. In colonial discourse the widow is a prominent figure representing the power of tradition, epitomized in the behavior of the *sati,* who immolates herself on the pyre of her dead husband. Legal reform became preoccupied with this symbol of victimhood and oppression. This representation established tradition as the simple negative of modernity, contrasting the freedom of the modern subject to the traditional woman bound by the past, whom the law can liberate and thus make modern. The reformist discourse on widowhood coexisted, however, with a literary genre in which the widow came to stand for the modern, expressivist subject. In a series of turn-of-the-century Bengali novels, the widow's unrecognized desire, which social custom denies her the opportunity to express, comes to represent the self-expression of the modern subject.

At a first reading, this subjectivity seems to be staged in terms very similar to those that define the representation of the bourgeois individual of modern Europe. Subjectivity is presented as a struggle between reason and passion. Reason is a shared, and therefore public, faculty, which attempts to discipline and educate the self, whereas passion or desire is private, interior, and thus the source of individuality and of the difference from one person to the next. Yet these apparent similarities conceal important differences. In the first place, the struggle between reason and passion is staged around questions about the purity of body, questions drawing on local debates that reach back to elements of Vedantic philosophy and Bengali poetic tradition. The modern subject emerges not through the simple adoption of European categories of thought but through a continuous process of cultural translation. Second, the faculty of reason that defines the modern subject is understood in these writings not as a generalized and abstract intelligence but as a kind of worldly common sense about the duties of the householder in the context of an extended family. This larger context of obligation-in-kinship is very different from, for example, the triangular struggle of mother-father-child theorized and popularized by Freud. In the Freudian understanding, the nuclear unit replaces the extended kin group, and sexuality is invented as the domain that mediates between physical desire and its psychological management. The theory of the private management or "repression" of desires that cannot be accommodated to the laws of public life becomes critical, as Foucault has shown, to the birth of the modern European subject, helping to maintain the new public and private spheres in alignment with one another. In the Bengali case the same alignment does not occur, leaving open alternative sources of collective and individual selfhood.

By attending to such differences in the constitution of what he calls "the Bengali-modern," Chakrabarty suggests that we can conceive of the modern collective subject as "a mobile point on something like a relay network in which many different subject-positions and even non-bourgeois, non-individualistic practices of subjectivity intersected." Thus the public sphere in Bengal opened up a space for a modern subject defined in part through extended kinship, making room for "practices of the self that call us to other ways of being civil and humane." European-modern practices were present at the colonial birth of the modern subject, and colonialism has made European narratives a global heritage that inevitably structures any subsequent account of this modernity. Yet the heterogenous genealogy of the Bengali-modern leaves "an intellectually unmanageable excess" when approached with the secular analysis of European social thought.

A theme that emerges from studies of this kind is that in the production of modernity, the hegemony of the modern over what it displaces as "traditional" is never complete. As a result, modernizing forces continuously reappropriate elements that have been categorized as non-modern, such as religious elements, in order to produce their own effectiveness. This question of modernizing religion has been explored extensively in the work of Talal Asad.[6] The modernization of religion is said to require its separation from politics, the economy, and scientific knowledge and its placing in a separate sphere that the law defines as private. But this "secularization," Asad argues, has never in practice separated religion from politics or other social spheres. The meaning of the term *secular*, moreover, is not something self-evident or universal. The concept emerged as part of the modern development of Christianity and defines not only the non-religious sphere but also the concept of religion. Religion is thus a modern and originally Christian category. It was formed through changes not in the things people believed but in the ways their lives were disciplined, both by methods of self-discipline and by the emergence of modern collective discipline in such forms as schooling and the law.[7]

This view of secularization contributes to alternative understandings of the production of colonial modernity. In the case of nineteenth-century Egypt, for example, Asad proposes that we should trace the process that created religion in relation to the emergence of colonial governmentality, emphasizing the importance of the institution of secular law with its highly mobile powers of discipline. Legal and other forms of modernization did not encounter a traditional sphere of religion but rather constructed the realm of religion, together with the problem of its secularization, as part of the process of instituting new forms of discipline and methods of governance. This approach offers an alternative way of seeing the apparent failures of secularization in contemporary politics. Such failures do not indicate the inability of modern, secular politics to delimit the traditional powers of religion. They show that producing a colonial modernity requires the production of groups and forces designated as non-modern yet able to contest the hegemony of the modernist politics that called for them.[8]

Lila Abu-Lughod's essay in this volume (chapter 4) also deals in part with the question of secularism, in a study of the construction of modern national subjects in contemporary Egypt. She examines this topic through a study of television dramas and their widely popular reception among different audiences. Treating the everyday lives and dilemmas of common citizens, focusing on what appears as their heightened emotionality, and always reaching a denouement that offers an unambiguous moral resolution, the television serials appear to share the characteristic conventions of modern melodrama. Abu-Lughod refers to Peter Brooks's argument that the melodramatic imagination played a central role in European modernity, providing a "post-sacred era" with a means of revealing the moral order in quotidian experience. For this reason, Brooks views melodrama as "the central fact of the modern sensibility."[9] But if this characterization of melodrama and the modern is useful for understanding nineteenth-century Europe, what explains the power and popularity of a particular kind of melodrama in contemporary Egypt, where the modern era is, among other differences, not unambiguously a post-sacred one?

Abu-Lughod argues that television melodrama in Egypt can indeed be seen as a technology for the production of new kinds of sensibility, and thus new kinds of selves. But it is a technology caught up in a different configuration of political projects and imaginative alternatives than those that may have defined the melodramatic imagination of nineteenth-century Europe. On the one hand, she shows, the television programs reflect the agendas and assumptions of the nationalist intellectuals who write and produce them. These intellectuals understand their role in relation to a post-independence project of nation-building, and they consciously attempt to use television drama to educate what they see as a less enlightened public and to inculcate a particular moral and political sensibility. On the other hand, Abu-Lughod argues, in seeking to develop this sensibility, the melodramatic genre employs a distinctive quality of emotionality and a way of telling personal life-stories that may be more significant in the shaping of personhood and sensibility than the producers' overt educational agendas.

The Egyptian television serials draw partly on a prior tradition of theater, film, and song, but these also cross-reference other expressive forms, such as epic poetry, laments, and folk stories. Such popular genres often expressed strong emotion, but emotion was not constructed as the pervasive interior state of a feeling subject. Sentiment in other genres, Abu-Lughod argues, was attached to specific contexts and took forms appropriate to that context and genre. In contrast, the sentiments of television melodrama cover a wide emotional range and are located in the quotidian, the personal, and the domestic. In narrating the lives of their protagonists in such terms, the serials locate emotionality in the sphere of everyday personal relations and construct the modern subject as a psychosocial being shaped and given meaning by this conflicted inner world.

Television drama, however, is not the only social force shaping a modern sense of personhood. In ethnographic studies of particular individuals, Abu-Lughod explores how the kinds of self-fashioning encouraged by the conventions of melodrama interact with other social forms, such as the importance of kinship in constructing and maintaining a social standing, and the new forms of women's piety and self-discipline developed through an increased involvement in religious devotion. Such social forces offer overlapping and sometimes alternative technologies of the self. These pull in a variety of directions, Abu-Lughod concludes, offering more complex trajectories than the singular story of modernity told on the basis of European history.

Several other essays in this book examine the heterogenous social forms and complex modernity that unilinear histories of the modern disavow. As with the preceding chapters, these contributions move between what we describe nowadays as two distinct world regions, the Middle East and South Asia. Kept apart by the conventional boundaries of academic area studies and, to a lesser extent, by the national and regional forms of contemporary state politics, these regions share interlocking histories both of imperialism and earlier patterns of long-distance trade, intellectual exchange, and Islamicate rule—an interlocking past and contemporary disjuncture that are juxtaposed in Amitav Ghosh's imaginative historical-ethnographic exploration, *In an Antique Land.*[10] The purpose in bringing together in this book the two regions is not to suggest any simple sociological comparison between them but rather to emphasize the reasons for avoiding such comparison. Comparisons of this sort, once the great aim of studies of modernization, require one first to establish the nature of modernity in general, as a standard against which the variations among different world regions could be measured. Since, as we argue here, there is no simple modernization in general, this standard was always by default the history of the West. Even the critics of modernization theory, in arguing that the peripheral position of the non-West prevented it from repeating the history of the West, still represented the non-West in terms of its difference from the West, and thus within the West's universalizing narrative.

Stefania Pandolfo's essay, "The Thin Line of Modernity: Some Moroccan Debates on Subjectivity," like those by Abu-Lughod and Chakrabarty, deals with the construction of the modern subject, in this case connecting subjecthood to the question of memory and differing relationships to the past (see chapter 5). She begins by contrasting the different constructions of time in Abdullah Laroui's writing on the crisis of the Arab intellectual and Driss Chraïbi's novel *The Simple Past.* For Laroui, a leading historian and intellectual of post-independence Morocco, the past is available only as the traumatic memory of colonization or the inauthentic neo-traditionalism of post-colonial politics. Nothing less than a complete effacing of these pasts can enable the emergence of a modern, authentic self, defined by the self-mastery of a historical consciousness located unambiguously in the present. In Chraïbi's novel, one of the major works of modern North African fiction, no such "simple present" is available. The novel explores a different sense of historical memory, in which the present is experienced as what Chraïbi calls "a thin line" between tradition and modernity, the interstitial space that marks the cut or break between the two, neither disavowing one nor wholly located in the other.

Pandolfo uses these alternative constructions of the relation between past and present to explore a practical encounter with the discrepant temporalities of modernity. She examines the problems confronting Moroccan psychiatrists and psychoanalysts whose patients,
while acknowledging the efficacy of modern psychiatry, at the same
time persistently resort to the traditional therapies of spirit possession,
magic, and bewitchment. These therapies, Pandolfo suggests, might be
understood as techniques for displacing the self to another scene,
where the self appears as an other and the symbolic order can be rene-
gotiated. As such, there seems to be, at least in the abstract, an ethical
possibility of a dialogue between popular therapies and modern psychiatry. But like Laroui, and echoing the attitudes and practices of the
earlier French colonial health administrators and ethnologists, the
psychiatrists and psychoanalysts insist that traditional forms are incommensurable with the modern. They argue in Lacanian terms that
such therapies work upon the imaginary alone and never touch the
symbolic order, where the modern, responsible subject is constituted.
Pandolfo does not argue that these views are simply mistaken and that
the worlds of patient and psychiatrist are commensurable and ought
to result in a dialogue. Rather, drawing on her work in a public psychiatric hospital, she suggests that the psychiatrists' abstract intellectual positions are subverted in the actual encounter with patients.
Presenting their symptoms in the idiom of popular therapies, patients
invoke a set of forces, understandings, and senses of community to
which the modern psychiatrist no longer has access. Yet this loss, as
in Chraïbi's novel, haunts the modern sensibility. The force of their
patients' words, familiar yet strange, remote yet secretly close, draws
them into this interstitial place of loss, in which the possibility of alternative forms of subjecthood is posed.

The complexity and variety of relationships between past and
present—and of constructions of the subject—are also explored in the
essays here by Nick Dirks (chapter 6) and Veena Das (chapter 7). Examining representations of India's recent political past, Dirks suggests
that Indian nationalist and even post-nationalist discourse has inherited from British colonial accounts an almost entirely negative image of
India's recent past, a world of corrupt local despotisms and extrava-
gant princely power. As with the work of Laroui on the colonial history of the Arab world, examined in Pandolfo's essay, there is a sense
that nothing of value can be recuperated from this defeated political

order, engendering a certain intellectual embarrassment toward the immediate past, at least in its political aspects. When nationalism sought an Indian "tradition" to defend and celebrate, it usually imagined a more ancient past rediscovered through sacred and literary themes, rather than the political order compromised and overcome by colonialism. Indian postcolonial theory, Dirks argues, has sometimes inherited these positions and has not always been attuned to the complexity with which the past is constructed or disowned.

Dirks explores a more ambiguous representation of the old order in two of the films of Satyajit Ray, *The Music Room* and *The Chess Players*. Ray's evocation of the world of irresponsible feudal landowners and incompetent local kingship can be interpreted as an ambivalent one, he argues. The ambivalence reflects an attempt to navigate a contradictory position between tradition and modernity rather than a simple nostalgia for or renouncing of the past. Dirks invokes Bataille to suggest that the obsession of Ray's feudal heroes with self-destructive consumption and conspicuous displays can be read as indicating not the simple impotence and decay of tradition in the face of the modern world but as a deliberate transgression against capitalist modernity's naturalization of self-interest, calculation, and reason. The effect of this different representation of tradition, Dirks suggests, is to rework the past as a means of refusing the "self-legitimating masquerades" of colonial order and capitalist economy. He concludes that such reworkings, by writing histories that are positioned against inherited colonial categories, offer an essential means for opening up the ambivalent potential of the political present.

The essay by Veena Das, "The Making of Modernity: Gender and Time in Indian Cinema," places in question the conventional idea that in the passage from tradition to modernity the nature of time undergoes a simple transformation, from a conception of time as cyclical to the idea of linear time. Exploring different representations of time in Indian cinema, she argues that Indian modernity is marked by multiple ways of constituting the relationship between the present and its pasts. There is no single construction of time that defines the experience of modernity, and thus there is more than one possible way of representing and relating to the past.

Since cinema does not portray time overtly but represents it through the differing construction of its characters, these multiple temporalities correspond to different ways of fabricating the self, Das suggests, and in particular to different constructions of masculinity. Like a number of other scholars, she proposes that gender provides a critical field in which struggles over modernity are fought out. And like Abu-Lughod, she believes that the media, in this case the medium of film, play a critical role in shaping the transformation of the political subject and the building of the nation, providing "a form through which the nation produces its autobiography."

Thus, in Kamal Amrohi's 1949 film *Mahal* (Palace), the male protagonist's impossible quest for a woman-spirit, whom he is unable to see or know except in the forms in which he fantasizes her, provides an allegory for a male desire for an inner space, as a protection against the wounds of modernity. This space, imagined as a female spirit returned from another age, suggests an impossible link to the past. The past is a feminized interior world, and for the male protagonist of Indian modernity to recover this world, Das suggests, the woman must remain mute and unable to engineer her own identity. In other cinematic works the gendered past is constructed differently, for example, as a decayed "past present" for which the subject experiences a fierce nostalgia yet which must be violently renounced out of fidelity to the present; or as a world of nature, from which modernity departs as a journey of the self into an unknown future.

Das emphasizes how the multiple registers of cinematic representation, in which dialogue, movement, camera angle, and music can tell different stories, make possible disjunctive images that offset and sometimes contradict one another. Instead of a neat account of tradition and modernity, with determined roles for women in relation to men, cinema offers a medium in which these categories are continually negotiated and displaced.

This question of the renegotiation and dislocation of the categories of colonial modernity is taken up from a different angle in the final essay of this book (chapter 8). There, Gyan Prakash analyzes the deployment of modern medical science in colonial India. Colonization developed, he argues, often well ahead of their development in the metropole, the new methods of biopolitics, which take as their concern the life and health of the population. To this end the colonial state introduced a series of institutions and procedures concerned with the physical condition of its subjects' bodies. Public health regulations and new therapeutics made the body visible to political authority and subject to its examination. Such innovations played a role in producing Indians as political subjects. The role differed from that of similar biopolitical procedures that Foucault analyzes in northern Europe, Prakash argues, and was perhaps more significant. In Europe, the large-scale operations of biopower functioned alongside small-scale, "capillary" forms of power that encouraged the production of modern, self-disciplining political subjects. The biopolitical management of the bodies of the population coexisted and competed with the sphere of autonomous interest-bearing subjects formed by the institutions of modern discipline. In the colonial state, as we have already seen in Chatterjee's essay, this "civil society" was much weaker and sometimes absent. However, this weakness or absence was not a restrictive liability, Prakash argues, but a generative dislocation.

The aim of colonial sanitary and medical procedures was, as it were, to modernize the body and thus make it healthy and productive, by cleansing it of indigenous habits and diseases. It follows that the body could emerge as a political object only from a space of difference, the same fissured space that Pandolfo's essay examines between modern psychiatry in Morocco and local therapeutics. In an earlier colonial period, before the mid-nineteenth century, European medicine in India had often drawn upon local medical knowledge and practice. But in the later part of the century, the development of biopower demanded the organization of medical procedures based upon an absolute distinction between Western medicine and local practice, between the modern and the traditional, between science and superstition. Once again, however, this differentiation must be understood as a process of renegotiation and translation, for in invoking the non-modern to perform its authority, the modern is always open to contagion, to dissemination. In particular, it opened up the space for an Indian nationalist elite to oppose colonial governmentality with a specifically "Indian" understanding of the body and mode of governance, invoking ayurvedic and yunani medical traditions. Since it was intervening in a field shaped by colonial governmentalization, however, this opposition was not an external act of negation but rather a process of reappropriation and relocation, operating "upon the very body that colonial governmentality made available." The result was what Prakash calls a disjunctive modernity, fabricated upon the fissure that appears to separate the Western and the native, the modern and the traditional, its authority perpetually unstable.

The arguments of these essays are too many to recapitulate in a short introduction, and the reader should be careful not to take these summaries as an adequate account. Nevertheless, certain common themes and approaches do emerge. First, each author moves the focus away from the general history of modernity in South Asia and the Middle East, to look at particular examples of the local articulation of modernity, the way the modern is staged and performed. This focus enables the account to break with the historical narrative that always locates the origins of modernity in the West and represents the non-West only in terms of its efforts to copy or resist an imported, second-hand modernity. Staging the modern has always required the non-modern, the space of colonial difference. Second, concentrating on the local articulation and dissemination of modernity means paying less attention to the grand designs of the colonial or modernizing state and more attention to the myriad local sites where the modern is realized and continually translated, in its articulation with and production of the non-modern. Third, the categories and oppositions that are rene-gotiated in these sites produce particular transformations shaped by specific fields of force. Such local dislocations can represent points of weakness, where the strategies of modernity are renegotiated, its bi-nary oppositions displaced, and its apparently fixed and overarching identities disturbed.

Notes

1. See Timothy Mitchell, *Colonising Egypt,* 2nd ed. (Berkeley: University of California Press, 1991).

2. Partha Chatterjee, *Nationalist Thought and the Colonial World: A Derivative Discourse?* (Minneapolis: University of Minnesota Press, 1993), and *The Nation and Its Fragments: Colonial and Postcolonial Histories* (Princeton: Princeton University Press, 1994).

3. Dipesh Chakrabarty, "The Difference-Deferral of a Colonial Modernity: Public Debates on Domesticity in British Bengal," in *Subaltern Studies VIII,* ed. David Arnold and David Hardiman (Delhi: Oxford University Press, 1994), 50–88; reprinted in *Tensions of Empire: Colonial Cultures in a Bourgeois World,* ed. Frederick Cooper and Ann Laura Stoler (Berkeley: University of California Press, 1997), 373–405.

4. Chakrabarty, "The Difference-Deferral of a Colonial Modernity," 81.

5. Dipesh Chakrabarty, "Witness to Suffering: Domestic Cruelty and the Birth of the Modern Subject in Bengal," this volume, ch. 3, citing Michel Foucault, "Nietzsche, Genealogy, History," in *Language, Counter-Memory, Practice: Selected Essays and Interviews,* ed. Donald Bouchard, trans. Donald Bouchard and Sherry Simon (Ithaca: Cornell University Press, 1977), 139–84.

6. Talal Asad, *Genealogies of Religion: Discipline and Reasons of Power in Christianity and Islam* (Baltimore: The Johns Hopkins University Press, 1993).

7. Ibid. Similar arguments have been made in relation to South Asia by Spivak and

Chatterjee, among others. Thus Spivak writes, "Even 'the secular' carries upon its exergue the history of a 'world' facing a specific 'ecclesia,' that inscription now effaced into the universal name of an enlightened world that has sublated religion. Assimilated polytheist excolonials were brought up to presuppose that the European 'secular' imagining of ethics, which has not lost touch with its God even in His Death, is the only space, of critique *or* dogma" (Gayatri Chakravorty Spivak, "Not Virgin Enough to Say That [S]he Occupies the Place of the Other," *Cardozo Law Review* 13, no. 4 [December 1991], reprinted in *Outside in the Teaching Machine* [New York: Routledge, 1993], 173). See also Partha Chatterjee, "Religious Minorities and the Secular State: Reflections on an Indian Impasse," *Public Culture* 8, no. 1 (1995): 11–39.

8. Talal Asad, "Modernizing Religion and the Law in Nineteenth-Century Egypt," communication presented at the conference "Questions of Modernity," New York University, April 1997.

9. Peter Brooks, *The Melodramatic Imagination* (New Haven: Yale University Press, 1976), 15, 21.

10. Amitav Ghosh, *In an Antique Land* (New York: Vintage, 1994).

One

The Stage of Modernity

Timothy Mitchell

Our sense of ourselves as modern, of our time as the era of modernity, is today open to two kinds of question. One is the now familiar debate about whether modernity is a stage of history through which we have already passed. The global mobility of finance, the world-encircling webs of image-making, the contingency of social identities, and the collapse of emancipatory visions have produced in recent decades an increasing confidence that modernity has given way to a new condition. The name it is given, the postmodern, identifies it only in terms of the stage it claims to move beyond. But analyses of postmodernism have ignored another kind of question about modernity, and in this respect have inherited and passed on some very modern ways of understanding the world. The second question is concerned not with the passing of modernity but with its placing, not with a new stage of history but with how history itself is staged. Modernity has always been associated with a certain place. In many uses, the modern is just a synonym for the West (or in more recent writings, the North). Modernization continues to be commonly understood as a process begun and finished in Europe, from where it has been exported across ever-expanding regions of the non-West. The destiny of those regions has been to mimic, never quite successfully, the history already performed by the West. To become modern, it is still said, or today to become postmodern, is to act like the West.

Locating the origins of capitalist modernity entirely within the West has always been open to question. Marx saw the "rosy dawn" of capitalism not in England or the Netherlands but in the production, trade, and finance of the colonial system.[1] The Egyptian economist Samir Amin pioneered the study of capitalism "on a world scale," arguing that conditions in the periphery represent not an earlier stage of development but an equally modern consequence of the continuous "structural adjustment" (Amin's 1957 phrase) to which societies outside the West have been subjected.[2] Wallerstein traced the beginnings of this world-system to the transformation of a pattern of trade (from luxuries to essentials) that was already global. A proper image of its development, therefore, was "not of a small core adding on outer layers but of a thin outer framework gradually filling in a dense inner network."[3] More recently, Janet Abu-Lughod has shown how this global network operated in the thirteenth and fourteenth centuries, long before the rise of Europe, while Andre Gunder Frank presents evidence that Europe continued to be peripheral to an Asian-centered world economy until the mid-eighteenth century or even the start of the nineteenth.[4]

These more global pictures make possible a less Eurocentric account of the formation of the European modern. If modernity had its origins in reticulations of exchange and production encircling the world, then it was a creation not of the West but of an interaction between West and non-West. The sites of this interaction were as likely to lie in the East Indies, the Ottoman Empire, or the Caribbean as in England, the Netherlands, or France. Presenting what he admitted might be "a topsy-turvy view of the West," to give one example, Sidney Mintz argued that modern methods of industrial organization were developed first not for making textiles in Manchester but sugar in the Caribbean. Sixteenth- and seventeenth-century sugar production demanded strict labor discipline, careful scheduling and time-consciousness, and the division of labor into work units by age, skill, and gender, to an extent as yet unknown in mainland Europe.[5] The discipline and coordination, as a historian of French colonial slavery remarks, made this "a new type of work, an element of social revolution."[6] Another study of capitalism's Caribbean origins argues that the very distances involved in colonial trade caused the development of the modern, bureaucratic supervision of labor, on ships and in port cities, that enabled finance capital to extract surplus value.[7] And turning from the supervisors to the slaves, Paul Gilroy suggests we see the slave ships as "the living means" for articulating the new modes of political dissent and cultural production that he calls the Black Atlantic. Getting on board, as it were, "promises a means to reconceptualize the orthodox relationship between modernity and what passes for its prehistory."[8]

Beyond the constitutive role of slavery, the sugar plantation, and the shipping industry, many other forms of social organization and cultural production that, since *Discipline and Punish,* we have come to consider as important as wage labor and the factory system in the emergence of European modernity were first developed well beyond the northern Europe of Michel Foucault's analyses.[9] The principle of self-monitoring embodied in Bentham's Panopticon was designed by his brother Samuel while assisting Russia's colonization of Ottoman territory, while monitorial schooling was invented in early nineteenth-century Bengal.[10] The emergence of "the population" as the primary object of governmental power, as Partha Chatterjee notes in his essay in this volume, and certainly the invention of "culture" as the features embodying the identity of a population group, probably first occurred in the colonization of non-European regions.[11] Uday Mehta shows that India played a sustained role in the theoretical imagination of nineteenth-century British liberalism (and in its authors' careers), exposing it to a constitutive ambivalence.[12] The cultural field we know as English literature was constructed as a curriculum and tool of character formation in colonial India before its appearance in England.[13] Colonial medicine, as Gyan Prakash examines in his chapter to this book, pioneered the extended governmental control of the body.[14] The methods of managing persons, self-identities, space, and movement that Foucault presents as essential to the formation of European modernity in many cases came to Europe from its encounter with what lay beyond.

To see modernity as a product not of the West but of its interaction with the non-West still leaves a problem. It assumes the existence of the West and its exterior, long before the world's identities had been divided into this neat, European-centered dualism. It might be better to propose that it was in the building of slave factories in Martinique, prisons in the Crimea, and schools in Calcutta that the decisive nature of the distinction between European and non-European was fixed. Edward Said's *Orientalism* stands as the most powerful account of how

Europe's sense of cultural identity was constructed in the business of colonizing and getting rich overseas.[15] Ann Stoler has argued that Dutch settlers in the East Indies, anxious to secure their identity in relation both to those of mixed blood and to poor whites, developed a new image of themselves as European. This identity prefigured the emergence of a bourgeois, European sense of self in the metropole and was subsequently imported into the Netherlands under the influence of colonial developments.[16] Similarly, the importance of Benedict Anderson's landmark study of nationalism lies in showing not so much that modern collective identities are constructs of the imagination but that the most important of these imaginings, territorial nationalism, was first elaborated not, as was always assumed, in Europe but in the creole communities of the Caribbean and South America. Creoles were those local-born "whites" whose displacement overseas meant they could never quite be Europeans yet who feared the contamination of Indian, Negro, or mestizo identities. In such mixing of populations lay the origins of the desire to fix political identity in the racial categories of modern nationalism.[17] White and non-white, European and non-European, West and non-West, were identities often elaborated abroad and only later, like nationalism itself, brought to Europe.

Even when the term "nationalism" came into currency in Europe, at least in English, it appeared only after the spread of the term "international" and was coined by an anticolonial movement. The idea of "the international" was popularized in London in 1862, when the world exhibition of that year was named the Great International Exhibition. The new word evoked the global order of imperialism that the exhibition was intended to represent. A delegation of Parisian workers sent to the exhibition met with London trade unionists and borrowed the new word, forming the Working Men's International Association under the leadership of Karl Marx.[18] The word "nationalism" appeared two decades later, introduced by the Irish Nationalist party as it launched the struggle against British colonialism.[19] The trajectory of the term followed the earlier itinerary of its sister term "liberalism," which was also coined on the continent's colonized periphery, in the latter case in the Spanish rising against French occupation during the Napoleonic wars. The periphery, in these matters, as Perry Anderson remarks, "pioneered the terms of metropolitan advance."[20]

Such questions about the role of the periphery (an increasingly inappropriate term) in the genealogy of modernity have shown that we need to reexamine much of the critical writing on the European modern that has shaped our thinking about its passing. *The Postmodern Condition*, Jean-François Lyotard's seminal essay, allows no place for the non-West in the defining of modernity and hence in the appearance of the postmodern.[21] Jean Baudrillard's account of the historical passage from the age of production and reproduction to the age of simulation has the same narrowness.[22] David Harvey's more broadly conceived work, *The Condition of Postmodernity*, makes occasional reference to imperialism and its crises but pays no direct attention to the world beyond the West, and the same is true of Jameson's commanding essay on the cultural logic of late capitalism.[23] This logic, according to Jameson, represents a new, globalized form of capitalism, in which all "enclaves of precapitalist organization" have been swept away, including the peasantry and other non-Western "residues."[24] Thus the non-West appears in such writing only at the point of its disappearance, when finally "everything has reached the same hour on the great clock of development."[25] In the work of Foucault, the absence of the larger world is even more striking. His genealogies of modern methods of knowledge, power, and selfhood provide no account of how France and northern Europe came to be defined as modernity's location. Despite his frequent interest in how the spacing of social practice can be the source of forms of power, his writing only reinforces our sense that the place of modernity is to be taken for granted.

This limitation of Foucault is especially marked in his genealogy of that emblem of modernity, the bourgeois individual. Stoler's important study of Foucault shows how *The History of Sexuality* entirely overlooks the colonial projects and apprehensions that paralleled and often prefigured the development of middle-class sexuality and selfhood in Europe.[26] The silence in Foucault now seems remarkable, yet before Stoler none of the major studies of his work had brought into view what Gayatri Spivak memorably refers to as his "sanctioned ignorance."[27] Whether one looks at Dutch settlers in Indonesia, the English in India, or the mixture of French and other European colonizers in Algeria, colonial society was experienced as an often threatening intermixture of social ranks, genders, and skin colors. To govern these new forms of disorder, colonial discourse became preoccupied with establishing distinctions of race, sexuality, culture, and class. These thematics were then available to be transferred back to the metropole, where in the later nineteenth century they helped form the racial, cultural, class, and sexual identities that defined the modern bourgeois self. For Foucault, race has only an oblique and unhistorical role to play in the emergence of bourgeois sexuality. By relocating modernity within empire, Stoler shows that the history of sexuality is interwoven with that of race and that the emergence of modern forms of selfhood cannot be accounted for within the boundaries of Europe alone.

These absences in Foucault and other recent theorists of modernity are doubly marked when one realizes, as Perry Anderson points out, that the idea of postmodernism itself, like the earlier idea of modernism (which did the work of the term postmodernism for a previous generation, evoking the ambivalence and contradictions of modernity) was born "in a distant periphery rather than at the centre of the cultural system of the time."[28] The concept of *modernismo* was coined in 1890 by "a Nicaraguan poet, writing in a Guatemalan journal, of a literary encounter in Peru," announcing a declaration of cultural independence by Latin American writers against the authority of Spanish literature. So too, Anderson adds, "the idea of a 'postmodernism' first surfaced in the Hispanic interworld of the 1930's, a generation before its appearance in England or America."[29] Moving to another interwar interworld, it was Ihab Hassan, the son of a provincial governor in northern Egypt (the father notorious for his violent suppression of an anticolonial revolt in 1930) who gave postmodernism its more recent currency in the United States.[30] Beyond Hassan, one could trace the decisive role of a 1940s–1950s Arab-Mediterranean borderland, located on the historical and cultural boundary of colonialism, from the Cairo of Edward Said and Anouar Abdel-Malek (and, briefly, Roland Barthes), the Istanbul of Auerbach's exile, the Tunis of Albert Memmi and Michel Foucault, the Constantine where Lyotard began his teaching career, the Morocco of Juan Goytisolo and Abdel Kabir Khatibi, and the Algiers of Jacques Derrida, Frantz Fanon, and more indirectly a generation of Parisian intellectuals.[31] The critique of the European modern, like so much of the modern itself, seems continually to have emerged from Europe's borders.

Relocating the question of modernity beyond the limits of the West brings a certain risk. There is a danger that instead of decentering the categories and certainties of modernity, one might produce a more expansive, inclusive, and inevitably homogenous account of the genealogy of modernity.[32] Appadurai suggests that we should dispense altogether with the picture of the globe divided into a Western core and non-Western periphery, or any other fixed geographical image, and think instead in terms of overlapping, disjunctive landscapes whose centers and perspective shift according to the different kinds of cultural, financial, and political forces one considers.[33] Stoler is careful not to propose a simple extension and reversal of the narrative of modernization, in which in place of modernist forms arising in the West and being extended abroad, they emerge in the colonies and are reimported to the metropole. She emphasizes instead, as does Foucault in other contexts, a mobile process of rupture and reinscription. When themes and categories developed in one historical context, such as a region of the colonial world, are reused elsewhere in the service of different social arrangements and political tactics, there is an inevitable process of displacement and reformulation.[34] At issue, then, is whether one can find a way to theorize the question of modernity that relocates it within a global context and, at the same time, enables that context to complicate, rather than simply reverse, the narrative logic of modernization.

The Force of History

To disrupt the powerful story of modernity, rather than contribute to its globalization, it is not enough to question simply its location. One also has to question its temporality. One must abandon its neat image not just of geographical space but also of historical time. The modern age presents a particular view of geography, in which the world has a single center, Europe—a Eurasian peninsula, as Marshall Hodgson remarked, that imagines itself a continent—in reference to which all other regions are to be located; and an understanding of history in which there is only one unfolding of time, the history of the West, in reference to which all other histories must establish their significance and receive their meaning.[35] These conceptions of history and geography are related. Historical time, the time of the West, is what gives modern geography its order, an order centered upon Europe. Accounts of the modern world that introduce a topsy-turvy view of this geography, by locating important developments outside the West, typically reestablish the order of modernity by removing these irregularities from any determining local context, or any non-European regional or global context, and repositioning them within the West's uniform and singular history. The discipline of historical time reorganizes discordant geographies into a universal modernity.

Take the example of how Mintz explains the origins of capitalism in Caribbean sugar production. *Sweetness and Power,* as the subtitle tells us, is about "the place of sugar in modern history." The book expands the history of capitalism to bring to light "a precocious development outside the European heartland," yet must return this aberrant development to its place, by putting it "in modern history."[36] Modern history means the development of capitalist modernity in Europe. Even when the history of modernity extends to the Caribbean, it must remain the history of the West. It is the West that defines the Caribbean as precocious, something advancing ahead of its time, where time means the movement of the West.

What does the story of slave plantations tell us about the history of capitalism? I leave aside here the long debates over the significance of the Caribbean and the Atlantic trade to the growth of European capitalism, except to note that Blackburn has recently confirmed that their contribution was "decisive," and that Frank argues that plundering the New World enabled Europe not to create a world economy but to buy into an existing Asian-centered one.[37] My concern here is with the way in which these developments outside "the West" are reorganized as part of its own history. Thus Mintz tells us that Caribbean slave plantations are important for understanding "the chain of causation that leads from one stage of development to another." Arguing that "it would be wrong to treat the plantation system as 'capitalistic' in the same way that the British factory system of the nineteenth century was capitalistic," he concludes that nevertheless "these curious agro-industrial enterprises nourished certain capitalist classes at home *as they were becoming more capitalistic.*"[38] Caribbean agro-industry was not capitalism, in other words, for the meaning of capitalism is defined by the factory system of nineteenth-century England; but it can have a place in modern history, because it nourished the formation of that system. Historical time, in such an account, is singular, moving from one stage of development to another. There is no possibility of more than one history, of a non-singular capitalism. The Caribbean slave plantation, although longer lasting than the nineteenth-century English factory, can be no more than a curious form of what later emerged in its normal form in the West.

The conception of historical time renders history singular by organizing the multiplicity of global events into a single narrative. The narrative is structured by the progression of a principle, whether it be the principle of human reason or enlightenment, technical rationality or power over nature. Even when discovered acting precociously overseas, these powers of production, technology, or reason constitute a single story of unfolding potential.

The use of the idea of a singular historical time to reorganize the dispersed geographies of modernity into stages of Europe's past finds its first clear expression in the work of Marx, where discrepant developments outside Europe are translated into something else: expressions of time itself. More forcefully than any other nineteenth-century writer, Marx constructs an idea of "Europe"—defined by the emergence there of modern bourgeois society—as the singular center of all other histories. The singularity of history, in Marx's case, derives from the development of the material forces of production, which periodically outgrow the social relations in which they are organized.[39] Singular does not mean uniform. In different countries, the historical process "assumes different aspects, and runs through its various phases in different orders of succession, and at different periods."[40] But these differences can only be thought of as different in relation to an underlying uniformity. One can gather together a diversity of local histories and describe them as different, in sequence, aspect, place, and period, precisely because they are imagined as the possible variations in a single process of development.[41] Presenting them as variations establishes the concept of a universal history, in relation to which all local histories—delayed, displaced, blocked, or rearranged—receive their meaning.

When he comes to explain capitalism's origins, however, Marx is forced to step outside this singular time. The step is taken at the very point where his narrative is pushed for the first time outside the boundaries of Europe. The general law of capitalist accumulation explains how capital produces surplus value and surplus value in turn produces further capital. But the law cannot escape this "vicious circle" to explain how capital is produced in the first place.[42] After six hundred pages on the workings of capitalist society illustrated almost exclusively by the case of England, the final section of volume one of *Capital,* on the origins of industrial capitalism, moves outside Europe and locates its beginnings in the colonial system.[43] "The discovery of gold and silver in America," a familiar passage explains, "the extirpation, enslavement, and entombment in the mines of the aboriginal population, the beginning of the conquest and looting of the East Indies, the turning of Africa into a warren for the hunting of blackskins, signalised the rosy dawn of the era of capitalist production."[44] The production of wealth overseas then gave rise to the protection of trade by the state, the colonial wars, the creation of a national debt, and the introduction of taxation to service it. In the systematic combination of these different colonial elements lay the beginnings of industrial capitalism.

This original accumulation of capital, however, did not seem to derive from any general principle of the development of the material forces of production. Its origins were dispersed around the globe and required a variety of new social forms and processes: slave-based production, colonial ports and settlements, genocide, international finance, modern warfare, and the organized power of a central state. How could such a dispersed multiplicity of social and political developments be turned into "economic phenomena," meaning not events related to the economy (a conception that does not exist in Marx's writing) but events revealing the economy of history—history's singular logic? How could these global influences and innovations be gathered back into the linear story of capital?

Marx's answer to this problem is first to leave aside an economic explanation for the origins of capital accumulation and to focus on what he calls the means. This enables him to find a single factor that characterizes all these developments: the use of force. "We leave on one side here the purely economic causes," he says. "We deal only with the forcible means employed."[45] His account then presents the origins of capitalism by describing it as a system of force. It consists of both "brute force, e.g., the colonial system," and what he describes as "concentrated and organized force," namely "the state power."[46] The narrative moves between descriptions of colonialism's physical violence—capital comes into the world "dripping from head to foot, from every pore, with blood and dirt"—and precise images of mechanical force, especially the metaphor of the lever: the colonizing corporations are "powerful levers for concentration of capital," the national debt becomes "one of the most powerful levers" of capital accumulation.[47] This focus on the image of force may seem unremarkable. Marx's preceding analysis of capitalism, after all, brings to light all the machinery of compulsion and forms of barbarism concealed within the free exchanges of the market system. In the explanation of original accumulation, however, every factor is reduced to a question of force. There is no analysis of the social organization, the methods of discipline, or the techniques of production that characterize the slave plantation, the shipping industry, the colonizing corporation, the colonial settlement, or the power of the army, to compare with his painstaking analysis of the nineteenth-century English factory. There is nothing except the use of force.

The absence of detail is not, I would argue, an innocent one, for characterizing the colonial system solely in terms of force has an important consequence. It enables Marx's writing to fold these heterogeneous overseas developments into the history of the West. Having told us first that force is just a means, not an historical-economic cause, he reveals at the end that force operates upon history itself; contributing to the movement of history, it is therefore something "economic" after all. The effect of colonial force, Marx explains, is "to hasten, hothouse fashion, the process of transformation . . . and to shorten the transition. Force is . . . itself an economic power."[48] The unusual social forms of the colonial system—slave production, protectionism, colonial militarism, the new compulsions of state power—are not diversions from the singular path of capitalism's history. Deprived of their complexity and diversity and reduced to mere expressions of force, they serve the purpose of *forcing* history, the way a greenhouse forces plants. Colonial developments whose difference in social form, disrupted timing, or displacement across the globe seem to undermine the effort to make history homogenous become simply the unlawful force that forces history ahead. Their separation abroad appears as no more than the mechanical distance of a lever, whose very length enables an outside event to propel the West forward.

It is not a matter of rejecting, in the terms in which he says it, the truth of what Marx tells us about the violence of modernity's origins. It is a question of asking what other histories must be overlooked in order to fit the non-West into the historical time of the West. To acknowledge the constitutive role of these other histories, as Ernesto Laclau among others has argued, would be to deny history—and capitalism—its singularity and to see modernity instead as a contingent process.[49] This does not mean arguing that its history is random, or simply "repudiat[ing] . . . the capitalist restructuring of the modern world," as critics of this kind of questioning have argued, or treating capitalism as a "potentially disposable fiction" held in place only by our acceptance of its categories.[50] Whether we want to or not, we accept these categories into our argument the moment we attempt to question them. They are fictions, if one wants that word, of the nondisposable sort. But even if we cannot escape the necessity of writing history as the story of capitalism, even if we must give in to it, as Derrida says in another context, it does not follow that all ways of giving in to it are of equal significance.[51] A writing that simply documents in increasing detail an ever-expanding globalization of capital, as Prakash argues, simply reiterates and reinforces the process one wants to question.[52] The alternative is to borrow from capitalism the tools with which to deconstruct it. In particular, one can borrow capitalism's notion of the non-capitalist, the West's notion of the non-West, and modernity's notion of the non-modern, and ask what these nondisposable fictions suppress.

The apparent rationality and coherence of capitalist modernity can be constructed only through an interaction with forces and events that seem to stand outside its own development. This "constitutive outside," however, cannot be referred back to any unfolding principle or internal contradiction, or be contained by an underlying causal or dialectical pattern.[53] If Caribbean slavery, for example, introduced into what we call capitalism's development, among other things, the dynamics of West African societies, the ecology of the Caribbean, the culture of slave households, the politics of genocide, and mass addiction to sugar, then that development can no longer be predicted or accounted for in reference to the endogenous unfolding of a rationality or potential, which would provide capitalism's essence and make modernity something monadic and fundamentally the same everywhere. Developments and forces external to any possible definition of the essence of capitalist modernity continually redirect, divert, mutate, and multiply the modernity they help constitute, depriving it of any essential principle, unique dynamic, or singular history.

A Specter Haunting—Europe

The concept of historical time recaptures histories happening overseas and returns them to the historical home of the West. Such representations construct the capitalist modern as a temporal object as much as a spatial one, giving it the coherence of a single parentage and unique abode. Uncovering the plural genealogy and ecology of what we unify under names such as capitalism or modernity puts this coherence in question. Each new context can reveal another parent, another logic. The identity claimed by the modern is contaminated. It issues from too many sources and depends upon, even as it refuses to recognize, forebears and forces that escape its control. To overlook these differences requires a constant representing of the homogenous unity of modernity's space and time. More precisely, it can be argued, the experience of modernity is constructed as a relationship between time and space. It is a particular way of expressing one in terms of the other. A way to begin to uncover this interdependence of space and time in the construction of the modern is to ask whether Foucault's failure to engage with the colonial genealogies of modernity is merely an oversight. There are enough occasional references to French colonialism in Foucault's work to suggest that his writing was silently aware of the significance of empire in the origins of modernity. Is it possible, then, that the silence is not accidental but plays a role in the production of Foucault's argument? Foucault's genealogy of sexuality and the bourgeois self does not entirely ignore the question of race—the element that provides the critical link with empire. Instead, as Stoler points out, he treats race as an anachronism, representing a pre-modern aristocratic concern with the purity of blood and the legitimacy of descent. In his 1976 lectures at the Collège de France, Foucault expanded this idea, arguing that a pre-nineteenth-century debate about purity of aristocratic descent was recovered and reinscribed in the late nineteenth century to serve the new technology of biopower (the large-scale management of life and death) developed as the characteristic governmental technique of the modern state.[54] This argument represents a double overlooking of empire, for eighteenth-century racism, as much as the later nineteenth-century forms, was a product of colonialism. As Rolph Trouillot tells us, Buffon, Voltaire, and other figures of the Enlightenment helped shape a scientific racism whose impetus came from Caribbean and North American opposition to the abolition of slavery.[55] Homi Bhabha has suggested that it is Foucault's very treatment of race as an anachronism, rather than a discrepant yet very contemporary discourse developed beyond Europe, that provides a clue to the significance of this silence about colonialism.[56] Treating race as an anachronism preserves a particular way of thinking about modernity, in which the modern is constructed not just as an historical era but as a particular relationship between space and time.

A distinctive feature of many experiences of modernity is what can be called its contemporaneity or presence. The modern occurs as that form of temporality that Walter Benjamin calls homogenous empty time, in which time is apprehended as the uniform, unfilled spaces marked out by the calendar, the timetable, and the clock.[57] Developing this notion, Benedict Anderson suggests that it gives rise to a new experience of simultaneity, in which people living unconnected lives can feel themselves joined by occupying the same homogenous temporal moment. His now-familiar argument proposes that this simultaneity is represented in the structure of the nineteenth-century European novel, in which characters whose lives never meet play roles together in the same narrative, and in the phenomenon of the mass-circulation daily newspapers of the same period, through which thousands of readers shared the experience of reading the same ephemeral material on the same day.[58] What underlies these apprehensions of simultaneity or co-presence is that both the characters in the novel and the readers of the newspaper can be thought to share the same *space*. They can be imagined as members of the same sociological entity, Anderson suggests, defined as a geographical space in which all co-exist at the same moment.

Benjamin seems to have borrowed the idea of homogenous empty time from Henri Bergson. In his *Essai sur la données immediates de la conscience* (1889), Bergson discusses the Kantian theory of space and time, in which these apprehensions are considered not properties of things in themselves but the two pure forms of human intuition. Bergson agrees that space is "the intuition, or rather the conception, of an empty homogeneous medium," but argues that temporality consists of heterogeneous, interpenetrating moments of duration, which our consciousness can reconfigure as homogenous time only by laying out in a *spatial* sequence.[59] Through this mental contrivance, "in place of a heterogeneous duration whose moments permeate one another, we thus get a homogenous time whose moments are strung on a spatial line."[60] The conception of time in "the illusory form of a homogenous medium," Bergson argues, "is nothing but the ghost of space haunting the reflexive consciousness."[61] In contrast to Bergson and following Benjamin and Anderson, I would attribute the modern apprehension of time as a homogenous medium to new forms of social practice, rather than to the tricks of a universal Kantian consciousness.[62] But it is useful to borrow from Bergson the insight that the experience of homogenous empty time rests on giving temporality a spatial expression. As Anderson's examples of this temporality seem to suggest, the contemporaneity of time is haunted by the ghost of space.

One can ask whether, in fact, the multiple social experiences of modernity are all expressed within a single conception of time, as Veena Das does in chapter 7 of this book.[63] One can also question, as several critics have, Anderson's focus on print culture as the most important mechanism of the experience of contemporaneity. Indeed, the second edition of *Imagined Communities* widens this focus by pointing in later chapters to the significance of such practices as census taking and map making in constructing the homogenous space of modernity and hence (it could be added) its temporality. Anderson's argument, moreover, is concerned with one specific consequence of these practices, the emergence of territorial nationalism. The more general point I want to draw from his analysis, however, is that modernity can be characterized, among other ways, by a sense of presence or contemporaneity created by the spatialization of time.

Putting empire back into the history of Europe, we first suggested, enables us to reverse the narrative of modernization and see the West as the product of modernity. We might rephrase things again now and suggest that modernity is produced *as* the West. The "now" of modernity, its culture of contemporaneity, the particular sense of simultaneity that is taken as modernity's experience, depends upon the representation of an homogenous space. The inhabitants of this space, almost all of whom never meet one another, can be conceived as living the same empty moment, as occupying the same time-space. This effect of simultaneity makes it possible to construct the idea of historical time: history is the story of a civilization, culture, or people whose diverse lives are imagined to share a singular epoch and to progress as a unit from one contemporaneous moment to the next. It is only this effect of a unitary, punctual, contemporaneous present, as Bhabha points out, that enables Foucault to present racism as an "anachronism." Race is an element recuperated from a pre-modern past and reinscribed in an otherwise homogenous present. The West is the space that haunts this presence.

This is the clue to Foucault's spectral silence about colonialism. The narrative of history, even in the brilliant revisionism of Foucault, is the story of Europe. To stage this homogenous time-space, there can be no interruptions from the non-West. The non-West must play the role of the outside, the otherness that creates the boundary of the space of modernity. This otherness, Bhabha argues, takes two forms. The non-West, as its name implies, represents the non-place, terra incognita, the wasteland "whose history has to be begun, whose archives must be filled out." But it also stands for the place of time-lessness, a space without duration, in relation to which the temporal break of modernity can be marked out.[64] In this sense, the colonial is not something absent from the story of modernity that Foucault tells. Or rather, Bhabha suggests, the colonial is a constant absence essential to Foucault's text. By relegating the non-West to the margins and foot-notes of his account, Foucault reproduces the spatialization of moder-nity. The homogenous time of modernity, its characteristic contem-poraneity, is preserved by the way Foucault respects the territorial boundaries of the modern. Thanks to the boundaries of this time-space, he can portray a synchronic discourse around the theme of the bourgeois individual and see race as an anachronism, rather than as the discrepant product of colonial developments whose otherness, in announcing the homogeneity of the modern, haunts it.

The Stage of Modernity

"What is this 'now' of modernity?" asks Bhabha. "Who defines this present from which we speak? . . . Why does it insist, so compulsively, on its contemporaneous reality, its spatial dimension, its spectatorial distance?"[65] How can one approach such questions in a way that does not simply produce a more global and more homogenous narrative of modernization, and inevitably end up retelling the story of the West? Is there some way to address the time-space of European modernity that does not end up remapping, as Foucault seems to, the contours of that time-space? Any adequate response to this problem must begin from what I would argue is the most powerful aspect of the produc-tion of the European-modern, and what at the same time exposes it to specters of difference and displacement that deny it the originality and coherence it claims: the way in which the modern is staged as repre-sentation. There is a tendency in recent scholarship to see the prolif-eration of media images, sign systems, simulations, and other forms of representation as the defining characteristic not of modernity but of the postmodern. Jameson defines the era of postmodernism or late capitalism as the age of the simulacrum, in which the real has been transformed into so many pseudo-events.[66] Baudrillard describes it as the age of simulation.[67] It is no doubt the case that what Appadurai usefully calls "the work of the imagination" plays an increasingly important role in the postelectronic age.[68] Yet it is important to remember that the orchestrating of image and imagination, the managing of the place of meaning in the social world and the experience of personhood, and the manipulating of populations and ecologies by their reduction to technical schemes and disciplinary programs, were already characteristic features of modernity in the colonial period. As I have argued in *Colonising Egypt,* consumerism and the great world exhibitions, tourism and Orientalism, urban planning and compulsory schooling, forced migration and mass conscription, global militarism and imperial commerce—all the novel institutional forms and political practice of late nineteenth-century Paris and London, or Cairo and Calcutta—were organized around the simulation, diagramming, and replication of the real.[69] From this perspective, the postmodern would have to be understood not as a disruption of meaning or loss of certainty that comes after the modern but as an instability always already at work in the production of modernity.

To claim that the modern is always staged as representation is not to argue that modernity is concerned more with image-making than with reality. It is to argue that the colonial-modern involves creating an effect we recognize as reality, by organizing the world endlessly to represent it. Representation does not refer here simply to the making of images or meanings. It refers to forms of social practice that set up in the social architecture and lived experience of the world what seems an absolute distinction between image (or meaning, or structure) and reality, and thus a distinctive imagination of the real. This dualism of the real can find certain roots, no doubt, in early modern social thought and practice and may draw upon and transform earlier traditions. Since the nineteenth century, however, it has been generalized in modern architecture and urban planning, social engineering and the management of nature, organized schooling and literature, entertainment and tourism; in military order, imperial pomp, and the disciplines of colonialism and nation-making; in all the mundane forms of self-monitoring and self-presentation that shape the lives of modern subjects; and, quite pervasively, in the organization of production and the prestidigitations of the market mechanism. In sphere after sphere of social life, the world is rendered up in terms of the dualism of image and reality. This corresponds, in turn, to a series of other simplifications, each of which stages the complexities and antagonisms of social experience in terms of a simple binarism: life and its meaning, things and their exchange value, activity and structure, execution and plan, content and form, object- and subject-world. In each case an immediacy of the really real is promised by what appears in contrast to be the mere abstractions of structure, subjectivity, text, plan, or idea.

The passage from pre-modern to modern is always understood as a rupture and separation, whether of a rational self from a disenchanted world, of producers from their means of production, or of nature and population from the processes of technological control and social planning. Each of these so-called ruptures is a way of accounting for a world increasingly staged according to the schema of object and subject, process and plan, real and representation.

The significance of this world-as-picture for understanding the colonial-modern lies in the fact that representation always makes a double claim. On the one hand, something set up as a representation denies its own reality. The representational text, image, model, game, structure, or project, however realistic, always asserts that it is only a text, a mere picture, a copy, a play, a scheme, a framework, an abstraction, a projection, not something real. It defines itself by what it lacks, its missing originality, its immateriality, its want of immediate presence, by the gap in time, space, and substance that separates it from the real thing. On the other hand, in asserting its own lack, a representation claims that the world it replicates, projects, reorganizes, enacts, or endows with meaning and structure must be, by contrast, original, material, immediately present, complete in itself, without lack, undelayed, filling its own time and space—in a word (what we imagine as) real. Colonial European modernity stages the endless set-up that pictures and promises us this complete, unmediated, self-present, immediate reality.[70]

If we return for a moment to Anderson's examples illustrating the creation of homogenous empty time, it is clear that they all share a common feature: the modern novel, newspaper, census, map, and museum, as well as the many other, more invasive practices that create the punctual time-space of modernity, are all methods of representation, in the specific sense just defined. The newspaper claims to capture a record of the present and make this passing presence available through a form of replay. The map and census provide figures that are imagined to picture the nation as a real and knowable totality. The theater, novel, and museum stage objects and characters to create simulations of a real world. Anderson considers the significance of these proliferating representations to lie in the experience of replication, meaning not simple copying but endless serialization. In its new social practices the modern state does more than count and classify the elements of the nation, he says. Since almost every state by the late colonial period was beginning to replicate similar procedures of statistical and cultural representation, the idea could emerge that the nation exists as a particular instance of an almost infinitely replicated series of nations.[71] More recently, he has argued that the logic of serial replication underlies the creation of all modern political identities and is therefore essential to the modern "imagining of collectivity."[72]

I do not doubt that the representation of community is made more effective by the repetition of such representations from one country to the next, across a world that can now be imagined for the first time as a horizontal plane of equivalent social units. The effect is probably stronger in the case of numerical representations of the nation, which make it possible repeatedly to compare nation states and arrange them in groups and sequences. The twentieth-century invention of national-income accounting and the idea of the "national economy" is the most important example of this.[73] Representation always gathers its strength from the way one picture is echoed and confirmed by another, so that each image forms part of a world-encircling web of signification. Yet the effectiveness of this world-as-picture lies not simply in the process of serialization. It lies in the apparent contrast created between images, which are repeatable, serializable, hyperlinked, open to endless imitation, and the opposing effect of an original, of what appears to be the actual nation, the people itself, the real economy. The act of representation, constantly repeated, makes each of these referents—nation, people, economy—appear as an object that exists prior to any representation, as something given, material, fixed in its unique time and space, not fissured by replication, not open to serialization and interlinking, and to the difference, instability, and misrepresentation that endless repetition might introduce.

It is this novel myth of immediate presence, of an original, material reality, a world prior to and apart from all work of replication, difference, antagonism, meaning, management, or imagination, that defines the peculiar metaphysic of modernity. It is this metaphysic in turn, that theories of postmodernity in most cases continue to reproduce.

The postmodern is typically understood as a world of images and replications that have lost touch with this supposedly original reality. The real, it is said, has been replaced by the pseudo-real. In other words, such accounts continue to assume the unproblematic nature of a distinction between the real and represented, even as they announce its historical disappearance. For this reason, most theories of postmodernity remain within the binary metaphysics of the modern.

The Mysterious Thing

If the presence of modernity occurs only as *re*presentation, this representing is not a phenomenon limited to the deliberate methods of making meaning on which accounts of the modern and the postmodern tend to focus, such as the modern novel, news reporting, museum displays, mass media, or the organization of medical, statistical, and other forms of official knowledge. Much of the best recent writing on modernity and postmodernity has been developed in the field of cultural studies, which tends to focus on these intellectual and cultural forms of representation, together with related spheres such as architecture, music, and fashion. As I have already suggested, however, modernity's methods of staging and representation structure much more than what we designate as the cultural and intellectual spheres. I will briefly discuss three broader aspects of the experience of modernity that can be understood in relation to the staging of the world as representation. Representation is the key, first of all, to how we imagine the construction of modern selfhood. On the one hand, the world-as-picture demands a spectator. It typically positions the person as the subject for whom the social world seems to exist as a view to be observed, an experience to be had, a set of meanings to be interpreted, or a code to be followed or deciphered. On the other hand, in the Western philosophical tradition, as Dipesh Chakrabarty's essay in this volume reminds us, the modern individual came to be defined as the one who could occupy such a position of disembodied observer of the world. Freed in this way from the traditional constraints of habit or belief and transcending their localism, it was said, modern subjects could discover a universal faculty of reason and employ it to represent to themselves the experiences and feelings of others and to submit their own interior life to its pedagogy. These individual powers of representation, moreover, were to be cultivated through literature and other imaginative social forms, shaping the modern sensibility through a further recourse to the process of representation.[74] Conversely, in the racialist discourses of colonialism, the backwardness of the native population could be analyzed in terms of a weakness of the mental power of representation. French colonial psychiatry in North Africa, as Stefania Pandolfo explains in her essay here, diagnosed the pathology of the indigenous mentality as an inability to symbolize. Unable to produce abstract representations, the colonized mind was said to be trapped in the mimetic faculty, the prisoner of images from which it could not obtain a spectatorial distance and thereby establish itself as a subject. Such analyses opened up the space for the twentieth-century project of psychiatry to produce the modern subject, by freeing the mind from this imprisonment in images and enabling it to represent truthfully the self and others. Similarly, Lila Abu-Lughod's essay on television considers how the contemporary powers of the mass media seem to produce a subject defined by what Raymond Williams has called "the dramatisation of consciousness." Under the influence of mass media, and television drama in particular, selfhood comes to be understood as something fashioned by staging one's life as a story, in a continuous representation of oneself to oneself and to others.[75]

Second, among the most pervasive examples of the way experience is rendered up in the dualism of image and reality is the simple, seemingly material form of the commodity. The system of commodities, Marx pointed out, is an arrangement of production and exchange in which objects present themselves to us always as representations of something else. "The mystical character of commodities," as he called it, arises from the fact that nothing can become a commodity, a thing of value, by standing for itself. An object can acquire value only by appearing to embody, or represent, some quality beyond itself.[76] "A commodity is therefore a mysterious thing," as Marx says, because it can never be just "a thing" but always appears, like a character on stage, as something representing something further.[77] Yet as Derrida has written, if the commodity is never single but occurs as a relationship between "a thing" and the value that it promises, then the possibility of anything being merely a thing, of standing only for itself, of having only one, natural use, is compromised. Why should one suppose that an object can exist as pure use-value, if the possibility of exchange, of one thing standing in for another, is always already part of its potential?[78] The system of commodities is not a masquerade or fetish ceremony in which the true nature of objects is disguised or misunderstood. It is that theater in which all the characters assure us that they are merely standing in for something else, so that we leave the performance reassured of the real world outside, seldom noticing that the illuminated exit signs lead only to other, much larger theaters.[79]

If this effect of real versus represented is embodied in the exchange of commodified objects, it is far more extensively inscribed in the larger theaters of consumption, services, entertainment, and manufactured experience that, even in Marx's day, were beginning to constitute the social worlds of modernity. The processes we simplify under the name of commodification transform the nature of labor and exchange but also encompass the birth of modern schooling, science, and entertainment and the transformation of leisure and personal relations. In every sphere, objects and experiences come to be organized as systems of consumption, requiring them to represent some value, idea, or imaginative realm beyond themselves. The proliferating commodifications of life entail the staging of social relations and realities, so that everything presents itself as the *re*presentation of some prior value, some larger meaning, or some original presence.[80]

In the third place, representation is the novel method of creating colonial modernity's distinctive apprehensions of space and time. What distinguishes the experience of modernity is not simply, as we suggested above, its sense of contemporaneity. It is not just a particular effect of shared presence within a common social space, the homogenous space of the nation or the West. What is distinctive is that such contemporaneity or presence is an effect that can be rendered up to experience only through the structure of a replication—through a representation of the social, a mapping of the nation, a narrative of its history, a set of statistical images, or the varieties of representational practice that structure modern politics. It occurs only as something staged. This, it should be noted, is a somewhat different formulation from those, such as David Harvey, who follow Henri Lefebvre and discuss modernity in terms of changing ways in which space is produced. In *The Condition of Postmodernity,* Harvey analyzes the history of capitalism in terms of increasing speeds of communication and the increasing physical space that technology can control. He calls this changing power over time and space a process of "space-time compression" and analyzes the shift from modernity to postmodernity as the transition of this process to a new stage.[81] Such arguments capture much of the dynamic of recent history. Yet they overlook what is most distinctive in the modern, a difference on which the new compression of space and time depends: what occurs is not simply a change in the way space and time are produced but the production of the apparent difference between space (or time) and its representation. Modern social and political practice realizes a distinction between what might now be called not only "abstract empty time" but also "abstract empty space" and its meaning. This distinction makes space and time appear for the first time as inert, contentless scales or dimensions. As mere scales or frames, they can then be made to compress, expand, or speed up, and to carry different meanings.

Modernity, we have said, seems to form a distinctive time-space, appearing in the homogenous shape of the West and characterized by an immediacy of presence that we recognize as the "now" of history. This time and space are the products of an endlessly replicating system of representation. Modernity's present is not that immediate experience of the real imagined by phenomenology but a present displaced and replayed through the time lag of representation.[82] Its location is not the plenitude of immediate surroundings but the homogenous, empty coordinates produced in the modern diagramming and programming of space. Capitalist modernity reproduces social worlds whose characteristic historical immediacy and spatial extension are generated only through their proliferating forms of representation, that is, through forms of replay, replication, and staging.

What conclusions can we draw from this for thinking about the place in modernity of the non-West? If modernity is not so much a stage of history but rather its staging, then it is a world particularly vulnerable to a certain kind of disruption or displacement. No representation can ever match its original, especially when the original exists only as something promised by a multiplicity of imitations and repetitions. Every act of staging or representation is open to the possibility of misrepresentation, or at least of parody or misreading. An image or simulation functions by its subtle difference from what it claims to simulate or portray, even if the difference is no more than the time lag between repetitions. Every performance of the modern is the producing of this difference, and each such difference represents the possibility of some shift, displacement, or contamination.

Once one places at the center of an understanding of modernity the process of representation and insists upon the importance of displacement, deferral, and delay in the production of the modern, the non-West emerges as a place that makes possible the distance, the difference, and the time lag required for these forms of displacement. In Bhabha's analysis, the non-West is not a place that is entirely outside the West, not a site of pure difference. The difference between West and non-West must be constantly produced, through a process of disavowal, "where the trace of what is disavowed is not repressed but repeated as something *different*—a mutation, a hybrid." The hybrid forms of colonial modernity return to disrupt the West's claim to originality and authority, disturbing it with "the ruse of recognition."[83]

Modernity must be staged as that which is singular, original, present, and authoritative. This staging does not occur only in the West, as we saw, to be imitated later in the non-West. Its authority and presence can be produced only across the space of geographical and historical difference. It is this very displacement of the West that enables modernity to be staged as "the West." If colonial modernities often prefigure the emergence of modern forms and programs in the West, as I suggested at the start of this chapter, their significance is not in enabling us to revise the narrative of the West and to provide an alternative history of origins and influences. Nor should a more global view of the modern encourage us to talk simply of alternative modernities, in which a (fundamentally singular) modernity is modified by local circumstances into a variety of cultural forms. As with the discussion of different paths of capitalist development, the pluralist language of alternative modernities always presupposes an underlying unity in reference to which such variations can be discussed. Rather, the significance of allowing the non-West to disrupt the history of the West is to show that the West has no simple origin, despite its claims to uniqueness, and its histories cannot adequately be gathered into the form of a singular narrative. It is not that there are many different modernities, any more than there are many different capitalisms. Modernity, like capitalism, is defined by its claim to universality, to a uniqueness, unity, and universality that represent the end (in every sense) of history. Yet this always remains an impossible unity, an incomplete universal. Each staging of the modern must be arranged to produce the unified, global history of modernity, yet each requires those forms of difference that introduce the possibility of a discrepancy, that return to undermine its unity and identity. Modernity then becomes the unsuitable yet unavoidable name for all these discrepant histories.

The Double Difference

The limits to this process of displacement and rearticulation are likely to be as varied as the political and discursive contexts in which the modern is produced. To conclude, however, I want to argue that the staging of modernity is characterized by another kind of limit, one that is not related to specific discourses but to a more general way, within the worlds of modernity, in which systems of meaning are produced. Oppositional discourse must intervene in a field already shaped by the highly mobile powers of government that mark out the terrain of modern politics. But this is also a terrain shaped, as I have suggested, by the distinctly modern techniques of representation. These techniques define not only the ground over which modern politics will be fought but also the nature of its objects.

We can take the example of colonial medical practice, which Gyan Prakash discusses in his essay (see chapter 8), to examine what this means. Colonial power defines the body as an object of hygienic regulation and medical intervention, Prakash argues, a body that is marked by its difference from indigenous discursive treatments of the person. But one could add that this process also creates what appears as a second form of difference: the new difference between "the body itself" and its meanings. Modern medical practice creates a network of significations in terms of which the body can be diagnosed, monitored, and administered. Other forms of biopower produce further representations of the body. Schooling, public health, economic planning, industry, and the labor market each develop their systems of measurement and evaluation, all seeming to refer to the same object. This proliferation of representations produces numerous different images of the body but also produces something further: the apparent distinction between the body and its image. The very multiplication of significations generated by modern governmental power, each presented as a mere representation of the same physical body, appears to establish the object quality of the body. This is a modern effect, presenting the body as an inert, material object, not possessed of any inherent force or significance. The difference between the body and its meanings will be increasingly accepted as the fundamental difference, and political debate will begin to occur only between alternative representations of the body. The debate will come to accept the underlying assumption of capitalist modernity—that social reality is to be ordered according to the principle of representation.

The production of modernity involves the staging of differences. But there are two registers of difference, one providing the modern with its characteristic indeterminacy and ambivalence and the other with its enormous power of replication. The modern occurs only by performing the distinction between the modern and the non-modern, the West and the non-West, each performance opening the possibility of what is figured as non-modern contaminating the modern, displacing it, or disrupting its authority. But the performance of modernity also stages the difference between what is staged and what is real, between representation and reality. The effect of this staging is to generate a new world of multiple significations and simulations. But its more profound effect is to generate another realm that appears to precede and stand unaffected by these proliferating signs: reality itself—what now appears as a material order that preexists the constitution of the social, an order that is only reflected by the processes of signification, never shaped by them.

This effect of the real will appear, as we have suggested, in the difference between the "physical" body and the meanings through which biopower organizes its management. It is in this sense that biopower does not simply provide new significations for the body but produces the body. In the staging of modernity, however, the real will be produced in countless other ways as well. What will appear especially real is the modern production of the social as a *spatial* object. Just as medical practice produces the modern difference between the body as physical object and its meanings, other social practices of modernity establish what appears as the difference between physical space and its representation. The closed, imaginary space of the modern nation-state is produced through forms of mapping, boundary making, border control, and the management of cultural forms and economic flows that create what Thongchai Winichakul calls the "geo-body" of the nation.[84] Like the medical body, the geo-body appears as a physical object that preexists its social constitution, rather than as the effect of a process of difference. This process is also at work in the cadastral surveys and legal arrangements that produce the modern institution of landed property, understood not as a network of social relations among multiple claimants to the land's productivity but as an individual right over a physical object.[85]

This brings us back to the theme with which we began: the spatialization of modernity. Even in some of the most critical studies of modernity, the geography of the modern is not in question. Modernity is staged as the West, and each account of the modern and the postmodern reenacts this staging. We have argued that this is only a particular representation, produced out of an imperial past and present, eliding the role of the non-West in the production of the West and ignoring the constant displacements involved in staging the difference between the two. But we have concluded by suggesting a further problem with this spatialization of the modern and a reason for its persistence. Modernity presents not only a particular version of the production of space, a particular image of the spatial order. The modern is produced as the difference between space and its representation. It is not a particular representation of space that characterizes the production of the modern but the organization of reality as a space of representation. The questioning of modernity must explore two forms of difference, both the displacements opened up by the different space of the non-West, and the ways in which this space is made to appear different. Modernity is the name we give the stage where this double difference is performed.

Notes

1. Karl Marx, *Capital: A Critique of Political Economy*, 3 vols. (New York: International Publishers, 1967), 1:703.

2. Samir Amin, *L'Accumulation à l'échelle mondiale* (Paris: Anthropos, 1970), Eng. trans. *Accumulation on a World Scale*, 2 vols. (New York: Monthly Review Press, 1974). The book was first written as a doctoral thesis in economics in Paris in 1957 under the title "On the Origins of Underdevelopment: Capitalist Accumulation on a World Scale." For its history, see Samir Amin, *Re-Reading the Postwar Period: An Intellectual Itinerary*, trans. Michael Wolfers (New York: Monthly Review Press, 1994), chs. 2 and 3.

3. Immanuel Wallerstein, *Unthinking Social Science: The Limits of Nineteenth-Century Paradigms* (Cambridge, Eng.: Polity Press, 1991), 75. For another important recent study of the rise of the European world economy, see Giovanni Arrighi, *The Long Twentieth Century: Money, Power, and the Origins of Our Times* (New York: Verso, 1994).

4. Janet Abu-Lughod, *Before European Hegemony: The World System, A.D. 1250–1350* (New York: Oxford University Press, 1989); Andre Gunder Frank, *ReOrient: Global Economy in the Asian Age* (Berkeley: University of California Press, 1998). Another notable critique of Eurocentric world history is Peter Gran, *Beyond Eurocentrism: A New View of Modern World History* (Syracuse: Syracuse University Press, 1996).

5. Sidney Mintz, *Sweetness and Power: The Place of Sugar in Modern History* (New York: Viking Penguin, 1985), 46–52, 55–61. The quotation is from p. 48.

6. Gabriel Debien, *Les engagés pour les Antille, 1634–1715* (Paris: Société de l'histoire des colonies françaises, 1952), 257, quoted in Robin Blackburn, *The Making*

of New World Slavery: From the Baroque to the Modern, 1492–1800 (London: Verso, 1997), 333.

7. Arthur L. Stinchcombe, *Sugar Island Slavery in the Age of Enlightenment: The Political Economy of the Caribbean World* (Princeton: Princeton University Press, 1995), 57–58.

8. Paul Gilroy, *The Black Atlantic: Modernity and Double Consciousness* (Cambridge: Harvard University Press, 1993), 17.

9. Michel Foucault, *Discipline and Punish: The Birth of the Prison* (New York: Pantheon Books, 1977); Ann Laura Stoler, *Race and the Education of Desire: Foucault's History of Sexuality and the Colonial Order of Things* (Durham: Duke University Press, 1995). The colonial origins of European modernity are also explored in Paul Rabinow, *French Modern: Norms and Forms of the Social Environment* (Cambridge: MIT Press, 1989).

10. Timothy Mitchell, *Colonising Egypt,* 2nd ed. (Berkeley: University of California Press, 1991), 185. On Samuel Bentham, see Matthew S. Anderson, "Samuel Bentham in Russia," *American Slavic and East European Review,* 15 (1956): 157–72. On monitorial schooling in Calcutta, see Henry Binns, *A Century of Education, Being the Centenary History of the British and Foreign Schools Society* (London: J. M. Dent, 1908), 110–11.

11. Partha Chatterjee, "Two Poets and Death: On Civil and Political Society in the Non-Christian World," this volume, ch. 2. On the colonial invention of culture see Mitchell, *Colonising Egypt,* 61–2, 101, 104–5, and Nicholas B. Dirks, ed., *Colonialism and Culture* (Ann Arbor: University of Michigan Press, 1992), 3–4.

12. Uday Singh Mehta, *Liberalism and Empire: A Study in Nineteenth-Century Liberal Thought* (Chicago: University of Chicago Press, 1999).

13. Gauri Viswanathan, "Currying Favor: The Beginnings of English Literary Study in British India," *Social Text* 7, nos. 1–2 (Fall 1988): 85–104, reprinted in *Dangerous Liaisons: Gender, Nation, and Postcolonial Perspectives,* ed. Anne McClintock, Aamir Mufti, and Ella Shohat (Minneapolis: University of Minnesota Press, 1997), 113–29. The beginnings of English literature have also been traced in another imperial context—the English subjugation of Scotland in the eighteenth century. See Robert Crawford, *Devolving English Literature* (New York: Oxford University Press, 1992), and Robert Crawford, ed., *The Scottish Invention of English Literature* (Cambridge: Cambridge University Press, 1998).

14. Gyan Prakash, "Body Politic in Colonial India," this volume, ch. 8. See also the major study by David Arnold, *Colonizing the Body: State Medicine and Epidemic Disease in Nineteenth-Century India* (Berkeley: University of California Press 1993); Megan Vaughn, *Curing Their Ills: Colonial Power and African Illness* (Stanford: Stanford University Press, 1991); and the essays collected in *Warm Climates and Western Medicine: The Emergence of Tropical Medicine, 1500–1900,* ed. David Arnold (Amsterdam: Rodopi Press, 1996).

15. Edward Said, *Orientalism* (New York: Pantheon, 1978); see also his *Culture and Imperialism* (New York: Knopf, 1993).

16. Ann Laura Stoler, "Rethinking Colonial Categories: European Communities and the Boundaries of Rule," *Comparative Studies in Society and History* 13, no. 1 (1989): 134–61, reprinted in Dirks, ed., *Colonialism and Culture,* 319–52; idem, "Sexual Affronts and Racial Frontiers: European Identities and the Cultural Politics of Exclusion in Colonial Southeast Asia," in *Tensions of Empire: Colonial Cultures in a Bourgeois World,* ed. Frederick Cooper and Ann Laura Stoler (Berkeley: University of California Press, 1997), 198–237; and idem, *Race and the Education of Desire,* 44–45, 102–23.

17. Benedict Anderson, *Imagined Communities: Reflections on the Origin and Spread of Nationalism,* 2nd ed. (New York: Verso, 1991), 47–65. See also Claudio Lomnitz-Adler's study of the emergence of modern Mexican identity in *Exits from the Labyrinth: Culture and Ideology in the Mexican National Space* (Berkeley: University of California Press, 1992).

18. Karl Marx, *Address and Provisional Rules of the Working Men's International Association* (London, 1864), reprinted in Karl Marx, *The First International and After: Political Writings,* vol. 3, ed. with an introduction by David Fernbach (New York: Vintage, 1974), 73–84; see also Fernbach's introduction, 10–12. The inaugural meeting of the International Association was held in London on September 28, 1864. The coining of the term "international" is attributed to Jeremy Bentham, in his colonial projects for a system of "international law" (*Oxford English Dictionary,* s.v. "international").

19. See *Oxford English Dictionary,* s.v. "Nationalism," and *Oxford English Dictionary, Additions Series* (1993), s.v. "nationalist." The term *nationalisme* did not appear in French until around the same period. See Eric Hobsbawm, *Nations and Nationalism since 1780: Programme, Myth, Reality,* 2nd ed. (Cambridge: Cambridge University Press, 1992), 121.

20. Perry Anderson, *The Origins of Postmodernity* (New York: Verso, 1998), 3, which is the source of the comment on the term *liberalism.*

21. Jean-François Lyotard, *The Postmodern Condition: A Report on Knowledge,* trans. Geoff Bennington and Brian Massumi (Minneapolis: University of Minnesota Press, 1984).

22. Jean Baudrillard, "The End of Production" and "The Order of Simulacra," in *Symbolic Exchange and Death* (Thousand Oaks, Calif.: Sage, 1993), 6–49, 50–86.

23. David Harvey, *The Condition of Postmodernity: An Enquiry into the Origins of Cultural Change* (Cambridge, Mass.: Basil Blackwell, 1989); Fredric Jameson, *Postmodernism, or the Cultural Logic of Late Capitalism* (Durham: Duke University Press, 1991).

24. Jameson, *Postmodernism,* 36.

25. Fredric Jameson, "Secondary Elaborations," in *Postmodernism or the Cultural Logic of Late Capitalism* (Durham: Duke University Press, 1991), 297–418. In this essay Jameson repeats his argument that postmodernism is "a situation in which the survival, the residue, the holdover, the archaic, has finally been swept away without a trace. . . . Everything has reached the same hour on the great clock of development or rationalization," but then adds "(at least from the perspective of the 'West')." For an exploration of this note of uncertainty, see Santiago Colás, "The Third World in Jameson's *Postmodernism, or the Cultural Logic of Late Capitalism,*" *Social Text* 31/32 (1992): 258–70.

26. Stoler, *Race and the Education of Desire.* There is an equally remarkable neglect of colonial developments in Foucault's archaeology of modern medical practice, *The Birth of the Clinic* (New York: Vintage Books, 1994).

27. Gayatri Spivak, "Can the Subaltern Speak?" in *Marxism and the Interpretation of Culture,* ed. C. Nelson and L. Grossberg (Basingstoke: Macmillan Education, 1988), 271–313; reprinted in *Colonial Discourse and Post-Colonial Theory,* ed. Patrick Williams and Laura Chrisman (New York: Columbia University Press, 1994), 66–111. "Foucault is a brilliant thinker of power-in-spacing," Spivak writes, "but the awareness of the topographical reinscription of imperialism does not inform his presuppositions. He is taken in by the restricted version of the West produced by that reinscription and thus helps to consolidate its effects. . . . [T]o buy a self-contained version of the West is to ignore its production by the imperialist project" (85, 86).

28. Anderson, *Origins of Postmodernity,* 3. Conservative social theorists used the term "modernism" as a term of disapproval in the 1960s and 1970s, much as they would use the term "postmodernism" in the 1980s and 1990s. See, for example, Daniel Bell, *Cultural Contradictions of Capitalism* (New York: Basic Books, 1976). Marshall Berman recalls how certain Columbia University faculty described the 1968 student protest as "modernism in the streets" (*All That Is Solid Melts into Air: The Experience of Modernity* [New York: Simon and Schuster, 1982], 31).

29. Anderson, *Origins of Postmodernity,* 3–4.

30. Ibid., 17, citing Ihab Habib Hassan, *Out of Egypt: Scenes and Arguments of an Autobiography* (Carbondale, Ill.: Southern Illinois University Press, 1986), 46–48.

31. Anouar Abdel-Malek and Albert Memmi wrote early critiques of Eurocentrism and Orientalism. See Anouar Abdel-Malek, "Orientalism in Crisis," *Diogenes* 44 (1959–63), 103–40, and Albert Memmi, *The Colonizer and the Colonized* (rpr. Boston: Beacon Press, 1991). The novelist and essayist Juan Goytisolo, one of the most important critics of Spanish modernity, was drawn to North Africa after working on behalf of Algerian independence in Paris and later made his home Marrakech; see Randolph Pope, *Understanding Juan Goytisolo* (Columbia: University of South Carolina Press, 1995). For a discussion of these forms of cultural displacement, see Aamir Mufti, "Auerbach in Istanbul: Edward Said, Social Criticism, and the Question of Minority Cultures," *Critical Inquiry* 25 (Autumn 1998): 95–125.

32. These issues are examined in the important essay by Gyan Prakash, "Writing Post-Orientalist Histories of the Third World: Perspectives from Indian Historiography," *Comparative Studies in Society and History* 32, no. 2 (April 1990): 383–408, revised and reprinted in Dirks, ed., *Colonialism and Culture,* 352–88.

33. Arjun Appadurai, "Disjuncture and Difference in the Global Cultural Economy," in *Public Culture* 2, no. 2 (1991): 1–24, reprinted in *Modernity at Large: Cultural Dimensions of Globalization* (Minneapolis: University of Minnesota Press, 1996), 32. For a related view about the absence of clear spatial geographies and the consequent predicament of fluid, fractured cultures see James Clifford, *The Predicament of Culture* (Cambridge: Harvard University Press, 1988).

34. Ann Stoler and Fred Cooper also caution against the tendency to homogenize the diverse experiences of colonialism and to overlook its tensions, limitations, and contingencies, in an excellent review of recent writing on colonialism and empire: "Between Metropole and Colony: Rethinking a Research Agenda," in Cooper and Stoler, eds., *Tensions of Empire,* 1–56.

35. The Eurocentrism embedded in the idea that Europe is a "continent," while the larger and more culturally diverse area of South Asia is only a "subcontinent" (and China a mere "country"), was brilliantly explored more than a generation ago by Marshall Hodgson; see Marshall G. S. Hodgson, *The Venture of Islam: Conscience and History in a World Civilization,* 3 vols. (Chicago: University of Chicago Press, 1974), and "The Interrelations of Societies in History," in *Rethinking World History: Essays on Europe, Islam, and World History,* ed. Edmund Burke III (Cambridge: Cambridge University Press, 1993), 3–28. For a more recent discussion, see Martin W. Lewis and Kären E. Wigen, *The Myth of Continents: A Critique of Metageography* (Berkeley: University of California Press, 1997), and Frank, *ReOrient,* 2.

36. Mintz, *Sweetness and Power,* 55.

37. The classic twentieth-century statement of the economic significance of Atlantic slavery to the development of industrial capitalism in Britain is Eric Williams, *Capitalism and Slavery* (Chapel Hill: University of North Carolina Press, 1944). Revisionist works of the 1970s and 1980s disputed the argument that colonies and colonial trade

made a decisive contribution to Britain's industrialization, especially Paul Bairoch, "Commerce international et genèse de la révolution industrielle anglaise," *Annales* 28 (1973): 541–71, and Robert Brenner, "The Origins of Capitalism," *New Left Review* 104 (July-August 1977): 25–93. For a review of these debates, see Seymour Drescher, "Eric Williams: British Capitalism and British Slavery," *History and Theory* 26 (1987), 180–96. Robin Blackburn has recently refuted the revisionists, arguing that slave production in the Caribbean "decisively advanced" the process of capitalist industrialization in Britain (*The Making of New World Slavery,* 509–80, quotation from p. 572). See also Stinchcombe, *Sugar Island Slavery.* On earlier attempts to explain the theoretical place of slave economies in the development of capitalism, see J. Banaji, "Modes of Production in a Materialist Conception of History," *Capital and Class* 7 (1979):1–44. On the larger problem of Eurocentrism in economic history, see J. M. Blaut, *The Colonizer's Model of the World: Geographical Diffusionism and Eurocentric History* (New York: Guilford Press, 1993), and Frank, *ReOrient,* 258–320.

38. Mintz, *Sweetness and Power,* 59–61; emphasis in original.

39. Karl Marx, *A Contribution to the Critique of Political Economy* (New York: International Publishers, 1970), 20–21.

40. Marx, *Capital,* 1:669–70.

41. The presenting of contemporary differences as the simultaneous existence of different stages of a single history was elaborated in twentieth-century Marxism in formulations such as Trotsky's "combined and uneven development" and Ernst Bloch's "simultaneity of the non-synchronous." For the latter, see his "Nonsynchronism and Dialectics," *New German Critique* 11 (Spring 1977): 22–38.

42. Marx, *Capital,* 1:667.

43. The initial discussion of the original accumulation of capital (ch. 27), on the beginnings of agrarian capital in the clearing of the agricultural population from the land, continues at first to focus on England. But here too the real significance of these developments can only be found in colonial developments—the colonization of Ireland and, especially, Scotland. What the removal of the population "really and properly signifies, we learn only in the promised land of modern romance, the highlands of Scotland. There the process is distinguished by its systematic character . . . [and] by the magnitude of the scale on which it is carried out at one blow" (ibid., 1:681).

44. Ibid., 1:703.

45. Ibid., 1:676.

46. Ibid., 1:703. On "the state power," see also Karl Marx, "The Civil War in France: Address of the General Council," in *The First International and After,* vol. 3 of *Political Writings,* ed. with an introduction by David Fernbach (New York: Vintage, 1974), 187–268, at 208–9.

47. Marx, *Capital,* 1:712, 705, 706.

48. Ibid., 1:703.

49. Ernesto Laclau, "New Reflections on the Revolution of Our Time," in *New Reflections on the Revolution of Our Time* (New York: Verso, 1990), 3–85. For particular developments of Laclau's argument about capitalism, see J. K. Gibson-Graham, "Identity and Economic Plurality: Rethinking Capitalism and 'Capitalist Hegemony,'" *Environment and Planning D: Society and Space* 13 (1995): 275–82, and Timothy Mitchell, "The Market's Place," in *Directions of Change in Rural Egypt,* ed. Nicholas S. Hopkins and Kirsten Westergaard (Cairo: American University in Cairo Press, 1998), 19–40. Major contributions to the question of writing post-Marxist history include Gayatri Chakravorty Spivak, "Subaltern Studies: Deconstructing Historiography," in *Selected Subaltern Studies,* ed. Ranajit Guha and Gayatri Chakravorty Spivak (New

York : Oxford University Press, 1988), 3–32; Gyan Prakash, "Writing Post-Orientalist Histories of the Third World," *Comparative Studies in Society and History* 32, no. 2 (April 1990): 383–408, and "Can the 'Subaltern' Ride? A Reply to O'Hanlon and Washbrook," *Comparative Studies in Society and History* 34, no. 1 (January 1992): 168–84; and Dipesh Chakrabarty, "Marx after Marxism: History, Subalternity and Difference," *Meanjin* 52 (1993): 421–34.

50. These criticisms are made by Arif Dirlik, "The Postcolonial Aura: Third World Criticism in the Age of Global Capitalism," in *Dangerous Liaisons: Gender, Nation, and Postcolonial Perspectives,* ed. Anne McClintock, Aamir Mufti, and Ella Shohat (Minneapolis: University of Minnesota Press, 1997), 501–28, at 515; and Rosalind O'Hanlon and David Washbrook, "After Orientalism: Culture, Criticism, and Politics in the Third World," *Comparative Studies in Society and History* 34, no. 1 (January 1992): 141–67, at 147.

51. Jacques Derrida, "Structure, Sign and Play in the Discourse of the Human Sciences," in *Writing and Difference,* trans. Alan Bass (Chicago: University of Chicago Press, 1978), 278–93, see especially 282.

52. Prakash, "Writing Post-Orientalist Histories of the Third World," and "Can the 'Subaltern' Ride?"

53. See Laclau, "New Reflections on the Revolution of Our Time."

54. Stoler, *Race and the Education of Desire.*

55. Michel-Rolph Trouillot, *Silencing the Past: Power and the Production of History* (Boston: Beacon Press, 1995), 77–78, citing, among others, Gordon Lewis, *Main Currents in Caribbean Thought: The Historical Evolution of Caribbean Society in Its Ideological Aspects, 1492–1900* (Baltimore: The Johns Hopkins University Press, 1983), and Pierre Boulle, "In Defense of Slavery: Eighteenth-Century Opposition to Abolition and the Origins of Racist Ideology in France," in *History from Below: Studies in Popular Protest and Popular Ideology,* ed. Frederick Krantz (London: Basil Blackwell, 1988), 219–46.

56. Homi Bhabha, "The Postcolonial and the Postmodern: The Question of Agency," in *The Location of Culture* (New York: Routledge, 1994), 194–96.

57. Walter Benjamin, *Illuminations,* ed. Hannah Arendt, trans. Harry Zohn (New York: Schocken Books, 1969), 263.

58. Anderson, *Imagined Communities,* 22–36.

59. Henri Bergson, *Time and Free Will: An Essay on the Immediate Data of Consciousness,* trans. F. L. Pogson (London: George Allen and Unwin, 1910), a translation of *Essai sur la données immediates de la conscience* (Paris: 1889), 95. On the Kantian conception of space and time, see Immanuel Kant, *Critique of Pure Reason,* ed. and trans. Paul Guyer and Allen Wood (Cambridge: Cambridge University Press, 1997), 157–67.

60. Bergson, *Time and Free Will,* 237.

61. Ibid., 110, 99.

62. For an examination of social practices that give rise to the new apprehension of time as a pure medium of consciousness, see Mitchell, *Colonising Egypt,* 73, 120.

63. Veena Das, "The Making of Modernity: Gender and Time in Indian Cinema," this volume, ch. 7.

64. Bhabha, *The Location of Culture,* 246.

65. Ibid., 244.

66. Fredric Jameson, "The Cultural Logic of Late Capitalism," in *Postmodernism, or the Cultural Logic of Late Capitalism* (Durham: Duke University Press, 1991).

67. Baudrillard, "The Order of Simulacra."

68. Arjun Appadurai, "Here and Now," in *Modernity at Large: Cultural Dimensions of Globalization* (Minneapolis: University of Minnesota Press, 1996), 1–23, at 5.

69. Mitchell, *Colonising Egypt*.

70. See Mitchell, *Colonising Egypt,* ch. 1, for a further development of this argument, which draws, inter alia, on the work of Martin Heidegger, especially "The Age of the World Picture," in *The Question Concerning Technology and Other Essays* (New York: Harper and Row, 1977), and also the work of Jacques Derrida, beginning with *Speech and Phenomena* (Evanston, Ill.: Northwestern University Press, 1973).

71. Anderson, *Imagined Communities,* 184. His argument here draws on Benjamin's argument in "The Work of Art in the Age of Mechanical Reproduction," in *Illuminations,* 217–51.

72. Benedict Anderson, "Nationalism, Identity, and the World-in-Motion: On the Logics of Seriality," in *Cosmopolitics: Thinking and Feeling beyond the Nation,* ed. Pheng Cheah and Bruce Robbins (Minneapolis: University of Minnesota Press, 1998), 127.

73. See Timothy Mitchell, "Fixing the Economy," *Cultural Studies* 12 (1998): 82–101.

74. Dipesh Chakrabarty, "Witness to Suffering: Domestic Cruelty and the Birth of the Modern Subject in Bengal," this volume, ch. 3.

75. Lila Abu-Lughod, "Modern Subjects: Egyptian Melodrama and Postcolonial Difference," this volume, ch. 4, citing Raymond Williams, "Drama in a Dramatised Society," in *Raymond Williams and Television,* ed. A. O'Connor (London: Routledge, 1989), 3–13.

76. Marx, *Capital,* 1:76.

77. Ibid., 1:77.

78. Jacques Derrida, *Specters of Marx: The State of the Debt, the Work of Mourning, and the New International* (New York: Routledge, 1994), 160. Derrida's writing aims to show how the possibility of exchange, of value, and of meaning itself is always already present in the occurrence of any object and is therefore part of the condition of possibility of the appearance of an object world. However, he limits his dismantling of this metaphysics of presence largely to the writing of literature and philosophy, seldom examining the larger texts of the social world. He therefore offers no investigation of ways in which the reorganizing of the social world as a system of representation in the projects of colonial modernity has extended and reinforced but perhaps also made more vulnerable the Western metaphysics of presence. For an exploration of these questions, see Mitchell, *Colonising Egypt,* chs. 1, 5, and 6. On Derrida and Marx, see the insightful analysis of Gayatri Chakravorty Spivak, "Limits and Openings in Marx and Derrida," in *Outside in the Teaching Machine* (New York: Routledge, 1993), 97–119.

79. This argument about representation has been so frequently misunderstood that it is worth repeating here that I am not making some "postmodernist" claim that the real world does not exist. Such a simple dogma would leave the metaphysics of terms like "real" and "exist" unexamined. My argument is that in the modern world the real is increasingly rendered up to experience through binary strategies of representation, in which reality is grasped in terms of a simple and absolute distinction between the real and its image. Yet a rigorous ethnography of these strategies shows that the image is never just an image but is infiltrated and undermined by elements that belong to what is called the real world. And conversely, that what we call the real never stands alone but occurs in relationship to and is continually compromised by the possibility of representation. The problem of modernity is not so much, in Latour's terms, that "we have never been modern" (because, as he argues, the distinction between real and representation that defines the experience of modernity was never successfully established). The problem is to understand, given this failure, what forms of social arrangement have

persuaded us to believe in such a simple metaphysics. It is this arrangement and metaphysic that I refer to here as representation and elsewhere have called "enframing" (see Bruno Latour, *We Have Never Been Modern*, trans. Catherine Porter [Cambridge: Harvard University Press, 1993], and Mitchell, *Colonising Egypt*).

80. The argument is frequently made that post-structuralist analyses of the cultural aspects of modernity cannot be extended to the "more concrete" political forms of modern society, because of a fundamental difference between texts and institutions. Peter Dews, for example, argues that "institutions are not simply textual or discursive structures" but form a "non-textual reality . . . traversed by relations of force" (*Logics of Disintegration: Post-Structuralist Thought and the Claims of Critical Theory* [London: Verso, 1987], 35). I would argue that any adequate understanding of capital, the state, or any of the other "more concrete" institutional forms of modern politics must address the techniques of difference that make possible the very appearance of what we call institutions. For a development of this argument in relation to the modern state, see Timothy Mitchell, "The Limits of the State," *American Political Science Review* 85 (1991): 77–96; see also Ernesto Laclau and Chantal Mouffe, "Beyond the Positivity of the Social," in *Hegemony and Socialist Strategy* (London: Verso, 1985), 93–148.

81. Henri Lefebvre, *The Production of Space* (Cambridge, Mass.: Blackwell, 1991); David Harvey, *The Condition of Postmodernity*, 201–323.

82. Cf. Derrida, *Speech and Phenomena*.

83. Bhabha, "Signs Taken For Wonders," in *The Location of Culture*, 111, 115.

84. Thongchai Winichakul, *Siam Mapped: A History of the Geo-Body of the Nation* (Honolulu: University of Hawaii Press, 1994).

85. See Timothy P. Mitchell, "Making Space for the Nation State," in *Colonialism, Postcolonialism, and the Production of Space*, ed. Derek Gregory and Daniel Clayton (New York: Routledge, forthcoming).

Two

Two Poets and Death:
On Civil and Political Society
in the Non-Christian World

Partha Chatterjee

Bankimchandra Chattopadhyay, the most renowned modernist literary figure in nineteenth-century Bengal, died on April 8, 1894. Three weeks after his death, a memorial meeting organized by the Chaitanya Library and the Beadon Square Literary Club was held at Star Theatre.[1] It was decided that the speakers would be Rajanikanta Gupta, the historian; Haraprasad Sastri, the famous scholar of Buddhism and early Bengali literature; and Rabindranath Tagore, then a young but already much acclaimed poet. Nabinchandra Sen, one of the most respected senior figures on Bengal's literary scene and a younger contemporary of Bankim in the civil service, was asked to preside. To the surprise of the organizers, Nabinchandra refused. In his place, Gurudas Banerjee, judge of the Calcutta High Court, presided over the meeting. The address on Bankim delivered by Rabindranath that day went on to become something of a landmark essay in Bengali literary criticism. Memorized by generations of schoolchildren, it has been for more than a century a staple of the formation and transmission of aesthetic canons in Bengal's new high culture.

What will concern us here is not the assessment of Bankim's literary output or of his historical role, on which much has been written.[2] Instead, our concern will be the reasons for Nabinchandra Sen's refusal to come to Bankim's memorial meeting. The poet Nabinchandra was known to have been close to Bankim, and although he did not often share what he thought were the latter's excessively Westernized literary tastes, he clearly deferred to his superior erudition, intellect, and public standing. The reasons for Nabinchandra's refusal had nothing to do with Bankim. Nabinchandra objected to the very idea of a public condolence meeting.

"Imitating the English, we have now begun organizing 'condolence meetings,'" Nabinchandra wrote. "As a Hindu, I do not understand how one can call a public meeting to express one's grief. A meeting to express grief, think of it!" "How many buckets have you arranged for the public's tears?" he is said to have remarked to one of the organizers. "Our" grief, he claimed, was "sacred"; it drove one into seclusion. "We do not mourn by wearing black badges round our sleeves." A meeting in a public auditorium could only create, he thought, the atmosphere of a public entertainment; this was not "our way of mourning for the dead."[3]

Soon after the memorial meeting, Rabindranath Tagore wrote an essay published in the journal *Sādhanā*.[4] "The Condolence Meeting" began by mentioning the objection that had been raised to the public condolence of Bankim's death. It was true, he said, that the practice was hitherto unknown in the country and that it was an imitation of European customs. But, like it or not, because of our European contacts, both external conditions and subjective feelings were undergoing a change. New social needs were arising, and new ways would have to be found to fulfill them. Because of their unfamiliarity, these might seem artificial and unpleasant at first. But merely because they were European in origin was not a good reason for rejecting them outright.

The main point of objection to the idea of a public condolence meeting seems to have been its *kṛtrimatā*, artificiality. That which is *kṛtrim* is a product of human action: it is an artifice—fabricated, unnatural. Sometimes it indicated a "mere" form, empty within; sometimes it could even describe behavior that is insincere, false. This is what Nabinchandra would have meant when he referred to the showing of grief by wearing a black armband. The *kṛtrim* form of a public meeting was inappropriate, he must have said, for expressing an emotion as intense and intimate as grief at the death of a loved one.

In his essay, Rabindranath straightaway took up the question of artificial social forms. A certain *kṛtrimatā* was unavoidable if social norms were to be followed, he said. Surely, not everything could be left to individual taste and feeling. Artificiality could be said to be a defect in matters that were strictly internal to the self, where individual feelings reigned supreme. But society being a complex entity, it was not always easy to determine the boundary between the domain of the individual and that of society. In matters pertaining to society, certain universally recognized rules had to be followed if social relations were not to degenerate into anarchy. For example, Rabindranath pointed out, grief at the death of one's father, or—another example—the feelings of a devotee toward god, could be said to involve some of the most intimate and intense emotions in human life. And yet society claims to lay down the procedures of funerary and other associated rites to be followed on the occasion of a father's death, or, in the other case, the procedures of worship to be followed by all devotees, irrespective of individual preference or taste. This is so because society deems it necessary to regulate and order these aspects of life in a way that is beneficial for all of society.

Having made this general point about the necessary "artificiality" of all social regulations, Rabindranath then goes on to argue that Indian society was for long largely a "domestic society" or a "society of households" *(gārhasthyapradhān samāj)*, a society in which the strongest social bonds rested on the authority of parents and other elders within the family. The specific forms of social regulation in India reflect this domestic character of traditional society. But this was now changing.

> Recently there have been some changes in this society of households. A new flood has swept into its domain. Its name is the public.
> It is a new thing with a new name. It is impossible to translate it into Bengali. The word "public" and its opposite "private" have now come into use in Bengali. . . .
> Now that our society consists not only of households but also of an emergent public, the growth of new public responsibilities have become inevitable.[5]

One such new public responsibility was the public mourning of the death of those who had devoted their lives not just to the good of their own households but to the good of the public. The form of mourning was "artificial" as before, but it was now a form in which not just the members of the household but members of the public were required to participate.

What is interesting about this part of Rabindranath's argument is the explicit identification of a new domain of social activity involving "the public" and of new social regulations ordering these public practices. But he then goes on to make some observations about this emergent public domain that are still more interesting.

> I do not deny the fact that the public in our country is not appropriately grief-stricken by the death of great men. Our public is still young; its behaviour bears the mark of adolescence. It does not recognize its benefactors, does not realize the true value of the benefits it receives, easily forgets its friends and thinks it will only receive what is given to it but will not incur any obligations in return.
>
> I say such a public needs to be educated, and discussions in public meetings are a principal means of such education.[6]

What we have here is a public that is not *yet* a proper public and a group of social leaders who think of their role as one of guiding this public to maturity. Rabindranath, as we can now recognize easily, is only restating here the fundamental problematic of the nationalist project of modernity under colonial conditions. The driving force of colonial modernity is a pedagogical mission.

What a "proper" public must look like is also, needless to say, given by world history. Rabindranath has no doubt about this. The examples that come to his mind in the context of Bankim's death are from the literary world of Europe and the relationship there between eminent literary figures and the public.

> We do not have a literary society in our country and in society itself there is no cultivation of literature. Social practices in Europe make it possible for eminent persons to appear on numerous occasions at numerous public meetings. Their circle of acquaintances is not restricted to their family and friends; they are at all times present before the public. To their compatriots, they are close at hand and visible. Which is why at their death, a shadow of grief falls over the whole country.[7]

By contrast, great men in India, despite their greatness, are not similarly visible in public. "Especially since women have no place in our outer society, our social life itself is seriously incomplete." The kind of intimate knowledge of a great person's life, habits, and thoughts that can evoke love and gratitude among ordinary people is completely lacking in our society. Instead of loving and respecting our great men, we turn them into gods to be worshipped from afar. The condolence meeting, argued Rabindranath, was precisely the occasion at which those who were close to a great person could tell the public what he was like as a human being, with faults and idiosyncrasies. They could make the great man as a private person visible to the public.

It is easy to recognize the sort of public sphere Rabindranath was wishing for. It was a public sphere consisting of not only books and journals and newspapers but also active literary societies, literary gatherings, an involvement of the public with things literary and cultural, an interest of ordinary people in greatness not as a superhuman gift but as a human achievement. Following Habermas, we can even sense here a hint of that new conception of personhood where the private and the intimate are, as it were, always oriented toward a public.[8] Rabindranath, we can see, was imagining for his own country a world of literary activity embedded in a public sphere constituted by a variety of civil social institutions, the sort of world he himself had seen at first hand when, some fifteen years ago, he had lived in England for more than a year as a student.

Was Nabinchandra not appreciative of a public sphere of this kind? What was the older poet objecting to? Many years after this incident, when writing his autobiography, Nabinchandra Sen returned to the subject. He was, as can be expected, strongly derisive of literary societies and literary gatherings, dismissing them as places where people met for idle talk, or rather idle listening. His idea of commemorating great literary figures was a very different one.

> If instead of these utterly wasteful meetings and speeches, the organizers were to preserve the birthplaces of the ancient and [modern] poets of Bengal and hold a sort of religious festival *[debpūjār mata utsab]* every year at those places, then we can pay our respects to our great writers, hold a community gathering and at the same time bring credit to the cause of Bengali literature. Mendicant *bairāgis* and itinerant singers have in this way turned the birthplaces of the Vaisnava poets Jayadeva, Chandidas and Vidyapati into places of pilgrimage where they hold annual festivals. But we, instead of following this sacred and "indigenous" *[svadeśi]* path, thanks to English civilization and education, spend our time organizing these laughable condolence and memorial meetings devoid of all true compassion.[9]

He indeed suggested that like the Vaisnava poets of old, the birthplaces of modern writers like Madhusudan, Dinabandhu, and Bankim should be turned into places of pilgrimage where devotees would gather once every year.

Nabinchandra also gave in his autobiography a particularly caustic description of Bankim's condolence meeting.

> The condolence meeting was held. When Rabi Babu finished his long, meandering lament, wiped the tears from his eyes and sat down, the audience—so I was told—started shouting from all sides, "Rabi Thakur! Give us a song!" The eminent Gurudas Babu, who was chairing the meeting, was much annoyed by this and said that Rabi Babu had a bad throat and would not be able to sing today.... They say in English that people go to church not to worship but to listen to the music. Perhaps it is truer to say that they go there to display their clothes. Similarly in our condolence meetings, people walk in chewing *pān*, humming a tune from Amrita Babu's latest farce, asking for a song in Rabi Thakur's effeminate voice and generally expecting a good evening's entertainment.[10]

Nabinchandra seems clearly unwilling to accept that a public condolence meeting, like many other formal occasions in modern European social life (including going to church), has any significance apart from mere show. Indeed, he is unprepared even to accept that humanization of greatness which is part of the celebration of ordinary life that lies, as Charles Taylor has pointed out, at the heart of the transformation in social consciousness brought about by Western modernity.[11] Nabinchandra would rather have the great deified after their death, their birthplaces turned into places of pilgrimage, their statues "worshipped with flowers and sandalpaste." This, he would say, was "our" way of collectively expressing our gratitude to the great.

We have here the seeds of a serious disagreement. Does modernity require the universal adoption of Western forms of civil society? If those specific forms have been, in fact, built around a secularized version of Western Christianity, then must they be imitated in a modernized non-Christian world? Are the normative principles on which civil social institutions in the modern West are based so culturally particular that they can be abandoned in a non-Western version of modernity? These questions have been raised often enough in recent discussions. I wish to discuss here only a particular aspect of the matter.

I have not brought up this incident at the beginning of this paper merely to present one more curiosity from the history of colonial modernity in nineteenth-century Bengal. I think this largely forgotten disagreement can be shown to have an interesting significance for us today, one that was not clear to any of the antagonists a hundred years ago. In order to bring this out, let me first state that the question of condolence meetings is not, as far as I can see, a matter of debate today. Their form is largely the same as in the West, with the laying of wreaths, observing a minute's silence and memorial speeches. These practices of a secularized Western Christianity are rarely recognized as such in India today: they have been quite thoroughly domesticated in the secular public life of the country's civil institutions. Of course, it is not unusual to find a few indigenous touches added on, such as the garlanding of portraits or the burning of incense sticks. Music can be part of such a secular function: in West Bengal as well as in Bangladesh, by far the most likely music on such an occasion would be something composed by Rabindranath Tagore himself. However, the atmosphere would not be one of a public entertainment: Nabinchandra's fears on this count have proved to be unfounded. Rabindranath's hopes of grooming a public into maturity seem to have been borne out.

This, of course, only concerns public institutions of civic life, whose formal practices are recognized as being secular. In other collective institutional contexts, which it would be grossly misleading to call "private," there is, needless to say, on an occasion such as the death of a prominent person or of someone closely connected with the institution, the continued observance of practices that are clearly recognized as religious. In the domain of the state itself, however, the political pressure to be scrupulously "secular" requires state authorities to assemble, paradoxically enough, a representative collection of practices from a variety of religions. Each of these—recitations, prayers, discourses, music—is presented in a state mourning as representing a religion; what makes it a part of a "secular" state function is the simultaneous presence in one event of all of these representative religious performances. We will return to this difference between secular public practices in civil institutions and state institutions when we talk about the relation today between civil society and political society.

Let me bring these up here: family, civil society, political society, and the state. These are classical concepts of political theory, but used, we know, in a wide variety of senses and often with much inconsistency. I must clarify here the sense in which I find it useful to employ these concepts in talking about contemporary India.

Hegel's synthesis in the *Philosophy of Right* of these elements of what he called "ethical life" spoke of family, civil society, and the state but had no place for a distinct sphere of political society. However, in

understanding the structure and dynamics of mass political formations in twentieth-century nation-states, it seems to me useful to think
of a domain of mediating institutions between civil society and the
state. The sharpness of the nineteenth-century distinction between
state and civil society, developed along the tradition of European anti-
absolutist thinking, has the analytical disadvantage today of either regarding the domain of the civil as a depoliticized domain in contrast
with the political domain of the state, or of blurring the distinction
altogether by claiming that all civil institutions are political. Neither
emphasis is of help in understanding the complexities of political phenomena in large parts of the contemporary world.

I find it useful to retain the term "civil society" to those characteristic institutions of modern associational life originating in Western
societies that are based on equality, autonomy, freedom of entry and
exit, contract, deliberative procedures of decision making, recognized
rights and duties of members, and such other principles. Obviously,
this is not to deny that the history of modernity in non-Western countries contains numerous examples of the emergence of what could
well be called civil-social institutions, which, nevertheless, do not always conform to these principles. Rather, it is precisely to identify
these marks of difference, to understand their significance, to appreciate how by the continued invocation of a "pure" model of origin—the
institutions of modernity as they were meant to be, since that is how
they had been conceptualized in the great texts of the Western canon—
a normative discourse can still continue to energize and shape the
evolving forms of social institutions in the non-Western world, that I
would prefer to retain the more classical sense of the term "civil society" rather than adopt any of its recent revised versions.[12] Indeed, for
theoretical purposes, I even find it useful to hold on to the sense of
civil society, used in Hegel and Marx, as bourgeois society *(bürgerliche
gesellschaft)*.

An important consideration in thinking about the relation between civil society and the state in the modern history of countries such
as India is that whereas the legal-bureaucratic apparatus of the state
has been able, by the late colonial and certainly in the postcolonial
period, to reach as the target of many of its activities virtually all of
the population that inhabits its territory, the domain of civil-social
institutions as conceived in their classical sense is still restricted to a
fairly small section of "citizens." This hiatus is extremely significant

because it is the mark of non-Western modernity as an always incomplete project of "modernization" and of the role of an enlightened elite engaged in a pedagogical mission in relation to the rest of society.

But then, how are we to conceptualize the rest of society that lies outside the domain of modern civil society? The most common approach has been to use a traditional/modern dichotomy. One difficulty with this is the trap, not at all easy to avoid, of dehistoricizing and essentializing "tradition." The related difficulty is one of denying the possibility that this other domain, relegated to the zone of the traditional, could find ways of coping with the modern that might not conform to the Western bourgeois, secularized Christian, principles of modern civil society. I think a notion of political society lying between civil society and the state could help us see some of these historical possibilities.

By political society, I mean a domain of institutions and activities where several mediations are carried out. In the classical theory, the family is the elementary unit of social organization: by the nineteenth century, this is widely assumed to mean the nuclear family of modern bourgeois patriarchy. (Hegel, we know, strongly resisted the idea that the family was based on contract, but by the late nineteenth century the contractually formed family becomes the normative model of most social theorizing in the West as well as of reformed laws of marriage, property, inheritance, and personal taxation. Indeed, the family becomes a product of contractual arrangements between individuals who are the primary units of society.) In countries such as India, it would be completely unrealistic to assume this definition of the family as obtaining universally. In fact, what is significant is that in formulating its policies and laws that must reach the greater part of the population, even the state does not make this assumption.

The conceptual move that seems to have been made very widely, even if somewhat imperceptibly, is from the idea of society as constituted by the elementary units of homogeneous families to that of a *population,* differentiated but classifiable, describable and numerable. Michel Foucault has been more perceptive than other social philosophers of recent times in noticing the crucial importance of the new concept of population for the emergence of modern governmental technologies. Perhaps we should also note the contribution here of colonial anthropology and colonial administrative theories.

Population, then, constitutes the material of society. Unlike the family in classical theory, the concept of population is descriptive and empirical, not normative. Indeed, population is assumed to contain large elements of "naturalness" and "primordiality"; the internal principles of the constitution of particular population groups is not expected to be rationally explicable, since they are not the products of rational contractual association but are, as it were, pre-rational. What the concept of population does, however, is make available for governmental functions (economic policy, bureaucratic administration, law, and political mobilization) a set of rationally manipulable instruments for reaching large sections of the inhabitants of a country as the targets of "policy."

Civil-social institutions, on the other hand, if they are to conform to the normative model presented by Western modernity, must necessarily exclude from its scope the vast mass of the population. Unlike many radical theorists, I do not think that this "defect" of the classical concept needs to be rectified by revising the definition of civil society in order to include within it social institutions based on other principles. Rather, I think retaining the older idea of civil society actually helps us capture some of the conflicting desires of modernity that animate contemporary political and cultural debates in countries such as India.

Civil society in such countries is best used to describe those institutions of modern associational life set up by nationalist elites in the era of colonial modernity, though often as part of their anticolonial struggle. These institutions embody the desire of this elite to replicate in its own society the forms as well as the substance of Western modernity. We can see this desire working quite clearly in the arguments of Rabindranath Tagore quoted at the beginning of this paper. It is indeed a desire for a new ethical life in society, one that is in conformity with the virtues of the Enlightenment and of bourgeois freedom and whose known cultural forms are those of secularized Western Christianity. All of these are apparent in Rabindranath's argument for new secularized public rituals. It is well recognized in that argument that the new domain of civil society will long remain an exclusive domain of the elite, that the actual "public" will not match up to the standards required by civil society, and that the function of civil-social institutions in relation to the public at large will be one of pedagogy rather than of free association.

Countries with relatively long histories of colonial modernization and nationalist movements often have quite an extensive and impressive network of civil-social institutions of this kind. In India, most of them survive to this day, not as quaint remnants of colonial modernity but often as serious protagonists of a project of cultural modernization still to be completed. However, in more recent times, they seem to be under a state of siege.

To understand this, we will need to historicize more carefully the concepts of civil society, political society, and the state in colonial and postcolonial conditions.

The explicit form of the postcolonial state in India is that of a modern liberal democracy. It is often said, not unjustifiably, that the reason liberal democratic institutions have performed more creditably in India than in many other parts of the formerly colonial world is the strength of its civil-social institutions, which are relatively independent of the political domain of the state. But one needs to be more careful about the precise relationships involved here.

Before the rise of mass nationalist movements in the early twentieth century, nationalist politics in India was largely confined to the same circle of elites that was then busy setting up the new institutions of "national" civil society. These elites were thoroughly wedded to the normative principles of modern associational public life and criticized the colonial state precisely for not living up to the standards of a liberal constitutional state. In talking about this part of the history of nationalist modernity, we do not need to bring in the notion of a political society mediating between civil society and the state.

However, entwined with this process of the formation of modern civil-social institutions, something else was also happening. I have explained elsewhere how the various cultural forms of Western modernity were put through a nationalist sieve and only selectively adopted, and then combined with the reconstituted elements of what was claimed to be indigenous tradition.[13] Dichotomies such as spiritual/ material, inner/outer, alien/indigenous, etc., were applied to justify and legitimize these choices from the standpoint of a nationalist cultural politics. We would have noticed in the debate between the two poets cited above a clear example of this politics. What I wish to point out here in particular is that even as the associational principles of secular bourgeois civil institutions were adopted in the new civil society of the nationalist elite, the possibility of a different mediation between the population and the state was already being imagined, one that would not ground itself on a modernized civil society.

The impetus here was directly political. It had to do with the fact that the governmental technologies of the colonial state were already seeking to bring within its reach large sections of the population as the targets of its policies. Nationalist politics had to find an adequate strategic response if it was not to remain immobilized within the confines of the "properly constituted" civil society of the urban elites. The cultural politics of nationalism supplied this answer by which it could mediate politically between the population and the nation-state of the future. In the debate between the two poets, Nabinchandra's arguments anticipated this strategic answer. It would, of course, be explicated most dramatically and effectively in what I have elsewhere described as the Gandhian moment of maneuver.[14]

This mediation between the population and the state takes place on the site of a new political society. It is built around the framework of modern political associations such as political parties. But, as researchers on nationalist political mobilizations in the Gandhian era have shown repeatedly, elite and popular anticolonial politics, even as they came together within a formally organized arena such as that of the Indian National Congress, diverged at specific moments and spilled over the limits laid down by the organization.[15] This arena of nationalist politics, in other words, became a site of strategic maneuvers, resistance, and appropriation by different groups and classes, many of them unresolved even in the present phase of the postcolonial state. The point is that the practices that activate the forms and methods of mobilization and participation in political society are not always consistent with the principles of association in civil society.

What, then, are the principles that govern political society? The question has been addressed in many ways in the literature on mass mobilizations, electoral politics, ethnic politics, etc. In the light of the conceptual distinctions I have made above between population, civil society, political society, and the state, we will need to focus more clearly on the mediations between population on the one hand and political society and the state on the other. The major instrumental form here in the postcolonial period is that of the developmental state, which seeks to relate to different sections of the population through the governmental function of welfare. Correspondingly, if we have to give a name to the major form of mobilization by which political society (parties, movements, non-party political formations) tries to channel and order popular demands on the developmental state, we should

call it democracy. The institutional forms of this emergent political society are still unclear. Just as there is a continuing attempt to order
these institutions in the prescribed forms of liberal civil society, there
is probably an even stronger tendency to strive for what are perceived
to be democratic rights and entitlements by violating those institutional norms. I have suggested elsewhere that the uncertain institutionalization of this domain of political society can be traced to the absence
of a sufficiently differentiated and flexible notion of community in the
theoretical conception of the modern state.[16] In any case, there is much
churning in political society in the countries of the postcolonial world,
not all of which are worthy of approval, which nevertheless can be
seen as an attempt to find new democratic forms of the modern state
that were not thought out by the post-Enlightenment social consensus
of the secularized Christian world.

In conclusion, I wish to suggest three theses that might be pursued
further. These are three theses that arise from the historical study of
modernity in non-Western societies. I advance them on the strength of
my reading of the history of the institutions of the modern state and
the practices of modern representative politics in India in the last hundred years or so. But I also venture to suggest that they have a large
degree of general relevance to the history of other postcolonial countries in the contemporary world. The theses are:

1. The most significant site of transformations in the colonial period
   is that of civil society; the most significant transformations occur-
   ring in the postcolonial period are in political society.
2. The question that frames the debate over social transformation in
   the colonial period is that of modernity. In political society of the
   postcolonial period, the framing question is that of democracy.
3. In the context of the latest phase of the globalization of capital, we
   may well be witnessing an emerging opposition between modernity and democracy, i.e., between civil society and political society.

Before ending, I should make a final remark on my story about
the two poets and death. Rabindranath Tagore won the Nobel Prize
for literature in 1913 and went on to become by far the most eminent
literary figure in Bengal. In his long and active career, he steadfastly
held on to his early commitment to an ethical life of public virtue,
guided by reason, rationality, and a commitment to a modernist spirit
of humanism. Since his death in 1941, however, he of all modern literary figures has been the one to be deified. On the day he died, when

his body was taken through the streets of Calcutta, there was a huge stampede when people fought with one another in an attempt to collect relics from the body. Since then, his birthplace has been turned into a place of pilgrimage where annual congregations are held every year—not religious festivals in their specific ceremonial practices, and yet not dissimilar in spirit. We could easily imagine the older poet Nabinchandra Sen chuckling with delight at the predicament of his more illustrious junior. The disagreement over "our" way of mourning for the dead has not, it would appear, been resolved as yet.

Notes

1. All three institutions survive today, more than a hundred years later, although performances at the Star Theatre were stopped after a fire destroyed a part of the building a few years ago.

2. Most recently, and brilliantly, by Sudipta Kaviraj, *The Unhappy Consciousness: Bankimchandra Chattopadhyay and the Formation of Nationalist Discourse in India* (Delhi: Oxford University Press, 1995).

3. Nabinchandra Sen, *Āmār jīban*, vol. 5 (1913), in *Nabīncandra racanābalī*, vol. 2, ed. Santikumar Dasgupta and Haribandhu Mukhati (Calcutta: Dattachaudhuri, 1976), 253.

4. Rabindranath Thakur, "Śoksabhā" (May–June 1894), in *Rabīndra-racanābalī*, vol. 10 (Calcutta: Government of West Bengal, 1989), 291–99.

5. Ibid., 293.

6. Ibid., 293.

7. Ibid., 294.

8. Jürgen Habermas, *The Structural Transformation of the Public Sphere: An Inquiry into a Category of Bourgeois Society*, trans. Thomas Burger (Cambridge: MIT Press, 1989).

9. Sen, *Āmār jīban*, 208.

10. Ibid., 253. Sen's description of this incident, though colored by his prejudices, is not entirely far from the truth. Tagore's most recent biographer quotes another source that gives a similar account. See Prasantakumar Pal, *Rabijībanī*, vol. 4 (Calcutta: Ananda, 1988), 3.

11. Charles Taylor, *Sources of the Self: The Making of the Modern Identity* (Cambridge: Harvard University Press, 1989).

12. An account of some of these versions is given in Jean L. Cohen and Andrew Arato, *Civil Society and Political Theory* (Cambridge: MIT Press, 1994).

13. Partha Chatterjee, *The Nation and Its Fragments: Colonial and Postcolonial Histories* (Princeton: Princeton University Press, 1994).

14. Partha Chatterjee, *Nationalist Thought and the Colonial World* (London: Zed Books, 1993).

15. One set of studies of Indian nationalist politics that explicitly addresses this "split in the domain of politics" is contained in the volumes of *Subaltern Studies* and in several monographs written by historians contributing to that series.

16. Chatterjee, *The Nation and Its Fragments*, ch. 11.

Three

Witness to Suffering: Domestic Cruelty and the Birth of the Modern Subject in Bengal

Dipesh Chakrabarty

Modernity and the Documentation of Suffering

Ekshan, a Calcutta-based literary magazine, published a remarkable essay in 1991, "Baidhabya kahini" or "Tales of Widowhood."[1] The author was Kalyani Datta, a Bengali woman who, since the 1950s, had been collecting from older Bengali widows she personally knew, stories about the oppression and marginalization they had suffered as widows. Datta's article reproduced these widows' tales in their own telling, based on notes she had taken from informal interviews. Unfunded and unprompted by any academic institutions, Datta's research was a notable instance showing how deeply a certain will to witness and document suffering—in this case, the plight of the widow—for the interest of a general reading public has embedded itself in modern Bengali life. Both this will and the archive it has built up over the last hundred years are part of a modernity that British colonial rule inaugurated in nineteenth-century India.

What underlay this will-to-document was the general figure of the Bengali widow of upper-caste Hindu families as a figure of suffering. This figure itself is an abstraction of relatively recent times. There have been widows, of course, in Bengali upper-caste families for as long as such families have existed. It is also true that there have been, from time immemorial, pernicious little customs in place for regulating and dominating the lives of widows. It is not that every Bengali upper-caste widow has suffered in the same way or to the same extent throughout history, or that there have been no historical changes at all in widows' conditions. Many widows earned unquestionable familial authority by willingly subjecting themselves to prescribed regimes and rituals of widowhood. Many have also resisted the social injunctions meant to control their lives. Besides, factors such as women's education, their entry into public life, the subsequent decline in the number of child brides, and an overall increase in life expectancies have helped reduce the widows' vulnerability. Kalyani Datta's private act of (public) recording of some widows' voices is itself a testimony to these undeniable historical changes.

Yet there is no question that widowhood exposes women to some real vulnerability in the patrilineal, patrilocal system of kinship of upper-caste Bengali society. The prescribed rituals of widowhood suggest that it is regarded as a state of inauspiciousness (for the inauspiciousness of the woman is traditionally blamed for bringing death to a male member of the household). The rituals take the form of extreme and life-long atonement on the part of the widow: celibacy, ban on meat-eating, avoidance of certain kinds of food, frequent fasting. Unadorned bodies carrying some permanent marks (such as the lack of jewelry, shaved head or cropped hair, and white saris with no—or black—borders) aim to make widows unattractive, setting them aside from others. Stories recounted since the nineteenth century have revealed the element of torture, oppression, and cruelty that often, if not always, accompanied the experience of widowhood.

Until the coming of colonial rule, however, widowhood was not thematized as a problem in Bengali society. Pre-British Bengali literature and writing had concerned itself with many aspects of women's lives and suffering: the daughter-in-law's suffering at the hands of the mother-in-law and sisters-in-law, the question of chastity of women, jealousy and quarrel between co-wives, but seldom, if ever, did the problems of widowhood receive attention.[2] Yet colonial rule changed all that. From the question of *sati* (widow-burning) that raged in the 1820s and 1830s and the widow-remarriage act (1856), through to the early Bengali novels written between the 1870s and 1920s, the widow and her plight remained a subject of central importance in Bengali writing. Indeed, in the last hundred and thirty years or so, many Bengali

Hindu widows—both in life and in fiction—have told their own stories in the different genres of fiction, memoir, and autobiography. Ever since the nineteenth century, the question of the widow's oppression has remained an important aspect of modern critiques of Bengali kinship. Kalyani Datta's short essay in *Ekshan* was part of this continuing and collective act of documentation of the suffering that widowhood has traditionally inflicted on women.

Why the figure of the widow came to be the focus of so much attention has been addressed by many scholars critical of both Bengali patriarchy and colonial domination. They have demonstrated a connection between "colonial discourse"—in particular the British use of the "conditions of women" question as a measure for quality of civilization—and the beginnings of a modern form of social criticism in Bengal that focused on such issues as *sati* and widow remarriage.[3] The questions I want to pursue here are somewhat different. It is obvious that the general figure of the suffering widow was produced in Bengali history by creating a collective and "public" past out of many individual and familial memories and constructions of the experience of widowhood. This collective past was needed for the pursuit of justice under conditions of a modern public life. What kind of a subject is produced at the intersection of these two kinds of memories, public and familial? What does this subject have to be like in order to be interested in documenting suffering? How would one write a history of a modern and collective Bengali subject who is marked by this will to witness and document oppression and injury?

Compassion and the Subject of Enlightenment

Let me state in a schematic fashion and with brutal simplification how I understand the problem of suffering as it relates to the subject of modernity posited by thinkers of the European Enlightenment. The capacity to notice and document suffering (even if it be one's own suffering) from the position of a generalized and necessarily disembodied observer is what marks the beginnings of the modern self. This self has to be generalizable in principle; in other words, it should be such that it signifies a position available for occupation by anybody (with proper training). If it were said, for instance, that it was only a particular type of person—such as a Buddha or a Christ—who was capable of noticing suffering and of being moved by it, one would not be talking of a generalized subject-position, for to be a Buddha or Christ may not be within the reach of everybody. People could not be made into a Buddha or a Christ through simple education and training. So the capacity for sympathy must be seen as a potential inherent in the "nature" of man. Such a "natural theory of sentiments" was indeed argued by Enlightenment philosophers such as David Hume and Adam Smith.

A critical distinction also has to be made here between the act of displaying suffering and that of observing or facing the sufferer. To display suffering in order to elicit sympathy and assistance is a very old—and perhaps universal and still-current—practice. The deformed beggar of medieval Europe or of contemporary Indian or U.S. cities is a subject of suffering but he or she is not a disembodied subject. Their representation of suffering is through the semiotic of their bodies. The sufferer here is an embodied self. The embodied self as such is always a particular self, grounded in this or that body. Nor would the sympathy felt for only a particular sufferer (such as a kin, or a friend) be "modern" in my sense. It is the person who, without being an immediate sufferer himself or herself but with the capacity to become a secondary sufferer through sympathy for a generalized picture of suffering, and who documents this suffering in the interest of social intervention, it is such a person who occupies the position of the modern subject. In other words, the moment of the modern observation of suffering is a certain moment of self-recognition on the part of an abstract, general human being. It is as though one person who is able to see in himself or herself the general human also recognizes the same figure in the particular sufferer—so that the moment of recognition is a moment when the general human splits into the two mutually recognizing and mutually constitutive figures of the sufferer and the observer of suffering. It was argued, however, that this could not happen without the aid of reason, for habit and custom could indeed blunt the natural human capacity for sympathy. Reason, that is, education in rational argumentation, was seen as a critical factor in helping to realize in the modern person this capacity for seeing the general.

Something like this "natural theory of sentiments" was argued in effect by the two most important nineteenth-century Bengali social reformers who exerted themselves on questions concerning the plight of widows: Rammohun Roy (1772/4–1833) and Iswarchandra Vidyasagar (1820–1901). Roy was instrumental in the passing of the act that made *sati* illegal in 1829, and Vidyasagar successfully agitated for widows to have the legal right to remarry, a right enshrined in the 1856 Act for the Remarriage of Hindu Widows.

Consider, for instance, Rammohun Roy's well-known tract "Brief Remarks Regarding Modern Encroachments on the Ancient Right of Females," one of the first written arguments in modern India in favor of women's right to property. This interesting document on property rights also discusses the place of sentiments in human relations (such as "cruelty," "distress," "wounding feelings," "misery," etc.). Both strands were intertwined in Roy's argument:

> In short a widow, according to the [current] exposition of the law, can receive nothing . . . [unless her husband dies] leaving two or more sons, and all of them survive and be inclined to allot a share to their mother. . . . The consequence is, that a woman who is looked upon as the sole mistress of a family one day, on the next, becomes dependent on her sons, and subject to the slights of her daughters-in-law. . . . Cruel sons often wound the feelings of their dependent mothers. . . . Step-mothers, who are often numerous on account of polygamy, are still more shamefully neglected in general by their step-sons, and sometimes dreadfully treated by their sisters-in-law. . . . [The] restraints on female inheritance encourage, in a great degree, polygamy, a frequent source of the greatest misery in native families.[4]

There are two interesting features of this document that make it the work of a modern documenter of suffering. First, in observing this cruelty to widows and women, Roy put himself in the transcendental position of the modern subject. This becomes clear if we look closely at the following sentence of his text:

> How distressing it must be to the female community and to those who interest themselves in their behalf, to observe daily that several daughters in a rich family can prefer no claim to any portion of the property . . . left by their deceased father . . . ; while they . . . are exposed to be given in marriage to individuals who already have several wives and have no means of maintaining them.[5]

Roy presents himself here both as a subject experiencing affect—"distress"—as well as a representative subject, one who "interests [himself] in their [women's] behalf": "How *distressing* it must be *to the female community* and *to those who interest themselves in their behalf.*" The capacity for sympathy is what unites the person who represents with those who are represented; in this way they share the same "distress." This clause in the sentence about representation refers to a new type of representation: people who took an interest in women's condition on behalf of women. But who were these women? They were not particular, specific women marked by their belonging to particular families or particular networks of kinship. Women here are a collective subject; the expression "female community" connotes a general community. It is this "general community" that shares the distress of a Rammohun Roy, the observer who observes on behalf of this collective community. And therefore the feeling of "distress" that Rammohun Roy spoke of referred to a new kind of compassion, something one could feel for suffering beyond one's immediate family, for women to whom one was not tied through any bond of kinship. "Compassion in general," we could call it.

But from where would such compassion or sympathy spring? What made it possible for a Rammohun or Vidyasagar to feel this "compassion in general," which most members of their community (presumably) did not yet feel? How would society train itself to make this compassion a part of the comportment of every person so that compassion became a generally present sentiment in society? It is on this point that both Rammohun and Vidyasagar gave an answer remarkable for its affiliation to the European Enlightenment. Reason, they argued in effect, was what could release the flow of the compassion that was naturally present in all human beings, for only reason could dispel the blindness induced by custom and habit. Reasonable human beings would see suffering and that would put to work the natural human capacity for sympathy, compassion, and pity.

Rammohun raised the question of compassion in a pointed manner in his 1819 answer to Kashinath Tarkabagish's polemical tract "Bidhayak nishedhak shombad," directed against his own position on *sati.* "What is a matter of regret," he said, "is that the fact of witnessing with your own eyes women who have thus suffered much sadness and domination, does not arouse even a small amount of compassion in you so that the forcible burning [of widows] may be stopped."[6] Why was this so? Why did the act of seeing not result in sympathy? Rammohun's answer is clearly given in his 1818 tract "Views on Burning Widows Alive," which targeted the advocates of the practice. Here Rammohun refers to the forcible way in which widows were "fastened" to the funeral pyre in the course of the performance of *sati* and directly raises the question of mercy or compassion *(daya)*: "you are unmercifully resolved to commit the sin of female murder." His opponent, the "advocate" of *sati*, replies:

> You have repeatedly asserted that from want of feeling we promote female destruction. This is incorrect. For it is declared in our Veda and codes of law, that mercy is the root of virtue, and from our practice of hospitality, &c., our compassionate dispositions are well known.[7]

Rammohun's counterresponse introduces an argument for which he presents no scriptural authority and which went largely unanswered in the debates of the time. This is the argument about "habits of insensibility." Much like the Enlightenment thinkers, and perhaps influenced by them, Rammohun argued that once the practice of *sati* became a custom—a matter of blind repetition—people were prevented from experiencing sympathy even when they physically watched the performance of *sati*. The natural connection between their vision and feelings of pity had been blocked by habit. If this habit could be corrected or its veil removed, the sheer act of seeing a woman being forced to become a *sati* would evoke compassion. Roy said:

> That in other cases you show charitable dispositions is acknowledged. But by witnessing from your youth the voluntary burning of women amongst your elder relatives, your neighbours and the inhabitants of the surrounding villages, and by observing the indifference at the time when the women are writhing under the torture of the flames, habits of insensibility are produced. For the same reason, when men or women are suffering the pains of death, you feel for them no sense of compassion, like worshipers of female deities who, witnessing from their infancy the slaughter of kids and buffaloes, feel no compassion for them in the time of their suffering death.[8]

We encounter the same argument about the relationship between sight and compassion in the writings of Iswarchandra Vidyasagar, the aforementioned Bengali reformer responsible for the 1856 act permitting Hindu widows to remarry. Vidyasagar's fundamental reasoning as to the solution of widows' problems had some critical differences from the position of Rammohun Roy, but like the latter, he too argued that custom and habit thwarted the otherwise natural relationship between sight and compassion:[9]

> People of India! . . . Habit has so darkened and overwhelmed your intellect and good sense that it is hard for the juice of compassion to flow in the ever-dry hearts of yours even when you see the plight of the hapless widows. . . . Let no woman be born in a country where

the men have no compassion, no feelings of duty and justice, no sense of good and bad, no consideration, where only the preservation of custom is the main and supreme religion—let the ill-fated women not take birth in such a country.

Women! I cannot tell what sins [of past lives] cause you to be born in India![10]

What this amounted to was some kind of a natural theory of compassion, the idea that compassion was a sentiment universally present in something called "human nature," however blocked its expression might be in a particular situation. Recall Adam Smith, explaining his theory of "sympathy": "How selfish soever man may be supposed, there are some principles in his nature which interest him in the fortune of others. . . . Of this kind is pity or compassion, the emotion we feel for the misery of others."[11] Hume also defined "pity" as a general sentiment, as "a concern for . . . the misery of others, without any friendship . . . to occasion this concern," and connected it to the general human capacity for "sympathy": "No quality of human nature is more remarkable . . . than that propensity we have to sympathize with others."[12] It is only on the basis of this kind of an understanding that Rammohun Roy could claim that the physical act of witnessing *sati* could act as the trigger for the production of compassion in *all* human hearts, provided that this natural connection between sight and sympathy was not severed by habit. Hence the role they assigned to reason in fighting the effects of custom. Reason and sentiments here naturally fall in line with each other in a vision of humanity where, ultimately, being human could only be a universal way of being. Sentiments as such are not the target of reason's work. Reason simply helps in letting them take their natural course by removing the obstacle of mindless custom and thus allowing the modern human to be responsive to suffering.

Supplementing the Subject of Enlightenment: A Translation of Difference

There were two problems with the Bengali adaptation of a "natural theory" of compassion in dealing with the question of domestic cruelty toward widows. One was inherent in the theory itself. By making truly human sentiments natural and universal and hence embodied, it filled up what would later be regarded as the space of human subjectivity, with reason alone. But reason, being universal and public, could never delineate the private side of the modern individual. To this problem, I will turn in the next section.

Here, I want to draw the reader's attention to what remains an interesting fact in the history of Bengali attempts to answer the Enlightenment question "from where does compassion come?" The Bengali biographies of Rammuhun Roy or Vidyasagar often present us with an answer to this question that is very different from the answer Roy and Vidyasagar themselves proposed. A central question the biographers found themselves obliged to address in writing the life stories of a Rammohun or a Vidyasagar was, What made it possible for these two Bengali men to see the suffering of women that even many parents did not see ? What made them compassionate? The biographers gave two answers. One was the Enlightenment answer we have already discussed: the role of reason in freeing vision from the blindfold of custom. But they also provided another answer, which is interesting in the present context. And that answer was *hriday* (heart). They argued, in effect, that it was the "heart" that Rammohun or Vidyasagar was born with which made them compassionate.

Nagendranath Chattopadhyay's biography of Rammohun Roy, *Mahatma Raja Rammohon rayer jibancharit* (1881–82), sees "sympathy and compassion" *(shahanubhuti o daya)* as part of Roy's inborn character: "Rammohun Roy was full of sympathy *[shahanubhuti]* and compassion *[daya]* for the suffering poor. Their misery always made his heart cry."[13] Chandicharan Bandyopadhyay's biography of Vidyasagar, *Vidyasagar* (ca. 1895), describes several anecdotes to document the compassion that Vidyasagar felt for suffering humanity. Indeed, one of the most remarkable things about the biographies of this legendary Bengali public man of the nineteenth century is that they all, almost without exception, describe, with approval and in detail, his propensity to cry in public (not an admirable trait, as we shall see, by Adam Smith's standard). Crying stands as proof of his tenderheartedness. Incident after incident is recounted to document how plentiful was compassion (*daya* or *karuna*) in Vidyasagar's heart. A typical sentence, to quote another of his biographers, Subal Mitra, would run as follows: "We have already seen that, while a scholar in the Sanskrit College[,] he showed his kindness of heart by giving food and clothing to the needy."[14] Or consider this other example said to be typical of Vidyasagar's life. When Vidyasagar was still a student in Calcutta, a respected teacher of his, Shambhuchandra Bachaspati, who taught Vidyasagar Vedantic philosophy and who was by then an old, physically decrepit man, married a very young girl. Vidyasagar, it is said, was opposed to this marriage and advised his teacher against it. His biographers are unanimous in describing how on meeting this girl, Vidyasagar "could not hold back his tears" thinking of the widowhood she seemed destined to suffer.[15]

> Isvar Chandra only cast a glance at the beautiful girl's face, and immediately left the place. The sight move[d] his tender heart, and drew tears from his eyes. He foresaw the miserable, wretched life which the unfortunate little girl must have in a very short time, and he sobbed and wept like a child.[16]

Chandicharan writes of this event: "This one single incident helps us to understand how tender was Ishvarchandra's heart and how easily it was stricken by other people's suffering."[17]

The biographies thus explain Rammohun's or Vidyasagar's capacity to generalize their compassion by reference to the special quality of *hriday*, or heart. They could generalize their sympathies from the particular instance to all cases because the supply of sympathy in their hearts was plentiful. In this they were different from, say, people such as the eighteenth-century king Raja Rajballabh of Vikrampur, Dhaka, who, moved by the plight of his young and widowed daughter attempted, unsuccessfully, to get her married again; or somebody like "one Syama Charan Das" of Calcutta in the early 1850s, who tried to do the same and was foiled by the local pundits.[18] These people had compassion but did not have it in measures ample enough to move them to see their daughters' problem as a problem afflicting, potentially, all upper-caste women. A person like Rammohun or Vidyasagar, however, was capable of moving to the general case from the particular because they were born with plentiful measures of *karuna* (compassion). Vidyasagar, in fact, was christened *karunasagar* ("ocean of compassion," as distinct from *vidyasagar*, "ocean of learning") by the Bengali poet Michael Madhusudan Dutt.[19] Their biographers cite some critical evidence from stories of their childhood to establish this *karuna* as an inborn character trait. Rammohun's revulsion toward the idea of *sati* (widow-burning), we are told, arose first when he learned of a close female relative being forced to this fate by the men of the household.[20] Similarly, Vidyasagar's determination to fight for the amelioration of widows' conditions is traced back to a childhood experience, when he discovered that a young girl who was once a playmate of his had become widowed and was now subject to all the prohibitions of widowhood. "He felt so much commiseration for the little girl that he, there and then, resolved that he would give his life to relieve the sufferings of widows. He was at the time only 13 or 14 years old."[21]

Generalized sympathy here is seen as a gift on the part of Vidyasagar: "He would give his life to relieve the sufferings of the widows." It is a gift of his heart. This understanding of compassion as a person's inborn capacity for *shahanubhuti* (*shaha* = equal, *anubhuti* = feelings) was interestingly different from the Smithian or Humean position that pity was a part of general human nature. The Sanskrit-derived Bengali word *shahanubhuti* is usually translated in English as "sympathy." Yet there are some profound differences. The idea of "sympathy" entails the practice and faculty of (another very European word) "imagination." We sympathize with someone's misery because we can through the faculty of imagination place ourselves in the position of the person suffering; that is sympathy. As Adam Smith writes: "We sometimes feel for another . . . because, when we put ourselves in his case, that passion arises in our breast from the imagination."[22] This capacity to imagine was part of human nature in Smith's discussion: "Nature teaches the spectators to assume the circumstances of the person principally concerned."[23] The Bengali authors, however, in explaining Rammohun's or Vidyasagar's inborn character as *shahriday* (with *hriday* or "heart") and therefore with the capacity for *shahanubhuti*, were drawing practically but implicitly on Sanskritic aesthetic theories of the *rasa shastra* (in aesthetics, the science of *rasa* or "moods"), according to which it was not given to everybody to appreciate the different *rasas* of life (including that of *karuna* or compassion). The capacity for *shahanubhuti* was, unlike *sympathy* in European theory, not dependent on a naturally given mental faculty like "imagination" (for which there is no corresponding category in Indian aesthetics); it was seen rather as a characteristic of the person with *hriday*. The quality of being "with *hriday*" was called *shahridayata*. A *rasika* person, one who could appreciate the different *rasas*, had this mysterious entity called *hriday*. And it was in that sense a Rammohun or a Vidyasagar could be called a *shahriday vyakti* (a person with *hriday*).[24] There is no theory of a general human nature in the *rasa shastra* to explain why some people are born with *hriday* and others not. To have *hriday* was a matter of exception rather than the rule. A Rammohun or a Vidyasagar was born that way. That is what made them rare and godlike, and placed them above ordinary humans. There could not be, therefore, a natural theory of compassion from this point of view.

There were thus two separate and unconnected theoretical ways of looking at compassion and personhood jostling together in the Bengali biographies of Vidyasagar and Rammohun Roy. One was the European-derived natural theory of sentiments. The other, derived from Indian aesthetics, was inscribed in the Bengali or Sanskrit words used to describe the capacity for sympathy or compassion. Words derived from Sanskrit texts of *rasa-shastra* circulated in Bengali writing as a form of practical consciousness, as words belonging to the vocabulary of everyday relationships. But they represented, nevertheless, a different hermeneutic of the social that supplemented the one represented by European Enlightenment thought. After all, Adam Smith's or David Hume's theories—in their conscious appeal to experience as the ground for generalization—often offered as universally applicable hypotheses positions that were clearly derived from very particular and specific cultural practices of the societies they knew. Smith, for instance, would blithely assume it to be a universal proposition that "the man who, under the greatest calamities, could command his sorrow, seems worthy of the highest admiration," or that "nothing is so mortifying as to be obliged to express our distress to the view of the public." (This could never explain, for instance, why Bengalis valued the fact that a man of Vidyasagar's stature would cry in public.)[25] These statements were as much theories as they were matters of prejudice (in the Gadamerian sense) in that they were interpretations as well.[26] Between them and the already existing interpretations structuring Bengali lives was created the field of the politics of translating difference.

This politics may be seen in a duality of attitudes that authors of biographies often express. Nineteenth-century biographical writing in Bengal was inspired by the Victorian idea that biographies contributed to social improvement by providing models of characters that others in society could emulate. A natural theory of compassion was helpful in this regard, for modern education (i.e., training in rational argumentation) could then be seen as the prescribed weapon for fighting the blinding effects of custom. Biographies were meant to be tools of such education. But if, on the other hand, compassion in general was a function of such a contingent and rare factor, such as the *hriday* one was born with, and was therefore a quality that was by definition in short supply, how would one train people in the art of this sentiment? How could every person cultivate that which, by its own nature, could only be acquired as a special gift worthy of veneration? Biographers of compassionate Bengali social reformers were often caught in this contradiction.

A biographer such as Bandyopadhyay would have to make two contradictory claims at once. He would convey the impression that Vidyasagar's greatness lay in the natural rarity of his kind of people. Not everybody was born with a heart as full of *shahanubhuti* as Vidyasagar's. And yet at the same time he would want his biography to make an example of Vidyasagar's life that others—not as gifted— could follow. "The lord of our destiny willing," he says toward the end of his book, "may the reading of [Vidya]sagar's life . . . spread the desire to imitate [his] . . . qualities."[27] Sometimes his text would directly address the reader, exhorting him to exercise his "imagination" and emulate Vidyasagar's noble example.[28] Yet on other occasions, he would emphasize the inborn nature of Vidyasagar's compassion and sentiments, leaving a degree of ambiguity as to whether compassion for all was something that followed from the natural human capacity for sympathy triggered by sight or whether it was a feeling that only the very exceptional were capable of experiencing.

Unable to resolve this contradiction between a view of *hriday* as a quasi-divine gift, and their commitment to a Victorian understanding of social "improvement" through the remolding of individual characters by disseminating stories of good examples, Bengali biographies often fell somewhere between biographies and hagiographies. They remained, for all their secular humanism, expressions of *bhakti* (devotion), an act of worship, on the part of the biographer toward his or her subject. Bandyopadhyay indicates clearly in his preface that writing the life of Vidyasagar was for him an action of the same category as offering *puja* (worship). He adopts the gesture of the religious devotee *(bhakta)*, whose language of humility was necessarily a language of self-denigration as well:

> Vidyasagar deserves veneration from the community of learned people; unfortunately, his present biographer, in comparison, would

only count amongst the leaders of fools. . . . He was extremely affectionate towards me . . . and I will also do *puja* to him for that reason all my life. This biography began as part of that arrangement for *puja* and this is the only right I have to narrate the story of his very sacred life.[29]

This was quite in keeping with the understanding that an excess of compassion in one's character was a rare gift from the world of gods. This understanding had its historical genealogies in aesthetic theories and devotional practices unconnected to Enlightenment thought, but it shadowed and supplemented what came from Europe. On the question of seeing the widow, there were thus at least two answers given to the question: whose sight generated sympathy or compassion? Was it the sight of the Enlightenment subject or of the subject who, as a rare gift, possessed *hriday*? That we come across the answers in the same body of texts suggests the answers did not displace but supplemented each other, to constitute an intertwined strand in Bengali modernity.

The Widow as the Bengali Modern Subject

Rammohun or Vidyasagar saw the widow from outside herself. The archive of accounts of widows' suffering they helped to build did not include the widow's private experience of it. Her subjectivity was not in question. By the time Kalyani Datta published her essay in 1991, however, recording the widow's own voice was critical to the enterprise. It was not only Kalyani Datta, the observer, who was documenting suffering; the sufferer herself spoke of her conditions. She was her own observer of herself. One of the archival values of Datta's essay are the different older women who address the reader directly from within it. The archives of this history, in other words, now included the subjectivity of the widow. The widow was both the object and the subject of the gaze that bore witness to oppression and suffering.

This was in keeping with what a standard account of the modern subject in European political thought—a history of the figure of the citizen, say—would lead us to expect. The modern subject, as many analysts of modernity have suggested, requires social and political thought to construct categories by which it comes to recognize the subject as having subjectivity, so that desires and emotions could be a part, not of anything general or universal as the biological human body or innate human nature, but of individual subjectivity itself. In other words, subjectivity itself, or what many commentators would call the "interiority" of the subject, comes to be constituted by a tension between individual-private experiences and desires (feelings, emotions, sentiments) and a universal-public reason. One could say that it is this opposition that manifests itself in the split between the private and the public in modernity.

C. B. Macpherson's *The Political Theory of Possessive Individualism* traces one source of the modern subject to the rise in the seventeenth century of the idea of the right of private ownership in one's own person. The subject who enjoyed this right could only be a disembodied, private subject, for the object over which his right extended was his own body.[30] It was not imperative in the seventeenth century that this subject, grounded in the idea of natural rights, be endowed with a deep interiority. The "private" of such a subject may indeed have been empty. But from the late eighteenth century on, this private was filled up to create what eventually became the domain of subjectivity. The young Marx, in "The Jewish Question," a polemic against Bruno Bauer that built on Hegel's *Philosophy of Right,* drew attention to this public/private split in the very conception of the citizen as spelled out in the 1791–93 French Declaration of the Rights of Man and Citizen. The citizen was the public-universal and political side of the human, who retained "natural rights" to private interests as a member of civil society. Religion could only be part of his private, egoistic sphere of self-interest.[31] William Connolly's recent genealogy of the subject of European political thought, traced through the writings of Hobbes, Rousseau, the Marquis de Sade, and Hegel, tracks the process whereby in the very theory of the subject, accounts of "strife and conflict in civil society" are shifted to a "site within the individual itself," until the individual becomes, by the end of the nineteenth century, the more familiar figure whose private self, now regarded as constituted through a history of psychological repression, can be pried open only by the techniques of psychoanalysis. In Connolly's words:

> The modern theory of the stratified subject, with its levels of unconscious, preconscious, conscious and self-conscious activity, and its convoluted relays among passions, interests, wishes, responsibility and guilt, locates within the self conflicts which Hobbes and Rousseau distributed across regimes.[32]

The birth of the modern subject in nineteenth-century European theory required a conflicted interiority where reason struggled to bring under its guidance and control that which distinguished one subject from another and which at the same time was itself *not* reason: this is the (initially) conscious and (later) subconscious world of passions, desires, and sentiments making up human subjectivity. While reason is a human faculty, it cannot constitute individual subjectivity because it is by definition universal and public. Passions, sentiments, etc., themselves have to be located within the mind and within a very particular understanding of the relationship between sentiments/emotions and reason. This relationship is pedagogic. Passions and sentiments, to be modern, require the guiding hand of reason. At the same time, this is a relationship of struggle because the two are of opposed and contradictory character. This struggle is what marks the interiority of the subject. Connolly describes this transition in the writings of Rousseau:

> Rousseau . . . shifts strife and conflict from civil society to a site within the individual itself. Demanding more from the self than Hobbes did, he must identify the struggle within it which Hobbes identified, and he must seek a more complete victory for the interior voice of virtue. Politics become interiorized . . . Rousseau withdraws politics from the general will and relocates it quietly inside the selves which will these general laws.[33]

Why was it important that the modern individual be conceptualized in terms of this internal struggle between passion/sentiments and reason? Timothy Mitchell's discussion of Durkheim in *Colonising Egypt* offers a suggestive answer. The very conception of the modern individual, Mitchell says, in discussing Durkheim's texts, poses a threat to the conception of the social and the general: If individuals are endowed with infinite individuality (which is what the drama of passions is supposed to reveal, each person his or her own novelist and analysand at the same time), what is there to guarantee the unity of the social? What would prevent the social, made up of such individuals (i.e., people not simply subject to social practice), from descending into the nightmare of anomie?[34] At the level of the individual, the answer would be *reason*. Reason, by focusing the mind on the general and the universal, would guide the individual's passion into its rightful place in the social. This thought, taken by itself, was not necessarily modern, but its generalization through society, one could argue, marks the coming of modernity.

Archiving and observing the Bengali widow as the subject of modernity then meant documenting not just the external conditions of the widow's life but her internal suffering as well, the way passion struggled with reason within her to mark her as modern. A clue to what was missing, in terms of this schema, from the framework of Rammohun and Vidyasagar is provided by the statement of Vidyasagar quoted above. Let us read a portion of it again, this time with an eye on the question of the widow's desires and her consequent agency:

> People of India! . . . Open your eyes for once and see how India, once a land of virtue, [is now] awash with sins of adultery and foeti-cide. . . . You are prepared to consign your daughters . . . to the intol-erable fire and torture of widowhood. You agree to connive at their conduct when, under the influence of irresistible passions, they be-come the victims of *adultery.* You are prepared to help them commit *foeticide* throwing aside all fears of immoral conduct and only out of the fear of being exposed to the public eye, and yet—the wonder of wonders!—you are not ready to follow the injunctions of the *shas-tras,* get them remarried, and free them from the insufferable pain of widowhood and free yourselves from the risk of all kinds of danger. You perhaps imagine that *with the loss of their husbands, women's bodies turn into stone, that they do lose all feelings of pain and sad-ness, that their passions are eradicated once for all.* . . . Let no woman be born in a country where the men have no compassion.[35]

I should explain that the reason why feticide and adultery assume such a prominent place in Vidyasagar's text was because the addressee of this text—those whom Vidyasagar in a generalizing and inflationary move addressed as "people of India"—were middle-class Bengali male householders of Calcutta of the mid-nineteenth century. The text was about their newfound sense of respectable forms of domesticity. Their fear of unwanted and illegitimate pregnancies caused by sexual liaisons between young widows and men in or outside the family was what this text addressed. The scandals of adultery and feticide—the Bengali word is *kelenkari* (disgrace), derived from the word *kalanka* meaning, literally, a spot or a stain (the moon's dark spots are called in Bengali the moon's *kalanka*)—were the "danger" to which Vidyasagar alluded. With a young widow in their midst, a middle-class family ran the risk of such *kelenkari* and the widow of acquiring the stigma *(kalanka)* of illicit relationship, which would destroy the respectability of her family. Where in this text is the subjecthood/agency of the young widow locat-ed? Vidyasagar's answer was unambiguous: the real problems were in the widow's body, in the drives and passions of youth, which were too strong to be regulated by the purificatory and self-renunciatory rituals of celibacy customarily recommended for widows. What made young women vulnerable to the danger of illegitimate pregnancy was the very nature of the passion physical youth engendered in their bodies. Recall Vidyasagar's words: "You perhaps imagine that with the loss of their husbands, women's bodies turn into stone, that they do lose all feelings of pain and sadness, that their passions are eradicated once for all." Vidyasagar was not alone in thinking of the widow's passions as something arising from the youth of her body. Fictional literature composed at this time on the question of widow remarriage suggest that this understanding was a common one.[36]

To build the archive of the widow's interiority, to see into her deep and stratified self, to hear her own voice as it were, required the development of a set of observational techniques for studying and describing human psychology. This was a role performed primarily by the novel. It was the forbidden love of the widow that the three stalwarts of early Bengali fiction—Bankimchandra Chattopadhyay (1838–94), Rabindranath Tagore (1861–1941) and Saratchandra Chattopadhyay (1876–1938)—made the subject of their novels. The issue of romantic love was itself a problem in the history of the formation of the democratic subject in a society in which the idea of choosing one's life partner—or of love being an act of self-expression of the subject—came up against the norms of social regulation enshrined in the custom of arranged marriages. Indeed, one reason why the figure of the widow may have held a special fascination for the early Bengali novelists is that the unrecognized desires of the widow represented a case of complete subordination of the individual to society. In the widow one could see the expressivist subject clamoring for (self)recognition. To delve into the interior world of the widow, whose innermost feelings were denied recognition by society, was to write the desire for freedom and self-expression into the very structure of the new Bengali subject. In doing this, however, the Bengali novelists also brought the question of the widow's interiority into the general field of view. Thus, long before such disciplines as history and sociology expressed the familiar modern will-to-document oppression, humanist literature was experimenting and perfecting the tools of modern description of "experience."[37]

Interiority and the Problem of Purity

The terrain of this literary development is complex. But I will have to be schematic and simplify issues that have more twists and turns in them than I can accommodate here. It is in Rabindranath Tagore's novel *Chokher bali* (1903), focused on the problem of a young widow's unrequited love, that we see a self-conscious step being taken in the depiction of human interiority as an absolute and autonomous inside of the subject: a complete marginalization of the physical body and its relationship to desire. *Chokher bali* is the story of the passion of a young man, Mahendra, who was married to a woman named Asha and who fell violently in love with a young widow, Binodini, who came from a village to stay with Mahendra, Asha, and Mahendra's mother in Calcutta. It is also a story about Binodini's own feelings of love, her initial attraction to Mahendra being replaced by her eventual love for Mahendra's best friend, Bihari. Unlike the widow characters in Bankim's novels, Binodini is literate; she is, in fact, depicted as an avid reader of Bankim's *Bishabriksha*. In a preface written to a later edition of the book, Tagore described how, for Bengali literature, the appearance of this novel heralded a sudden change. Its novelty lay in its emphasis on the interior space of human beings. True, there was still a role for the sense organs, for the idea of *ripu* (the traditional Hindu view of six particular embodied passions that destroy man), but all this was now subordinated to the work of psychological forces. As Tagore himself put it:

> What drives the story of *Chokher bali* from inside and gives it its intensity is the jealousy of the mother. It is this jealousy that provided Mahendra's *ripu* with an opportunity to bare itself, all tooth-and-claw, which would not have happened under normal circumstances. . . . The method of new literature no longer simply delineates events in the right order, it analyses them in order to extract stories about the inside of human beings. [Tagore uses the expression "aanter katha."] This new method made an appearance in *Chokher bali*.[38]

One may read this statement as installing in Bengali fiction the modern subject endowed with an interiority. In Vidyasagar, the widow's desire was understood as lust, a purely physical passion of youth regulated by the laws of nature and hence powerful beyond human control. With Bankimchandra, Rabindranath, and Saratchandra, there began a new and self-conscious discussion of what romantic (heterosexual) love *(prem)* was, as distinct from the problem of lust. There is, however, a twist to this story of the birth of the modern subject in Bengali literature. That twist and its history are now condensed in a word that came into wide circulation in the period 1870 to 1920. This word was *pabitra,* used as a qualifier of secular, human love. Usually glossed in English as "pure," but connoting something of a combination of "sacred," "auspicious," and "unstained" or "untainted"—untainted, that is, by physical passion—this word has been used by many Bengali writers to signify love that transcends physical passion. The *prem* (love) that was *pabitra* was the highest kind of love. Bankimchandra defined *pabitra* as that which has conquered or transcended the senses *(jitendriya).* This was an ancient theme. As a way of thinking about the body, it reached back to certain strands of Vedantic philosophy; but it became central to nineteenth-century nationalist discussions of conduct and the self, where the ideal of self was posited as that of being *jitendriya,* literally someone who had conquered his or her physical senses.[39] The Bengali discussion of love, however, was more immediately indebted to medieval Vaishnava poetry (followers of the preserver-god Vishnu are called Vaishnava), which modern Bengali writers increasingly rediscovered from the 1870s onward.[40]

Much Vaishnava poetry was structured around the theme of the illicit love that Radha, the married heroine of this poetry, bore for Krishna, an incarnation of the god Vishnu in a human form. This extramarital love had brought on Radha the opprobrium of *kalanka,* which many Vaishnava poets exonerated by portraying Radha's love as symbolic of the devotee's spiritual longing for union with god and therefore as actually having very little to do with narrowly construed physical passion or self-indulgence. It was in this ideal of love as a spiritual sentiment, as something devoid of any hint of lust, that Bengali writers found an elaboration of desire between the sexes that could signify individual interiority and desires and yet at the same time seem socially respectable for avoiding any suggestion that love could also be about the body. In an essay comparing the two medieval Vaishnava poets Jayadev (twelfth century) and Vidyapati (fifteenth century), Bankimchandra made a distinction between two kinds of nature *(prakriti),* external *(bahihprakriti)* and internal *(antahprakriti).* The body and its passions belonged to external nature, to the realm of the senses. Interiority was the nature internal to humans, and it was there that one could get away from the rule of the senses and make love spiritual or *pabitra.* Bankimchandra wrote:

The writers of lyrical poetry in Bengali may be divided into two groups: those who look at man setting him in the context of natural beauty and those who attend solely to the human heart, keeping external nature at a distance. . . . It is external nature *[bahihprakriti]* that is predominant in Jayadeva and his likes while in the likes of Vidyapati we find the domain of nature that is internal *[antahprakriti]*. Jayadev and Vidyapati both sing of the love between Radha and Krishna. But the love that Jayadeva sings of obeys the external sense-organs. The poems of Vidyapati, and especially those of Chandidasa, transcend our external senses . . . and become *pabitra*, that is to say, devoid of any association with the senses or with self-indulgence.[41]

Vaishnava doctrines were mixed in with European romanticism—Bankim, for instance, refers to Wordsworth as the poet of the spiritual *antahprakriti* (internal nature) in the same essay—to arrive at the modern Bengali understanding of love as a formation of sentiment that combined recognition of individual desire with the middle class's need for respectability.

The story, apparently popular since the seventeenth century, of the socially scandalous love between the famous fifteenth-century Bengali poet Chandidasa, a Vaishnavite Brahman, and a low-caste washerwoman called Rami, was recycled time and again in modern Bengali writing to illustrate the ideal of romantic love.[42] In one of his poems on this subject—and in lines that Bengali literary criticism has made immortal since the end of the last century—Chandidasa himself compared Rami's love to something as pure as "gold without dross,"without, he said, even a scent of (physical) desire in it. When he was about twenty, Tagore wrote a highly influential essay in which he upheld these lines of Chandidasa as the ideal of love between men and women:

> How pure was Chandidas's love! He could separate love from self-indulgence. That is why he said of his lover's beauty, that there was not even a scent of [physical] desire in it. . . . I will be with her but not touch her body. . . . this is not a love of the external world, a love of seeing and touching. This is the treasure of dreams. It is wrapped up in dreams and has no relationship to the world which is awake. It is love in its absolute purity and nothing else. Chandidasa's statement does not belong [only] to the time when he wrote it.[43]

Historians of Bengali literature, from Dineschandra Sen at the beginning of this century to the more recent Asit Bandyopadhayay, have followed Tagore in this opinion.[44] Thus while the interior space of the widow—or of the human subject—opened up to the documentary gaze of Bengali novelists, love, being *pabitra,* emerged as a flight of the spirit, which was always struggling with the aid of moral reasoning to avoid any suggestion of physicality. This, I want to argue, determined to a large degree the nature of the Bengali modern and some of its significant specificities.

In Bankimchandra, Rabindranath, and Saratchandra, the body circulates as what threatens the domain of interiority. The body threatens its capacity to be pure, or *pabitra.* In Bankim, however, while reason struggles with passion and this struggle is the central fact of human interiority, the body still enjoys an autonomous existence—autonomous of the mind, that is, through Bankim's category of beauty or external appearance *(rup),* which belongs to his understanding of external nature *(prakriti).* According to Bankim, it is in the nature of man to be attracted to *rup.* In his novel *Bishabriksha* (The Poison-Tree), published in 1873, the *rup* of a young and beautiful widow called Kunda plays a critical role in drawing a happily married man, Nagendra, to itself like a moth to fire. Nagendra leaves his wife and marries Kunda. This fire-moth relationship was, for Bankim, a perfect image of the way external nature or *bahihprakriti* tempts humans to their ironic or tragic destiny. As he himself wrote in his ironic, witty, and humorous series of essays in the book *Kamalakanter daptar:*

> From now on it seemed to me that every man was but an insect. Each one of them had his own kind of fire in which he desired to die . . . Some do and some get stopped by the glass. Knowledge is one such fire, wealth another, status, beauty, religion, sense-organs are of other kinds—this world is full of fires. The world is also full of glass. The light that attracts us, the light into which we want to tumble down, drawn by that attraction—well, we do not reach it, do we? We buzz back and forth only to return again and again. If it had not been for the existence of [this] glass, the world would have been burnt down by now.[45]

The interiority of someone like Nagendra, the tragic hero of *Bishabriksha,* is made up of a story in which his reason/will struggles, unsuccessfully, with *bahihprakriti,* or external nature. Human freedom, suggests Bankim, lies in being able to distinguish—with the help of moral reasoning—between that which belongs to the interior space of the subject, the *prakriti* or nature of the interior *(antahprakriiti),* and that which belongs to external nature or *bahihprakriti.* Humans are apt to feel an attraction for physical beauty. Nagendra, the hero of Bankim's novel, calls it "chokher bhalobasha" (lit., love of the eyes).[46] To this "love of the eyes," Bankim opposed something one might call "love of the mind." The theory is elaborated by another character in the novel, Haradev Ghosal, Nagendra's brother-in-law, who says to Nagendra the following (and the reader will see how this ideal of pure love provided a framework through which Bengali authors consumed European literature as well):

> There are many sensations in the mind which people call love. . . . The desire to enjoy the beauty of a beautiful woman is not love. . . . This propensity . . . is sent by God; it is by means of it, too, that the world's desires are realised, and it fascinates all creatures. Kalidasa, Byron, Jayadeva are its poets. . . . But it is not love. Love is born of the faculties of the mind. [Its] result is sympathy, and in the end, self-forgetfulness and self-renunciation. This is truly love. Shakespeare, Valmiki and the author of the Bhagavat Purana are its poets.[47]

We would miss the complexity of Bankim's thought if we read him as simply reinventing the nature/culture distinction of European sociology and locating woman in nature. *Rup,* formal beauty, belongs to *bahihprakriti,* or external nature. Bankim, as I have said, makes a distinction between external and internal nature, *bahihprakriti* and *antarprakriti.* But the word *prakriti,* in Bankim, always resonates on two separate registers, symptomatic of the processes of cultural translation, which modernity essentially was in colonial Bengal. Bankim's category *prakriti* mediates between the modern scientific understanding of nature as a collection of inert bodies driven by blind, unconscious physical laws, and the older Tantric understanding of *prakriti* or nature as a form of consciousness, a feminine power animating the world, creating it in collaboration with *purush,* man or the masculine power, and tempting the latter to both live and die.[48]

One fundamental difference between Bankim's approach to desire in *Bishabriksha* and that of Tagore in *Chokher bali* is that there is no problem of *rup* or the "love of the eye" in *Chokher bali.* Physical beauty, as we have seen, remains a part of Bankim's cosmology; he warns against its impact on the mind precisely because he considers it genuinely powerful. Tagore leaves us in no doubt that his heroine Binodini is the new woman endowed with interiority and subjectivity. However physically attractive she may be, Binodini is a product of new education and enlightenment. Unlike in the novels of Bankim, reason in *Chokher bali* does not struggle to distinguish between love born of *rup* and love born of a "faculty of the mind." It was as if in response to Bankim's idea that love or attraction could be caused by the fact that human sight, independent of human morality, could not help being influenced by physical beauty *(rup)*, Tagore would quip (through the voice of Binodini): "Has God given men only sight and no insight at all?"[49] By thus subordinating sight to insight, Tagore shifted the drama of sentiments from the external space of physicality to the space of interiority in the subject.

Purity or *pabitrata* emerges in Bengali fiction as a set of techniques of interiority, the use of which could make one's innermost emotions (such as love) "pure" and thus help them transcend anything that was external to the subject's interior space—the body, interests, social dogmas, and prejudices. It created an extreme autonomy in the status of affect and a strong sense of resolve in the subject. For this acquisition of the quality of one's interiority being *pabitra* did not come without a determined struggle against the senses that connected one to the exterior world, and this battle was the spiritual struggle of an individual to be an individual. Tagore could thus create in his fiction extremely forceful characters of widows whose struggle against social injustice took on the halo of a spiritual vigilance. In *Chokher bali,* for instance, a character named Annapurna, an aunt of Asha's who, much like a "traditional" widow, decides to live in the holy city of Banaras, illustrates this point. An elderly person, she stays well outside the circuit of youthful romantic love in the novel. But her conversations with Asha leave us in no doubt that this widowed aunt was nothing but her own person. Her resolution to keep her innermost self pure or *pabitra* was at the same time her quiet defiance of social conventions:

> Asha one day asked her, "Tell me Auntie, do you remember our uncle?" Annapurna said, "I became a widow at eleven. My husband's image I can only recall as a shadow." Asha asked, "Then who do you think about, Auntie?" Annapurna smiled a little and said, "I think of Him in whom my husband resides now, I think of that god." Asha said, "Does that make you happy?" Annapurna ran her fingers through Asha's hair affectionately, and said, "What would you understand, my child, of what happens inside me? Only my mind knows it. And it is known to Him, He is who is in my thoughts. . . . There was a day when this aunt of yours, when she was your age, entered the commerce of give and take with the world,

just as you are doing now. Like you, I also used to think, why wouldn't my service and my nurturing give rise to contentment in the person I served? Why would I not receive grace from him whom I worshiped? . . . But at every step I saw that this did not happen. One day I left the world out of the feeling that everything in this world had failed for me. But today I see that nothing had failed. . . . If only I knew it then. If I had done my duties in the world as though they were my duties to Him, if I had offered my heart to this world only as a ruse for offering it to Him, then who could have made me suffer? . . . This is my advice: whatever the suffering you receive, keep your faith and devotion intact. And may your sense of *dharma* [proper action] be unflinching.[50]

The later writer Saratchandra Chatterjee espoused a view similar to Tagore's. In a move reminiscent of the way Tagore converted the problem of "sight" into that of "insight," Saratchandra effected a displacement of Bankim's problematic of *rup* (beauty) in order to make room for the idea of *prakrito rup* (true or real beauty), an inside to the human being that now seemed more beautiful than mere external beauty or outward appearance. Speaking in anger at the treatment of a young widow whom he knew from his childhood and who had lost all her social standing overnight simply because a man was one day found in her bedroom, Saratchandra said in 1932:

Perhaps she has nothing called chastity left any more. Suppose I accept that. But what about her femininity? Will her nursing of the sick for days and nights on end . . . and her unstinting giving to the poor receive no . . . consideration? Is the woman's body everything that matters, does her inside *(antar)* count for nothing? Even if this woman, widowed in her childhood and driven by the unbearable urging of youth, failed to preserve the purity *(pabitrata)* of her body, will that make all the qualities of her inside false? . . . Where do we get to see the true beauty *(prakrito rup)* of the human being? In the covering of his or her body or in the covering of his or her interiority? You tell me.[51]

The details of Saratchandra's argument here are worth some attention, for they help us see the working of "the aesthetic marginalization of the body" in early modern fiction in Bengal. Saratchandra does not argue against the idea of chastity as such; more typically and primarily, he sees it as a practice of the mind and not of the body. The young widow might have been with another man, but if anything, that only destroyed the purity of her body; the more valuable purity was the purity of her mind, which was reflected in her acts of compassion and self-sacrifice and which—and not her body—was what gave her real beauty *(prakrito rup)*. The argument about *pabitrata* or purity was about the interior self. Its cultivation made the woman her own person. Saratchandra saw the inner purity of the good woman as the sign of the woman's individuality. It was therefore also his ground for opposing men's unquestioned rights over women. He wrote to a woman correspondent about "[the idea] that she who became a widow at the age of sixteen or seventeen would have no right to love or marry anybody else." "Why not?" he asked and added, "It takes only a little thought to see that there is but one prejudice hidden in this [proposition], that the wife is a possession of the husband."[52]

The novels thus establish the idea of a private but communicable sphere of interiority—autonomous of the physical body—something that is critical to the category of the modern subject in European thought.[53] Bengali literary thought acknowledged lust, an animal passion residing in the body. To this it opposed the idea of *prem* or love. *Prem* came to mark the autonomy of the individual in the widow, precisely by putting a distance between itself and the body through the techniques of purity or *pabitrata*. Fiction thus shone a light by which to see and archive the widow as an individual subject endowed with interiority. The widow, qua widow, could now both write herself and be written about.

But the continuing theme of purity or *pabitrata* suggests that it was around the question of the body that the struggle of reason with passion was staged in this dramatization of human interiority. The body remains an unresolved problem in these novels. It is either completely marginalized as the seat of the lust that *pabitra prem* (true/pure love) conquers or it comes back (as in Bankim) in the problem of *rup* (form, appearance), as fate that teases and tempts the human's internal nature *(antahprakriti)*. In either case, nothing mediates between the body and the interior space of the subject. What was ideologically invested in the practice of *pabitrata*? How indeed was the theme of purity meant to capture the interior strife of the modern subject? What was the nature of this strife? In *Chokher bali*, Tagore gives a particular name to the form of reason that struggles with physical passion to produce the practices of purity: *kartabyabudhhi (kartabya =* duty; *budhhi =* intellect). This, in other words, was the mode of reasoning that kept one tied to one's worldly duties, a kind of common sense about the householder's life lived in a context where the extended family, even if unworkable in practice, constituted in ideal the horizon of well-being. As Tagore himself interjected in the course of narrating the novel:

> If love is ever plucked out and isolated—as one plucks a flower— from the difficult duties that make up the householder's world, it cannot sustain itself by [feeding] only on its own sap. It gradually wilts and becomes distorted.[54]

The struggle that constitutes the interiority of the subject is thus between passions on one side and familial obligations on the other, and it is in this struggle that sentiments need the guiding hand of (a moral) reason. It was the respectability of the extended family—and not just of the loving couple—that was at issue. Vidyasagar's problematic had thus indeed survived into Tagore's. The pursuit of *pabitrata* gave the modern subject an interior space of struggle, created an autonomy vis-à-vis the body and yet thereby sustained a Bengali "family romance" that was nothing like the European psychological triangle of the mother, the father, and the child that Freud both technicized and popularized in the early twentieth century. For the category of *pabitrata*, tied to an idealization of the extended family and kinship, obviated the emergence of a category such as "sexuality," which could have mediated between the physical basis of sexual attraction and its psychological superstructure in the individual.

The Archive of the Modern Subject: Who Gets Called to Witness Suffering?

Modern Bengali literature, then, played a crucial role in generalizing a will to document the suffering of the widow and in enabling certain ways of seeing. As a genre, the novel was particularly suited to the task of aiding in the reproduction of a general and generalizing sentiment while preserving and nurturing the idea of the individual-private. Its techniques of verisimilitude promoted a sense of the particular while at the same time creating a vision of the general. The growing and close connection forged between literature, middle-class reading practices, and new forms of personhood is a history still unexplored in the case of Bengal. But there are some suggestive pieces of evidence. By the 1930s, for example, it would appear that the readers of Bengali novels actually compared the different and many widow characters created in fiction and mentally placed them in a series signifying the progressive evolution of the modern individual, a progression from the stage of social conventions completely tying down the individual to the idea of the individual endowed with "free" interiority. The following lines from Suresh Samajpati, the editor of the Bengali literary journal *Sahitya,* addressed to Saratchandra, illustrates this mode of comparative and historicist reading:

> There is a substantial difference between the character of Rohini that Bankimchandra created and that of your Sabitri. Firstly, Rohini was the niece of Brahmananda, she had no lack of status in society. Her only crime was that in spite of being a widow, she loved Gobindalal. Your . . . Sabitri enjoys no such social standing. Secondly, it required a lot of arranging [of events] for the love-affair between Gobindalal and Rohini to look inevitable [in Bankim's novel], . . . At least in the eyes of society there is an excuse for the love between Rohini and Gobindalal. But there can be no such excuse possible for the love between Sabitri and Satish. One depends on the contingency of events, the other on desire alone.[55]

Individuals, including female readers of this humanist fiction, came to see their lives in the light of literature. In her autobiographical book *Kom boyosher ami* (The Me of Younger Years), the contemporary Bengali writer Manashi Dasgupta describes an older, widowed aunt, "Itupishi" (father's sister/cousin, called Itu) as being "somebody straight out of the pages of Bengali fiction." "She became a widow at a young age, now she worked for the government's education department having put herself through school. . . . With ease she would converse with my father on the subject of the failure of the United Nations while helping my mother cook *nimki* [popular savories]."[56] Kalyani Datta's research into the condition of Bengali widows in the 1950s and the 1960s were themselves inspired by fiction: "Widowhood has featured endlessly in Bengali literature over the last hundred and fifty years. . . . My interest in the lives of widows was aroused in my childhood as a result of meeting at close quarters characters in real life who resembled those encountered in stories and novels."[57]

If we assume that the different practices of writing about widows—fiction, autobiographies, diaries, reminiscences, and investigative reporting of the widow's suffering in the nineteenth and twentieth centuries—created in Bengal something like the European bourgeois public sphere inhabited by a discursive and collective subject of modernity, an interesting problem follows. How would we understand this collective subject? Was this subject the same as the citizen-subject of European political thought? There is no doubt that colonial quasi-modern law molded aspects of both action and subjectivity on the part of the widows. The Bengali poet Prasannamayi Devi (1857–1939), who herself became a widow at the age of twelve, tells the story, for example, of a brave nineteenth-century village woman called Kashiswari who, on becoming a widow at a young age, successfully sought legal intervention against possible oppression and harassment by men.[58] Widows' own accounts of domestic cruelty, however, bridge two kinds of memory that together form the modern archive of familial oppression in Hindu middle-class Bengal: social-public memory addressed by the citizen-historian who documents suffering and social injury in the interest of justice in public life, and addresses of familial memory articulated within specific locations of kinship.[59] Kalyani Datta's essay itself is an example of this, for she puts into print—and thus makes into public memory—memories she could sometimes access only as a member of a very particular network of kinship.

In standard narratives of European-bourgeois modernity, these two kinds of memories, the familial and the public, would eventually be aligned with each other. First, families based on modern romantic love would replace the extended kin structure with the Freudian oedipal triangle. And the unitary-expressive and rights-bearing bourgeois subject, split into his or her private and public selves, would eventually assimilate into a structure of private "repression"—that which could not align itself with the laws of public life. So the history of repression and sexuality would come to constitute the private history of the subject of public life. As Foucault's *History of Sexuality* shows, such a repressive hypothesis and a consequent incitement to speech were critical to the birth of the modern subject and the documentation of bourgeois interiority.[60] In the Bengali case, the addressees of these two memories—the social-public and the familial-private one, the citizen-subject and the subject of kinship—remain much less aligned with each other (a disjuncture similar to that examined in Egyptian television drama in the essay by Lila Abu-Lughod in this volume).[61] The collective subject whom we could call the Bengali-modern is perhaps better conceptualized as a mobile point on something like a relay network in which many different subject-positions and even non-bourgeois, non-individualistic practices of subjectivity intersected. Kalyani Datta's text murmurs with multiple, heterogenous voices she can collect together only in a general gesture of seeking justice. The discursive collective Bengali subject of modernity was made up of multiple and non-commensurable practices, some of them distinctly non-modern by the standards of modern political thought.

First, there was the voice of the archaic-modern subject, whose cry of pain—always public in an archaic sense—was indeed addressed to the exceptional subject (not the normalized citizen) who could both receive and appreciate the *rasa* of *karuna* (compassion): the reader here is called to the position of somebody with *hriday*—a Rammohun, a Vidyasagar, a Jesus, a Chaitanya, or a Buddha to hear this voice. Listen, for example, to this Bengali widow:

> A woman who has lost her father, mother, husband and son, has no-body else left in the world. It is *only if* others in the household are of a kind disposition that a widow's life can be happy. Otherwise, it is like being consigned to a hell-pit.[62]

The conditional clause in this statement—"only if"—makes it clear that to this speaker, compassion was not a part of the normal order of life. Its existence was unpredictable. This is the widow speaking indeed but not as a citizen-subject seeking the promise and protection of law.

Then there is the voice that addresses itself to gods in search of strength and support. Listen to the voice of Gyanadasundari speaking to Kalyani Datta sometime in 1965. A child widow who in fact had never met her husband, she was sent to her in-laws to spend the rest of her life as a widow. Here she recounts an experience of deprivation in which the Hindu goddess Kali plays a critical role helping her to survive:

> I entered the kitchen [she said, speaking of her daily round of activities] immediately after my morning bath [to cook for] this large family. By the time I was finished, it would be late afternoon. A room full of cooked food—I cannot describe how hungry the smell of rice and curry made me feel. Sometimes I felt tempted to put some in my mouth. But my [deceased] husband's aunt had told me the story of the wife of a certain [deceased] person—this woman had been struck down with blindness on account of eating stealthily in the kitchen. Stories of this kind helped me control my hunger. Every-day I would pray to [the goddess] Kali: Mother, please take away my greed. Perhaps it was through the grace of the goddess that I gradu-ally lost any appetite I used to have.[63]

What is the nature of the human subject here? In what mode do we recognize ourselves in Gyanadasundari Devi? How is Kalyani Datta—

and indeed, the reader—positioned by this text? In more ways than one, it would seem. Datta (or the reader) may have been there to document the subject of suffering in the interest of eventual social intervention. Her intended position may have been that of the modern, secular, historicizing, and ontologically singular human being. She may have indeed heard the religious reference to the goddess in light of the spirit of toleration with which the secular subject approaches religion: "It is the sigh of the oppressed, the soul of a soulless world."[64] But does not Gyanadasundari's voice also place us alongside another human, one who is *not* ontologically singular, the human who acts as though he or she implicitly knew that being human meant one could address gods without having to first prove their reality?[65] This positioning would take us beyond the logic of the social sciences.

The point is that operating as it did through the same connections that were expected to generate familial affection as well, cruelty toward widows in the context of extended kinship was something that constantly proliferated the positions and voices of both its agents and victims, and sometimes blurred the distinctions between the two. Kalyani Datta reports the story of both the victimhood and the agentiality that a mother took on herself when her daughter, a six- or seven-year-old child, lost her husband. To the mother fell the duty of ensuring that the girl, who did not even understand the change in her status, observed all the self-renunciatory rites of widowhood. The incident relates to fish, not allowed to widows but considered a delicacy in the cuisine of riverine Bengal. We have the story in Kalyani Datta's telling:

> [The young girl's] mother used to feed her widows' food. The boys of the household would sit on another side of the room and be served fish. They said to her one day, "How come you haven't got any fish?" Her mother pointed to fried lentil balls and said to her: "This is your fish." The mischievous boys would suck on fish-bones and ask the girl: "How come your piece of fish does not have any bones?" The girl would ask her mother, "Mother, why doesn't my fish have any bones?" . . . The mother later on used to break off bamboo slips from baskets and stick them into the lentil balls and the girl would proudly show them off to the boys. . . . It was long before she even realized the deception.[66]

The mother who administered the cruelty of deceiving her own child suffered—we assume—no less than her child. One can also read this story as a tribute to a loving mother's ingenuity—faced with the cruelty

of both custom and callous boys—in preserving her little child's digni-
ty. However we read it, clearly the actions of the boys (not necessarily
the mother's sons), the mother, and the child-widow in this anecdote
create a dynamic network of relationships that cannot be contained
within the figure of a single victim.[67]

Indeed, one of the most interesting aspects of widows' own
critiques—in the nineteenth and twentieth centuries—of the cruelty
they received at the hands of their relatives was an appeal to an ideal
subject of the extended family. How should a brother behave toward
a widowed sister, or a brother-in-law toward a widowed sister-in-law?
Or a nephew toward a widowed aunt? Putting widows' complaints
into print and the act of reading them were often part of a larger discussion about sentiments proper to the ideal Bengali family, which
was seldom seen as nuclear. A telling case in this regard is that of
Indumati, an aunt of Kalyani Datta. Indumati (born ca. 1872), a young
widow of a *zamindar* (landlord) family, decided to live in the holy city
of Banaras—a traditional refuge for many a hapless widow—on a
monthly allowance from her inheritance of the deceased husband's
estate. She was subsequently cheated out of her inheritance. Her allowance dwindled from Rs 250 a month to Rs 10, reducing her to the
status of a beggar. Kalyani Datta last saw Indumati in Benaras in 1955
(and we hear her in print in 1991). She had by then reached the depth
of her penury and was living in an institution. "I did not recognize
her," says Datta:

> Our aunt, the wife of a *zamindar* (landlord) family with fifty per
> cent share in the estate, sat naked in a dark room without windows,
> muttering curses addressed to . . . God. She could not see very well.
> Feeling helpless, I started yelling out my name and that of my father.
> She recognized me then and immediately started crying. . . . After a
> while, she asked me how long I had been in Kashi [Banaras]. When
> she realized that I had been there for twenty days and had come to
> see her only a day before my day of departure, her tears returned.
> "Here I am," she said, "hoping that I would [now] be able to shed
> some tears and spend some days in the comfort of your company,
> and all you offer me is this *fake* [perfunctory] *sense of kinship*. I
> don't even want to see your face." So saying, she turned her back
> on me.[68]

This entire passage, one could say, is a modern discussion of what
Bengalis call *atmiyata* (kinship, the quality of being one's own people),
a much-valued category in Tagore and other modern writers.[69] Notice

how in Kalyani Datta's telling of the story a subject voice emerges that absolutizes a modern and relational subject of kinship, and does so by placing the very sentiment of obligation in kinship over and above considerations of either interest or perfunctory social form. Indumati/ Kalyani Datta—for the two voices are actually indistinguishable here—obviously make a distinction between a fake show of kinship sentiment and a "real" one. But they do not require such a sentiment to be an expression of the personality of the individual expressing it, for the sentiment would be demanded of any member of the kin group without reference to the differences between their individual person-alities. And yet the language allows certain claims to be made on an-other person's affection in a way that, strictly speaking, would not be possible in the context of typically expressivist individualism where feelings, once dead to the individual concerned, are seen as inauthen-tic and hypocritical. The subject of this emotional transaction is mod-ern and yet, as I have said before, not like the bourgeois individual of Europe inscribed in the family romance of the typical triangle of the nuclear family.[70] I am not claiming that this idealized subject of kin-ship was necessarily a modern construction. What is modern is the way the coming of a public sphere opened up a space in public life for the modern subject of extended kinship alongside, say, the sphere of intervention made possible by law and the idea of the rights-bearing individual.

The subject of Bengali modernity who demonstrates a will to witness and document oppression is thus inherently a multiple subject whose history produces significant points of resistance and intracta-bility when approached with an apparatus of secular analysis that has its origins in the self-understanding of the European modern. Thus we may read the author Kalyani Datta in two different ways. As an au-thor and a person, it is indeed possible that in writing her essay docu-menting and recording for posterity the voices of individual widows, she performs as a citizen subject engaged in a struggle for democracy and social justice in the realm of the family. One could, in the same mode, read her essay as a chapter in the biography-history of some larger collective entity, such as "middle-class Bengali women" or "the Bengali *bhadramahila*" (as women of the respectable classes are called). But what is also documented in her essay and elsewhere, thanks to the resolute will to witness suffering that marks modern attempts at social justice, are practices of the self that call us to other ways of being civil

and humane. These are practices of the self that always leave an intellectually unmanageable excess when translated into the politics and
language of liberalism or Marxism that we owe to European modernity. At the same time, the very colonial crucible in which the Bengali
modern was originated ensured that it would not be possible to fashion a historical account of the birth of this modernity without reproducing some aspect or other of European narratives of the modern
subject. For the European modern was present at this birth. Colonialism guarantees a certain Europe of the mind—the Europe of liberalism or Marxism—this precedence. What a historian of a colonial modernity can do today—taught as he or she is in the (European) art of
historicizing—is to re-energize the word "birth" with all the motor
power of Nietzschean thought that Michel Foucault revived for us in
recent times.[71] To see "birth" as genealogy and not a clear-cut point of
origin, to make visible—as Nietzsche said—the otherness of the ape
that always gets in the way of any attempt to trace human descent directly from God, is to open up the question of the relationship between diversity of life practices/life worlds and universalizing political
philosophies that remain the global heritage of the Enlightenment.[72]
This account of the birth of the Bengali modern is, I hope, a step in
that direction.

Notes

Thanks are due to Arjun Appadurai, Homi Bhabha, Gautam Bhadra, Carol Breckenridge, Alice Bullard, Steve Collins, Faisal Devji, Ranajit Guha, Dipankar Gupta, Anne
Hardgrove, Uday Mehta, Bhaskar Mukhopadhyay, Klaus Neumann, Christopher Pinney,
Sheldon Pollock, Gyan Prakash, Asok Sen, and Sanjay Seth for conversations and comments on an earlier draft. It was Asok Sen's imaginative work on Rammohun Roy and
Isvarchandra Vidyasagar that awakened in many of us in Calcutta of the 1970s a sense
of the possibility that the history of modern colonialism in India could indeed be seen as
a series of shifts and reversals in the career of modern European reason. This essay is
dedicated to him in a spirit of affection and long-standing gratitude.

1. Kalyani Datta, "Baidhabya kahini" (Tales of Widowhood, in Bengali), *Ekshan*,
20 (Autumn 1991). This essay appears to have been reprinted in Kalyani Datta, *Pinjare
boshiya* [in Bengali] (Calcutta, 1997). Unfortunately, it has not been possible for me to
consult this later version.
2. See Muhammad Abdul Jalil, *Madhyajuger bangla shahitye bangla o bangali
shamaj* (in Bengali) (Dhaka, 1986), 149–67.
3. The historical question of the oppression of Hindu widows has been studied by
many scholars. Without any pretense to being exhaustive, I may mention the following
recent studies: Lata Mani, *Contentious Traditions: The Debate on Sati in Colonial India,
1780–1833* (Berkeley: University of California Press, 1998); Lucy Caroll, "Law, Custom
and Statutory Social Reform: The Hindu Widows' Remarriage Act of 1856," *Indian

Economic and Social History Review 20, no. 4 (1983); Sudhir Chandra, "Conflicted Beliefs and Men's Consciousness about Women: Widow Remarriage in Later Nineteenth Century Indian Literature," *Economic and Political Weekly,* 31 October 1987, 55–62; Rosalind O'Hanlon, "Issues of Widowhood: Gender and Resistance in Colonial Western India," in *Contesting Power: Resistance and Everyday Social Relations in South Asia,* ed. Douglas Haynes and Gyan Prakash (Delhi: Oxford University Press, 1991), 62–108.

4. Rammohun Roy, "Brief Remarks Regarding Modern Encroachments on the Ancient Rights of Females," in *Rammohan rachanabali* (Collected Works of Rammohun Roy, in Bengali), ed. Ajitkumar Ghosh (Calcutta, 1973), 496–97.

5. Ibid., 496–97, 500–501.

6. "Prabartak o nibartaker dvitiyo shombad," in Rammohun Roy, *Rammohun rachanabali,* 203.

7. Ibid., 575. This is Rammohun's own translation of his 1818 text, "Sahamaran bishaye prabartak o nibartaker shombad," ibid., 175.

8. Ibid. Hume, distinguishing between "custom" and "reason," equates the former with "habit": "Custom or Habit. For whenever the repetition of any particular act or operation produces a propensity to produce the same act or operation, without being impelled by any reasoning or process of understanding, we always say that this propensity is the effect of *Custom*" (David Hume, *Enquiries Concerning Human Understanding and Concerning the Principles of Morals* [1777], intro. L. A. Selby-Bigge [Oxford: Oxford University Press, 1990], 43, emphasis in original). Hume argues that it is "custom or repetition" that can convert "pain into pleasure" (*A Treatise of Human Nature* [1739–40], ed. L. A. Selby-Bigge, rev. P. H. Nidditch [Oxford: Oxford University Press, 1978], 422).

9. For a theoretically informed discussion of Vidyasagar's intellectual positions, see Asok Sen, *Iswarchandra Vidyasagar and His Elusive Milestones* (Calcutta: Riddhi-India, 1975).

10. Chandicharan Bandyopadhyay, *Vidyasagar* (ca. 1895; rpr. Calcutta, 1970), 266. I have followed and modified the translation provided in Isvarchandra Vidyasagar, *Marriage of Hindu Widows,* ed. Arabinda Poddar (Calcutta: K. P. Bagchi, 1976), 107–8.

11. Adam Smith, *The Theory of Moral Sentiments,* ed. D. D. Raphael and A. L. Macfie (Indianapolis: Liberty Fund, 1984), 9; see also 22. Raphael and Macfie explain (14n) that Smith's theories were in part a refutation of Hobbes's and Mandeville's contention that all sentiments arose from self-love.

12. Hume, *Treatise,* 316, 369.

13. Nagendranath Chattopadhyay, *Mahatma Raja Rammohon rayer jibancharit* (in Bengali) (1881; rpr. Calcutta, 1991), 273.

14. Subal Chandra Mitra, *Isvar Chandra Vidyasagar: A Story of His Life and Work* (1902; rpr. New Delhi: Ashish Publishing House, 1975), 116.

15. Bandyopadhyay, *Vidyasagar,* 48–49.

16. Mitra, *Isvar Chandra,* 78–79.

17. Bandyopadhyay, *Vidyasagar,* 49; see also 187.

18. Mitra, *Isvar Chandra,* 272–73.

19. See Binoy Ghosh, *Bidyasagar o bangali samaj* (in Bengali) (Calcutta, 1973), 363. Vidyasagar was sometimes called *dayar sagar* (ocean of kindness) as well.

20. Sivanath Sastri, "Rammohun Roy: The Story of His Life," in *The Father of Modern India: Commemoration Volume of the Rammohun Roy Centenary Celebrations, 1933,* ed. Satis Chandra Chakravarti (Calcutta, 1935), pt. 2, 20.

21. Mitra, *Isvar Chandra,* 261.

22. Smith, *Moral Sentiments,* 12.

23. Ibid., 22. Hume also saw sympathy as universal to human nature.

24. For a general discussion of the place of *hriday* in Sanskrit aesthetics, see Ranerio Gnoli's *The Aesthetic Experience According to Abhinavagupta* (Banaras, 1968).

25. Smith, *Moral Sentiments,* 45, 50.

26. See the discussion in Hans-Georg Gadamer, *Truth and Method* (London, 1979), 239–53.

27. Bandyopadhyay, *Vidyasagar,* 478.

28. Ibid., 278.

29. Ibid., preface, 6.

30. C. B. Macpherson, *The Political Theory of Possessive Individualism: Hobbes to Locke* (Oxford: Oxford University Press, 1974), 137–42.

31. See Karl Marx, "On the Jewish Question," in *Early Writings,* trans. Rodney Livingstone and Gregor Benton, introduction by Lucio Colletti (Harmondsworth, Middlesex: Penguin Books, 1975), 211–41.

32. William E. Connolly, *Political Theory and Modernity* (Oxford: Oxford University Press, 1989), 71.

33. Ibid., 57–58.

34. Timothy Mitchell, *Colonising Egypt,* 2nd ed. (Berkeley: University of California Press, 1991), 121.

35. Emphasis added.

36. See, for instance, contemporary plays written on the question of widow remarriage in which the widow's own problems are understood as *joubanjontrona* (lit., the agony of the body in youth) or *joubonjvala* (lit., the burning sensation produced by the onset of youth): Radhamadhab Mitra, *Bidhaba bisham bipod* (in Bengali) (Calcutta, n.d. [1856?]); idem, *Bidhabamonoranjan natak* (in Bengali) (Calcutta, 1857); Anon., *Bidhaba shukher dasha* (in Bengali) (Calcutta, 1864); Umacharan Bandyopadhyay, *Bidhabodbaho natak* (in Bengali) (Calcutta, n.d.); and Jadunath Chattopadhyay, *Bidhababilash* (in Bengali) (Calcutta, 1864).

37. For a somewhat parallel argument about the role of humanitarian and realist writing in eighteenth- and early nineteenth-century Europe, see Thomas W. Laqueur, "Bodies, Details and the Humanitarian Narrative," in *The New Cultural History,* ed. Lynn Hunt (Berkeley: University of California Press, 1989), 177–204.

38. Rabindranath Tagore, *Chokher bali,* in *Rabindrarachanabali* (in Bengali) (Calcutta, 1962), vol. 8, preface.

39. Dayananda, Vivekananda, and Gandhi were nationalist leaders who played a key role in disseminating these ideas.

40. The biographer of Tagore, Prabhatkumar Mukhopadhyay, writes: "It was the Bengali weekly *Amritabazar Patrika* (March 28, 1870) that first drew the attention of the education-proud Bengalis to Vaishnav poetry. But the first collection of these poems in a book-form was edited by Jagabandhu Bhadra (1870)" (Prabhatkumar Mukhopadhyay, *Rabindrajibani o rabindrasahitya prabeshak* [in Bengali] [Calcutta, 1960], vol. 1, 68). For an informative discussion of Vaishnavism in nineteenth-century Calcutta, see Ramakanta Chakravarti, *Vaisavism in Bengal, 1486–1900* (Calcutta, 1985), chs. 21 and 22.

41. Bankimchandra Chattopadhyay, "Bidyapati o Jaydeb," in *Bankimrachanabali* (Collected Works of Bankimchandra, in Bengali) (Calcutta, 1973), vol. 2, 191.

42. Sukumar Sen, *Bangla sahityer itihas* (in Bengali) (Calcutta, 1991), vol. 1, 126, says that the story of the love affair between Chandidasa and Rami became popular from the seventeenth century on.

43. "Chandidas o bidyapati," in *Rabindrarachanabali* (in Bengali) (Calcutta, 1962), vol. 13, 635.

44. See Dines Chandra Sen, *History of Bengali Language and Literature* (Calcutta, 1911), 149, and Asitkumar Bandyopadhyay, *Bangla shahityer shompurno itibritto* (in Bengali) (Calcutta, 1992), 100–101.

45. "Kamalakanter daptar," in *Bankimrachanabali* (in Bengali) (Calcutta, 1973), vol. 2, 58. See also the discussion in Sudipta Kaviraj, *The Unhappy Consciousness: Bankimchandra Chattopadhyay and the Formation of Nationalist Discourse in India* (New York: Oxford University Press, 1995).

46. Bankimchandra Chattopadhyay, *Bishabriksha*, in *Bankimrachanabali* (in Bengali) (Calcutta, 1985), vol. 1, 261. See Marian Maddern's translation of *Bishabriksha* (The Poison Tree), in Bankim Chandra Chatterjee, *The Poison Tree: Three Novellas,* trans. Marian Maddern and S. N. Mukherjee (New Delhi, 1996), 113.

47. Bankimchandra Chattapadhyay, *Bishabriksha,* 114.

48. See Mohitlal Majumdar's thoughtful discussion in *Bankimchandrer upanyash* (in Bengali) (Calcutta, 1979), 21–51.

49. Tagore, "Chokher bali," 316.

50. Ibid., 302–3.

51. Gopalchandra Ray, *Saratchandra* (in Bengali) (Calcutta, 1966), vol. 2, 201–2.

52. Cited in Khondkar Rezaul Karim, *Bangla upanyashe bidhaba* (The Widow in Bengali Literature, in Bengali) (Dhaka, 1979), 71.

53. Post-structuralist and feminist thought have made us skeptical of this fiction of the autonomous subject, but for the period we are considering this was the guiding fiction.

54. Tagore, "Chokher bali," 232.

55. Quoted in Ray, *Saratchandra,* vol. 2, 18–19.

56. Manashi Dasgupta, *Kom boyosher ami* (in Bengali) (Calcutta, 1974), 49.

57. Kalyani Datta, "Baidhyabar kahini," 41.

58. Prasannamayi Devi, *Purba katha* (in Bengali), ed. Nirmalya Acharya (1917; rpr. Calcutta, 1982), 80–81.

59. Drawing on the work of Maurice Halbwachs, Paul Connerton discusses this problem of articulation of social and familial memories in his *How Societies Remember* (Cambridge: Cambridge University Press, 1989), 38–39.

60. Michel Foucault, *History of Sexuality,* Vol. 1: *An Introduction,* trans. Robert Hurley (New York: Vintage, 1980), pt. 2, ch. 1.

61. Lila Abu-Lughod, "Modern Subjects: Egyptian Melodrama and Postcolonial Difference," this volume, ch. 4.

62. Datta, "Baidhabya kahini," 43, emphasis added.

63. Ibid., 50–51.

64. As the reader will recognize, these familiar words paraphrase Marx.

65. See Ramchandra Gandhi, *The Availability of Religious Ideas* (London: Macmillan, 1976), 9.

66. Datta, "Baidhabya kahini," 53.

67. For other similar accounts see also ibid., 49–50; Nistarini Devi, *Shekele katha* (1913) (in Bengali), in *Atmakatha,* ed. Nareshchandra Jana et al. (Calcutta, 1982), vol. 2, 33, 35.

68. Datta, "Baidhabya kahini," 48.

69. See the discussion in Ronald B. Inden and Ralph W. Nicholas, *Kinship in Bengali Culture* (Chicago: University of Chicago Press, 1977), 3–34.

70. A similar point is made in the autobiography of the mother of the Bengali

reformer Keshub Sen, Sarasundari Devi (1819–1907). When she suffered at the hands of her in-laws following the death of her husband, Keshub Sen suggested to his mother the solution of legally dividing up the family's property. "Keshub said to me," she writes, ". . . Mother, if you want, I can get your and Krishnabehari's [another son] shares, too, by getting a lawyer to write." I replied, "No. Is money the most important thing? Should *your uncle* [emphasis added] go to jail for the sake of money? Let it be, there is no need [to claim the money] at present" (Saradasundari Devi, *Atmakatha* [1913] [in Bengali], reprinted in *Atmakatha,* ed. Nareshchandra Jana et al. (Calcutta, 1981), vol. 1, 14, 26.

71. Michel Foucault, "Nietzsche, Genealogy, History," in *Language, Counter-Memory, Practice: Selected Essays and Interviews,* ed. Donald Bouchard, trans. Donald Bouchard and Sherry Simon (Ithaca: Cornell University Press, 1977), 139–84.

72. Nietzsche, cited ibid., 143.

Four

Modern Subjects:
Egyptian Melodrama and
Postcolonial Difference

Lila Abu-Lughod

In the late 1980s, a group of young university-educated Egyptians performed for their friends in Cairo a clever satire of local television. Recordings of the show later circulated informally on audio and video cassettes. The performance made fun of the language of state officials and religious authorities, whose frequent appearances on discussion programs are seldom popular. The final three sketches on the tape, however, took on Egyptian television's most popular programming, the dramatic serials and films. Two of these stories were set in the countryside, where the misdeeds of foolish or violent peasants were easily found out by more educated officers of non-rural origins. The third sketch enticed its imaginary viewers with a film that promised to be "full of tears and surprises." The story opened with two sweethearts declaring their mutual love. When the man suggested that they should get married, the woman protested that they were of different classes yet admitted that she had longed for the kind hand that would rescue her from the society that despised her. She explained that she was a dancer, forced to do this kind of work when she was driven out of her father's home by a stepmother. So the couple went off to the religious cleric to marry. There they discovered that they had the same last name. The young man was distraught: "The only woman I've ever loved turns out to be my sister?!"

The performance satirizes the major interpersonal themes of television melodrama and old films—love, family, and class differences—and recapitulates the politics that inform them: evil is represented as rural backwardness and good as urban modernity. It parodies the unlikely coincidences on which melodrama thrives, but in mimicking the expressive music and heightened emotionality of speech on which the effectiveness of these moral dramas depends, it also nicely captures two other key features—a strong moral message and what seems to be, to the university-educated satirists and to anyone more familiar with Western television drama, an excess of emotion.

Melodrama and Modernity

Melodrama has been the subject of a great deal of literary and media theory. The touchstone is Peter Brooks's *The Melodramatic Imagination,* which made a powerful case for the significance of melodrama as a literary/theatrical genre associated with the upheavals of the French Revolution and the onset of the crisis of modernity.[1] Brooks argued persuasively for a particular definition and understanding of the melodramatic imagination—as concerned with the revelation of the moral order in the everyday in a "post-sacred era."[2] Most intriguing was his claim that melodrama was "the central fact of the modern sensibility."[3]

What can the satirical performance in Cairo by a talented group of university students tell us about melodrama and modernity in Egypt? Brooks was concerned with theater and novels in nineteenth-century Europe. In the twentieth century, melodrama is more closely associated with forms of mass media like radio, film, and television. And in Egypt, as in other postcolonial contexts, cultural forms like television melodrama, projected by national television industries, are seen by state officials and middle-class professional producers as particularly effective instruments of social development, national consolidation, and "modernization."[4] This raises the question of what sorts of "modern sensibilities" television melodrama might mark in a place like contemporary Egypt, where those who make melodrama see themselves as trying to produce modern citizens and subjects.

I should note that there remains a good deal of confusion—or at least an enormous range of possibility—in the usage of the term "melodrama" in literary, film, and television studies today and some justification for questioning whether the term actually designates a single genre at all.[5] For Egypt, I would be happy to call television serials domestic dramas. But it is useful to keep the term "melodrama" to remind us of a few features. First, these serials are unquestionably "modern" in drawing directly upon modernist literature, film, and radio. They are mostly about the everyday and involve ordinary people. Their characters are not the universally known heroes of epic poetry or folktales but representations of the common citizen. Like Latin American *telenovelas* and unlike British, Australian, and American soap operas, the Egyptian serials are finite, generally running to either fifteen to thirty episodes. Like melodrama, they come to a resolution, something that some scholars of media consider crucial to ideological clarity.[6] What the television parody captured exquisitely, however, is that they are also more emotional and forthright in their moral lessons than contemporary Euro-American television dramas.[7]

It is the significance of these latter two qualities—the unapologetic moralism (apparent in the plots and storylines) and the quality of emotionality, with affect located in ordinary life (apparent in the genre conventions)—that I explore below, concerning how Egyptian television serials contribute to the creation of a "modern sensibility." But I will also explore the difference it makes when a modern sensibility is being crafted in a society for which notions of national development remain strong as part of a political legacy, where the embeddedness of individuals in kin and family remains ideal, and where secularism has been only ambivalently constructed as essential to modernity.[8]

Television serials in Egypt, I will argue, work with modernist projects at two levels: intentionally, through disseminating moral messages inflected by local political ideologies, thus attempting to set the terms of social and political debate; but also more subtly, through popularizing a distinctive configuration of narrative and emotionality.[9] In this latter way, as a genre with certain conventions, television melodrama in Egypt might be understood most directly as a technology for the production of new kinds of selves.[10] It is a technology, I will suggest, for staging interiorities (through heightened emotionalism) and thus constructing and encouraging the individuality of ordinary people.

Yet I also want to show that this technology is put to work in a local social and political context that differs in many ways from the context of soap opera production and viewing in Europe or the United States, particularly in the overt projects to produce citizens of the nation in a society in which kinship remains important and other forms of community and morality exist.[11] Moreover, the growing relevance of religious identity and the practices of self-monitoring being encouraged place the genre of television melodrama, though popular, in a field of other technologies of modern self-making, some pulling in the same direction, some not. This suggests that we should be wary of telling any unilineal stories of personhood and the coming to modernity.

Moral Vision as Political Ideology

In keeping with media ideology in postcolonial nations, television drama is viewed by most of its producers in Egypt not simply as entertainment but as a means to mold the national community. As Veena Das and others have begun to explore, national cinemas often represent and even help produce the sense of nationhood.[12] What has not been explored is how this ideology shapes the morality of melodrama. The Egyptian serials are concerned with morality—as Brooks' theory might lead us to expect—but this morality is social or community-oriented and thoroughly imbricated with the available political discourses. Like the Cameroonian miniseries *Miseria,* described by Petty, and perhaps much officially sanctioned Third World drama, many Egyptian serials privilege "dogmatic concerns at a social level." The morality is not so much that of the individual as the social. Or as Willemen says of Indian cinematic melodrama, of the individual as a member of a society undergoing transformations.[13]

A comparison of the storylines of Egyptian television writers illustrates the way morality is made social and the social is constructed in terms of political ideologies.[14] For a liberal feminist writer like Wafiyya Kheiry, who has written serials about women and work and the impact of migration to the Gulf, it is the educated middle classes or those whom she calls "the cultural elite"—families with long familiarity with literature and other cultural forms—who represent the embattled values.[15] She dreads the boor as much as the nouveau riche. For a progressive like Usama Anwar 'Ukasha, Egypt's best-known television writer, the hope in his serials usually lies in an alliance between the good authentic people—artisans, the honest hardworking poor devoted to family and community—and the modern educated classes with a commitment to progress, morality, and the good of the nation. Even aristocrats, such as "the pasha" in his most magnificent serial, *Hilmiyya Nights,* can be redeemed by nationalist sentiment. Many of his serials are concerned with the struggles of middle-class people to maintain principles and values and they often portray the poor as virtuous. Some of his serials even relate individual lives to political events such as the Palestinian *intifada,* the Gulf War, and the peace agreement with Israel. His intertextual references are with the political discourse of speeches, newspapers, and historical memory. He shares with other progressive producers like Muhammad Fadil, the director with whom he often collaborates, a sense that his art is for the "development" of Egypt. For example, in discussing a television film on the 1956 nationalization of the Suez Canal that he was directing in 1993, Fadil explained that his intention in portraying this historic national event was "to provide viewers with a sense of hope by communicating that, as Egyptians, we are capable of accomplishing things." The responsibility of art, he added, was to portray reality "as it ought to be."[16]

The link between moral vision and political stance is just as clear in the serials of a conservative writer like Tharwat Abaza. His work is distinguishable from the serials of liberal and progressive writers like 'Ukasha and Kheiry by its avoidance of reference to the national question, nostalgia for patriarchy and feudal values, and commerce with religion. Abaza frequently uses stories from the Quran or from Islamic history as inspiration—following plots or moral themes loosely while setting the stories in the present, complete with infertility clinics, apartments in Europe, Mercedes cars, land seizures, and crooked businesses. He generally ignores in his stories the anxieties and struggles associated with modernity or the burning social issues of the day that so intrigue writers like 'Ukasha and Kheiry. His politics are to appear distant from "the political"—as it is conventionally conceived in Egypt. He tends to avoid in his stories any reference to Egypt as a nation, or to its place in a larger world, and thus the main concern of contemporary political discourse—nationalism. If for other writers the city—the space of the modern—is the primary setting for the moral struggles of a complex new world, Abaza usually prefers the countryside, which can become a timeless, seemingly apolitical, locale for the play of good and evil, couched in the comforting tones of religious discourse.[17] Abaza is from one of the politically prominent old landowning families of Egypt but his own background is no less modern than that of Kheiry or 'Ukasha. He is a graduate of the Law Faculty of Cairo University and was, until recently, head of the Writer's Union. His nostalgia is a defensive product of the social and political transformations of the postcolonial age.

The three writers attribute good and evil to different social classes, deploy nationalist and religious discourses differently, and represent the past and future differently. In short, their visions of the moral order—that which Brooks saw as essential to melodrama—differ. This is evidence that the melodramatic genre may be a key site for contending visions of a moral universe, visions refracted, as in Egypt in the medium of state television, through the competing political ideologies of the age in that particular nation.

Because television is an (albeit complex) instrument of a state that is more ambivalently secular than the Europe Brooks describes as the context of the birth of melodrama, its drama does not always exclude religious referents or place morality solely within the non-sacred realm, as Abaza's serials show.[18] But on the whole, the moral visions are not defined by reference to religious truths. In fact, although many political ideologies do not find expression on state television, the most obvious exclusion is that of the Islamists, who, since media war was declared on them in 1993, are regularly represented in dramas as violent, immoral, and ignorant of religion. However, what seems distinctive about the moral referents of the Egyptian serials, compared to most U.S. melodrama, is that they are tied, in keeping with the sanctioned political ideologies, to the larger social good and the community. With consequences I will take up below, Egyptian television serials, modernist in their secularism and their concern for the nation, explicitly worried about the moral ills threatening the social fabric, also tend to place individual characters very much within their families and their communities.

Melodramatic Emotions

Viewers, whether ordinary television watchers or critics, recognize to varying degrees the ideologies informing these melodramas and react to them—either sympathetically or with hostility, depending on their own situations and political visions. Yet what viewers may be less conscious of—and thus less able to resist—is another aspect of televised melodramas that is actually widely shared: its placing of strong emotion in the everyday interpersonal world. This is a generic convention that cuts across content, that has its source in the genre itself (as adapted and developed over thirty years in Egypt) but is underwritten by the educated middle-class assumptions of those who produce television. This aspect of melodrama may be even more important to the projects of modernity than are the conscious political messages of the serials, because of the way it stages, and perhaps shapes, selfhood.

This is not the place to discuss general debates about reception and the effects of media, among the thorniest problems in media studies. I think it is abundantly clear that melodramatic texts can work on viewers in multiple ways. One cannot simply analyze the overt messages of plot and character. For example, as I have argued elsewhere, Egyptian television dramas whose storylines promote nationalist sentiment might fall on deaf ears yet be, as part of a national viewing experience, engendering a certain sense of national affiliation.[19]

What I want to explore here is how melodrama in Egypt might work on people's senses of self by the very way it represents characters as emotional. I will ask, in other words, about one of the distinctive features of melodrama: the purloined letter of its high emotionalism. If Feuer, in her classic article on melodrama, describes American primetime soap-opera acting as Wagnerian, it is difficult to know what to call the conventions of Egyptian melodramatic acting.[20] She argues that this overwrought acting style is necessary to distill and intensify emotion. Brooks, more cerebral, argues that the exaggerated emotions of early nineteenth-century melodramatic acting were expressionistic, their purpose being to clarify the moral message.[21] I think he overlooks the independent effects—or at least implications—of witnessing such "excessive" affect.

Critics in Egypt are fond of complaining about television. Many express weariness with the *nakad* (an untranslatable word referring to the piling on of troubles that I will translate as "misery"), calling for more comedy, more musicals. Cartoonists, often the most astute commentators on Egyptian life, caricature the experience of watching soap operas as being tied up with tears. Television writers even make fun of themselves about this. In a self-referential moment, one serial scripted a maid (the stereotypical soap opera viewer) inviting a student to come watch the serial with her so they could "get miserable together." But *nakad* is merely an aspect of the general emotionality of Egyptian television melodrama. Although Ang notes that melodrama may be characterized by its "tragic structure of feeling" and the sense that characters are "victims of forces that lie beyond their control"—favorite themes in the many Egyptian television dramas that treat the tribulations of good families facing the problems created by the shortage of housing, a Kafkaesque bureaucracy, or the forces of corruption—the most powerful and appealing dramas actually display a wide range of emotions.[22] Many people with whom I spoke described the good television serial as one that "pulls" *(bitshidd)*. It not only "pulls" audiences in but also "pulls" on their feelings. As one television producer put it, misery is just the easiest way to play on the emotions.

This emotionality, I believe, adds a crucial lesson to melodramas. Not only are they about the moral (and thus the social and political) order, as suggested above, but they provide an education in sentiment. By this I do not mean that they teach people how to feel. That is probably too crude, although they might indeed encourage certain public expressions of emotion or even sentimentality.[23] Rather, by attaching these strong sentiments to everyday life, melodramas fashion ordinary characters whose personhood is defined by what seems a rich inner life and an intense individuality.

This focus on the emotionally laden interpersonal domestic world, what in the United States and Europe is thought of as women's world, is what has made feminist media scholars take soap opera so seriously.[24] Yet the significance of the location of sentiment in the sphere of interpersonal relations has gone almost unremarked, perhaps because it is so taken for granted in our society, where women and emotion are so ideologically conjoined.[25] Modleski comes closest to noting what I would like to consider in more detail.[26] In her analysis of the link between daytime television and women's work, she argues that the narrative structures and close-up shots so favored by soap operas exercise women viewers' abilities to read how intimates are feeling. Their viewing experiences thus replicate their primary emotional work in the family: anticipating the needs and desires of others.

These ideas about emotions and personhood can be linked to Raymond Williams's hypothesis that the unprecedented exposure to drama that television has allowed has led to a "dramatisation of consciousness."[27] By this he means that television has led us to see our own daily lives as dramas. Although I would caution against some aspects of this, citing the methodological impossibility of gaining access to people's "consciousness" and a discomfort with the humanist assumptions of an unproblematic inner life such a term suggests, I think Williams's great insight is to suggest that something novel happens to subjectivity as a result of television drama.[28] And in Egypt the question is whether there has not developed a melodramatization of consciousness.

In other words, can the growing cultural hegemony of television melodrama (following lines laid down by radio serials and films) be engendering new modes of subjectivity and new discourses on personhood, ones that we could recognize as "modern" in their emphasis on the individual? The main features of the modern subject as it has been understood in the West—autonomous, bounded, self-activating, verbalizing him/herself—have been delineated in the philosophical and historical literature, with Foucault offering us the most interesting theories of the development of the technologies of the modern (bourgeois) self and their links to new forms of power.[29] In the introduction to the second volume of *The History of Sexuality,* he suggested that the discourse on sexuality has been crucial to the development of the modern self; one becomes the subject of one's sexuality. In later lectures he speculated on the relationship between the confession in Christianity and the modern forms of hermeneutics of the self.[30] Psychologizing, buttressed by the whole discourse of psychoanalysis with its vivid conjuring of a rich and conflictual inner world, is also instrumental in constructing modern subjects. And the discourse of feelings and emotion—the very stuff of melodrama—is essential to the psychological.[31]

What is interesting about Modleski's argument about television soap opera as that which trains women for interpersonal work is the assumptions it makes about selves and emotion. It presumes women who live in modern bourgeois families and have a vocabulary of sentiment attached to gesture. It also takes for granted that when sentiments are found, they are expressive of the inner feelings and personal truths of others. This set of assumptions about emotion and personhood must be recognized as historically and culturally specific. As Cvetkovich notes, nineteenth-century mass and popular culture played an important role in constructing the discourse of affect crucial to establishing the middle-class hegemony of a "gendered division between public and private spheres and the assignment of women to the affective tasks of the household."[32]

The untheorized corollary, however, of the discourse of affect is the discourse of the individual who is the subject of these emotions. It is, I want to suggest, the individual who is being highlighted in the heightening of emotionality in Egyptian melodrama. The serials are not only directed at women but men as well. And though they mark men as, on the whole, less emotional than women and the upper classes as less emotional than the lower, all characters are more emotional than might be thought appropriate by a bourgeois European or American self. In part, the extreme staging of melodramatic selves may seem necessary for those whose goal is to "modernize" a society whose dominant social form is still the family and kin network and whose cultural forms until quite recently (and even contemporaneously in some regions) could be understood to work in different ways and with differing constructions of personhood. So I first want to contrast the melodramatic "structures of feeling" to those of some other popular Arab cultural forms that might previously have provided materials for constructing or conceptualizing selves. One goal is to reveal the particularity of the relationship between modernity and melodrama in the formation of subjectivity. I further want to suggest that the forms of melodrama in Egypt, like the structures of the social and economic worlds in which people there find themselves, differ in crucial ways from the forms and the contexts of Western soap opera and life. In the final section of this chapter, I turn to the sensibilities and the life stories of a woman who was extraordinarily enmeshed in the world of television and radio serials in order to suggest how we might trace the distinctive affective and narrative forms of melodrama into forms of personal subjectivity in Egypt. I will also show, however, how other aspects of Egyptian modernity bolster, or undermine, the work of television melodrama.

Distinctive Subjectivities

Whatever its interreferences with or roots in other forms of cultural expression, Egyptian television melodrama is distinct in its structure and sentiment. The serials are created by people versed in modern literature, theater, and film—Egyptian, Arab and European.[33] Although occasionally drawing on what they would consider "folk" traditions for local color or regional identification, or to invoke the authentic (as when they have "simple" protagonists reciting proverbs), the primarily urban, middle-class producers of melodrama distinguish their work unambiguously from "traditional" Egyptian and Arab forms of cultural expression that have been, until quite recently, the popular and familiar forms in rural areas and among the uneducated. And the differences between the emotional styles and imaginaries created by these narrative and poetic traditions and those of television melodrama are striking.

This difference can be seen especially clearly in the adaptations to television of local folk forms. This happened in 1997, with the serialized dramatization during the month of Ramadan of the epic about Abu Zayd al-Hilali, considered by many the most magnificent work of Arab oral narrative poetry. The epic, which in its entirety runs to thousands of verses, follows the adventures across North Africa of the Bani Hilal, a Bedouin tribe driven by drought from their home in the Arabian Peninsula. As described by Slyomovics for Upper Egypt and Reynolds for Lower Egypt, it is recited professionally by socially marginal poets with astonishing verbal talents, not to mention prodigious memories.[34] Widely familiar, it is never performed in its entirety; but when listeners hear their favorite segments, they know the context and the shadow whole is evoked.[35]

In her analysis of the differences between oral and printed versions of the epic, Slyomovics has noted not only that printed versions (or studio-produced commercial recordings) are complete and sequential, rather than segmented and partial, but that they also lack the elaborate punning of the performed. This absence of punning indicates two things: a declining attention to the language itself, or poetics, in the printed versions; and a greater reliance on the story, rather than the multiple meanings of the puns, for establishing character.[36]

The television drama shared with the printed versions (on which the scriptwriter most likely relied) a chronological development and decreasing attention to linguistic play, and to the verbal itself. It further transformed the epic by turning it into a melodrama about interpersonal relationships and individual longings and passions, many set in the domestic sphere. The best illustration of these transformations—and thus the genre conventions of serialized melodramas—is how the serial dramatized the birth of the hero Abu Zayd. This opening section of the epic (rarely performed in Upper Egypt, according to Slyomovics, because it is never requested by local audiences, yet popular, according to Reynolds, in lower Egypt)[37] constituted the first and crucial week of the television serial, drawing viewers in. The story of Abu Zayd is that he is the son of Rizq of the Hilali Bedouin tribe and Khadra Sharifa, the daughter of the Sharif of Mecca, a descendent of the Prophet. Khadra is barren for many years (in some versions it is seven, in some eleven). Despite their happiness with each other, husband and wife are miserable because of the absence of a son. Finally, Khadra is taken to a pool to supplicate. She sees a powerful black bird driving away the other birds. She prays for a son as strong and ferocious as this bird. She then does miraculously bear a son—Abu Zayd, the hero of the epic. In the version performed for Slyomovics by an Upper Egyptian poet, the pregnancy and birth are described quickly, the love scene after Khadra's visit to the pool being slightly more elaborate:

> Khadra Sharifa had stopped bearing, but weak with desire
>   she came to the royal bed yearning.
> Rizq son of Nayil came to her after the evening prayer.
> Khadra wore silk brocade, she sat with him, she wore
>   brocade of silk, her best clothing.
> Rizq asked for union with her.
> She was happy! And the Lord of the Throne sent her an
>   infant who vexes the enemy!
> She bore an infant who vexes valiant men!
> Khadra passed the full nine months.
> They approached the Emir Abu Zayd, Emir of valiant men,
> they found the Emir Abu Zayd was blue-black, not
>   resembling his father,
> they found the hero, Abu Zayd the Hilali, the color of a
>   black slave.[38]

In a version recorded by Reynolds, the narrative is more elaborate and dramatic but the focus is on the reactions of others to the black infant and the anger and accusations of Rizq.[39] Neither version dwelt on the emotions of the protagonists just before the birth.

In the televised episode of the birth, covered in the Upper Egyptian performance in just the last six lines, we see Khadra going into labor, the anxious father just outside her door awaiting the birth, a desperate fight in the streets over the midwife (who is needed in three places at once), more agonies of labor, the husband praying to God, and later, when he hears the child has been born, falling to his knees, tears in his eyes, and raising his arms to praise and thank God. Then we see hushed arguments in Khadra's room between the midwife and the attendant women, the midwife refusing to give the father the news. What's wrong? The midwife points and says, "Look." They carefully lift the cover off the baby. In a close-up, with music, we see a black baby. The mother is sleeping, beatific. When she sits up and is confronted with this, she holds the baby lovingly, innocently saying, "The boy is our son, mine and Rizq's. Whether light or dark, he is a gift from God whom we accept." But then she too becomes alarmed. It dawns on her that the others are worried that she will be accused of adultery.

It is not that the television drama is emotional and the performed epic not. The performed epic too describes feelings, in the conventional formulas for such things. In an earlier segment, for example, Rizq and his wife Khadra cry over their inability to have a son. After several lines recounting how Rizq watched other men play with their sons, the Upper Egyptian poet's version goes:

> Rizq the Hilali eyed them and his wound increased
> Inside his tent tears poured again
> inside his tent tears poured again
> he cried, wet his cheeks and his handkerchief
> Khadra Sharifa left, her tears a canal.
> Beautiful as she was, she loved him to the point of death
> beautiful as she was, by God, unique
> she cried and felt hardship each night he was absent:
> "Tell me what is the reason for laments, O love, O Rizq,
>   you cry why, why?"

Similarly, a version recorded by Reynolds has Rizq saying:

> I am the last of my line, my spirit is broken
> I have spent my life and not seen a son, prosperous
> I have taken of women, eight maidens,
> And eleven daughters followed, princesses true!
> This bearing of womenfolk, ah!, has broken my spirit
> I weep and the tears of my eyes on my cheek do flow.[40]

But the televised drama focuses on the relationships among characters and the shifting emotions of a set of characters who often stare off into space while music evokes their inner feelings. Instead of formulaic phrases about tears and their plenitude, what could be thought of as the phenomenology of emotion, television drama tries to produce the inner beings who feel these emotions through close-ups of facial expressions and melodramatic acting. Moreover, the serial brings the mythic heroes down to earth and makes them ordinary people, in line with the process of "descending" individualization Foucault has described as so characteristic of modern disciplinary regimes.[41] This is reinforced by the overwhelming visual presence of interior worlds and domestic spaces (always the case, of course, with soap operas, for obvious budgetary and technical reasons).[42]

Like all "folk" traditions, the oral epic's main intent is not the development of the inner life of characters. Most of the epic, like folktales told all over Egypt, consists of what characters did and said and includes little "emotion language" or the gestures and music that substitute for it in melodrama. This is not to say that one cannot find in the cultural traditions the elaboration of sentiment. The poetic, rather than the narrative, genres are the place to look for this. Yet I would argue for a fundamental difference in the localization—or locatability—of the emotions in melodrama and poetry. For example, the *ghinnaawas*, or little songs of the Awlad 'Ali Bedouin that I have written about, are short expressions of sentiment.[43] Although people recite them as part of stories, to express the sentiments of particular characters, and otherwise in the contexts of intimates to express their own sentiments about particular life events, they are conventional and formulaic. They are thus, in a sense, depersonalized. They are repeated and appropriated by others and thus are also disembodied. Furthermore, much of the appreciation of these poems, like the performed Hilali epic, comes from the poetry of their language.

Ritual lamentation of the dead in Egypt, as in other parts of the Arab and circum-Mediterranean world, is another highly developed poetic art that is quintessentially emotional.[44] In Upper Egypt, where many of the television viewers with whom I have been working live, the 'adida, as the lament is called, is performed at the funeral by women specialists. The mournful chanting is extremely emotional in its presentation and also evokes strong sentiment through its imagery. However, as Elizabeth Wickett has shown, despite this potent imagery, "few references to emotional states can be found in the laments, either ascribed to the lamenter or to the feelings of the deceased after death."[45] Laments are, she adds, "ritual texts performed in an emotional arena" and therefore, I would argue, differ significantly from melodrama in being limited in context and sentiment. They are specific to the ritualized context of the funeral. In contrast, the emotions of melodrama cover a wide range and are attached to individuals and embedded in the everyday, the ordinary, and the domestic.

By establishing these contrasts, I am not trying to assert the existence of a rigid distinction between modernity and tradition, the "folk" art inhabiting (and defining) the traditional past and the melodrama the contemporary present. All sorts of cross-referencing and transformations occur, especially as "traditional" forms aggressively enter the mass media world contemporaneous with the melodrama.[46] What I am saying is that television melodramas offer distinctive constructions of the world and images of persons, especially within a context defined by "traditional" forms and "traditional ways of life" from which modernist writers and directors are distancing themselves. Their specificity is in the emotionalization of the quotidian world, which in turn works to enforce a sense of the importance of the individual subject—the locus and source of all these strong feelings.

Heroine of Her Own Melodrama

One evening, as I sat watching television with a poor Upper Egyptian village family in the midst of various crises, the mother joked, "We are a soap opera!" *(ihna tamthiliyya)*. In this comment, one can see that television melodrama had come to inform her perceptions of her own life. I think this occurs on a much more intimate and individual level as well. To illustrate how this might work, I want to discuss a person I knew in Egypt who was deeply involved with television and radio melodramas: an unmarried domestic servant in Cairo I call Amira.[47] She listened to her transistor radio while she cooked for her employers. When she could, she stopped to watch the noon serial on television. She always watched the evening serials when she got home. She was knowledgeable about the actors and actresses; she had watched most serials and films. Intelligent and articulate, she could summarize plots easily and remember most. She rarely watched foreign imports although admitted that the American serial *Knots Landing,* which she claimed to have been able to understand, even though she could not read the subtitles, had been an exception.

Unmarried and with no children, she was both freer to follow television and more dependent on it for companionship and emotional-social involvement than most women I knew in Egypt. She was somewhat isolated socially because she lived on her own. Her mother and brothers still lived in the countryside in Manufiyya. She had two sisters in Cairo. One was married with children, and she saw her little. Besides the people she worked for, some of whom she could not communicate with (they did not speak Arabic), her main contacts seemed to be her unmarried sister, with whom, however, she had frequent conflicts, and one friend, a single woman who also had come to Cairo from the countryside and like her worked as a domestic servant. With both, she watched television.

Amira was both more sentimental and more volatile than many women I have come to know. She was often moved by the serials she watched. When we watched television together, her explanations of who particular characters were carried moral and emotional valences. This scene, she once said of an episode of *Hilmiyya Nights* (a serial she had watched several times, though it ran to more than a hundred episodes), reveals the worthy from the unworthy. With pity, she explained to me who a character in another serial written by 'Ukasha *(Honey and Tears)* was. This is a poor young man who is sickly because his mother keeps marrying and abandoning him. She puts herself first. When she gets divorced she takes him back; but then she goes and marries again. This has ruined his health and made him very sensitive. Amira had concluded her summary of the plot of this serial with admiration for the heroine: "Zaynab is strong and willful in the cause of right. She's not strong for an immoral end."

But this sentimentality extended to other areas. Once when we turned on the television in 1990 and saw a clip of people in Iran crying after an earthquake, this triggered her memory of having wept "for an hour" after the Egyptian soccer team lost the World Cup match. She had kept herself awake until the early hours of the morning to watch the game on television. She was upset because "they worked so hard and got so tired and then God didn't reward them." She had wept when they lost, and then wept again when she saw the Egyptian players crying. "It really hurt."

Amira was also often embroiled in conflicts and arguments—with her sister, her employers, and her neighbors. She told stories about how angry she was, how wronged she had been. Her neighbors kept a dog on the roof who bothered her. She fought with her landlords because she had to wake up at 3:00 A.M. to fill her water cans and haul them up to the third storey. There was no water at other times in her building. She fought with employers who left her sitting on their doorstep with cooked food for a party, having refused to give her a key to their apartment and having promised to be home to receive the food.

Although I cannot argue for a direct causal link between her involvement with television serials and her emotionality I suspect there is one. There is, however, another more obvious link between television melodrama and the ways she constructed herself as a subject. This link is through the ways she made herself the subject of her own life stories. I found it striking that of all the women whose life stories I have heard, Amira was the one whose tales took most clearly the form of melodrama. Hers was a Manichean world with good, kind people who helped her and were generous, and greedy, stingy, or cruel people who victimized her.

One can see this in the way she constructed her story of coming to Cairo to find a better life. A local labor contractor found her first job. She came from a poor family and she had worked on construction sites, hauling dirt and sand, for a daily wage. She wanted to go to Cairo because she saw her sisters, who had gone there to find work, coming home dressed well and wearing gold. She was nineteen when she first went. But she lasted only a month in the first job. The family mistreated her. They woke her up at six in the morning, they didn't feed her, and they kept the food locked up. She was paid five or six pounds per month (about nine dollars, at that time). She cried and cried and finally persuaded her sister to call and say that she was needed back at home to tend a sick relative. She found another employer and another. Each time, she would find some excuse to go home to the village, and she would not return. Eventually, she found a job with a good family as a cook and stayed with them for eight years. The themes repeat: exploited and mistreated, the innocent victim escapes until fate deals her some kind people.

It is when she talks about her brief marriage, however, that all the elements of drama crystallize. At thirty-seven, she realizes that she is too old to hope for marriage. She declares herself ugly anyway—"Who would want to marry me?" But someone did, in 1985, when she was about thirty. The marriage lasted twenty-nine days, and she had to get her sister's husband to pay the man a thousand pounds (approximately seven hundred dollars at the time) to divorce her. She told the story easily; perhaps it was a well-rehearsed story. He was a plumber who saw her at work. When he asked her about the possibility of marriage, she sent him to discuss it with her brother-in-law. They were engaged for four months but she never went anywhere with him. When she would suggest it, he would refuse. She claims it was because he didn't want her to know what he was like or to know anything about him.

Once they were married he began beating her. He wanted her to hand over her wages. She refused, saying she had a loan to pay off, and then she planned to stay at home. A man, she explained, is supposed to support his wife. He locked her in the house. All she wanted was to be rid of him and so she got her brother-in-law, whom she held responsible since he was supposed to have looked into the man's background, to pay him money to leave her alone. It turned out he was a tough from a poor quarter. Amira is convinced that he wanted to kill her to take her apartment.

Bitterly she added, Egyptian men are no good. Lots of men have asked her to marry them. Men on the streets, men she meets at work. But they all want her money. Actually, it is her apartment they want. When they discover that she has an apartment and furniture they know they will only have to contribute inexpensive things as a dowry. Her husband, for example, had provided the living-room furniture but she already had the bedroom furniture and the apartment. (Given the severe shortage of housing, the exorbitant "key money" that must be paid to get a rental unit, and the expenses of furnishing the apartment, considered the responsibility of the groom, many young men find it difficult to marry.) When I asked what would then happen, she explained, "Then they'll take a second wife. Once they have the apartment and money."

If we ask, as the anthropologists Ruth Behar and Laurel Kendall have, about the narrative qualities of life stories, we see that if Behar's Mexican informant's life story was shaped by the Christian model of suffering and redemption, Amira conforms more closely to the model of melodrama.[48] Like the television dramas, the themes of her story are money, with the villain trying to cheat her out of hers, and the secret, with the truth about her sinister husband discovered too late. The melodramatic heroine, innocent and good, is wronged and victimized. Seeking a better life, symbolized by her sisters' good clothes and gold, she leaves the village and home to find herself overworked, underpaid, and hungry in a house where the food is locked up. Seeking love, companionship, or respectability—whatever it is that marriage is supposed to bring—she finds herself betrayed and beaten.[49]

What I think is most significant about this way of telling her life stories, however, is that through it Amira makes herself the subject, the melodramatic heroine, in fact, of her own life. Perhaps in part by her love of television melodrama, she has been encouraged to see herself as the subject of the emotions that sweep her and thus as more of an individual. This puts her in a better position to be a modern citizen, something the television producers want from their melodramas. For Amira, this position is reinforced by the structures of her life: her migrant status and separation from her family, her reliance on her own labor for survival, her private apartment with its own electricity and water bills, and her subjection to the law and to taxation as an individual.

Postcolonial Differences

Yet Amira's story and her life present certain complications for a straightforward narrative of coming to modern individual subjecthood as we might tell it along familiar Western lines. First, Amira's tragic story is marked by critical absences and failures. The most specific is the failure of her brother-in-law to have taken seriously his family responsibility of protecting her from a bad marriage. More generally, she suggests that her vulnerability is caused by the absence of a strong family that could have supported her and kept her from having to work as a maid. Her emptiness is related to the failure to have married and, as most women do, to have a family of her own. In all the life stories of domestic servants I have recorded, it is always a rupture to the ideal of women's embeddedness in family and marriage that accounts for their positions doing work that is both hard and not respectable, and for their not being, in a sense, full persons.[50] Amira's story, while told mostly in terms of herself as an individual moving through life, evokes the ideal she cannot have—the ideal of being a fulfilled person defined by kinship and family.

To note that kinship remains crucial for Amira is not to say that television melodrama is not producing its effects. After all, as I noted earlier, even while the genre conventions encourage individuality and the political messages include citizenship and wider social belonging, television melodramas do not overtly challenge the ideal of family so taken for granted in Egypt. In keeping with urban middle-class ideals, the nuclear family gets more play than the extended, but women and most men characters are still placed within families.

However, there is something else of great importance in Amira's day-to-day life that does not derive from television melodrama and that in some, but not all, ways undermines the processes television encourages. In part because she is cut out of family life and cannot rely on kin to provide community, purpose, and social respectability, Amira is attracted to the new path to individual expression and respectability opened up to women in the last two decades by the movement to make Islam more central to everyday life and politics. Recognizing this further complication, along with acknowledging the continuing centrality of kinship and the ways that Egyptian melodramas embed morality in the social, reminds us of the difference it makes that a modern form of drama and the forms of selfhood it encourages are being produced in a postcolonial nation with its own specific history and, as Chakrabarty has argued for Bengal, its own form of modernity.[51]

As much as work and watching television, religious practice organizes Amira's schedule, informs her sense of self, and colors her understanding of her world. Because mosques have flourished in the last decade and a half, and because it has become much more accepted in that period that women should pray in them and attend religious lessons, Amira's regular attendance is not uncommon for lower-class and middle-class urban women. However, the same structural features that make her more dependent on television and free to follow it—living alone, being unmarried, and without children—enable her to pray more regularly, go to mosque on Fridays and sometimes even after work, and to participate in the special mosque prayers of Ramadan, the month of special devotion and fasting as well as heavy television watching. Similarly, that she wears the *higab,* the modest head covering that has become a fashionable sign of piety and middle-class respectability in the towns and cities, is not unusual. But Amira's regular participation in lessons at the mosque has intensified her identity as a Muslim and given meaning to the wearing of this item of clothing, including a terror that the fabric of her *higab* might have a pattern of crosses on it. As a result of her involvement in these religious practices and identifications, Amira is pulled very much into a community, and not the national community to which individual citizens are, according to television writers, supposed to relate themselves.[52]

Yet many of Amira's religious observances are self-oriented and thus might be thought of as running along the same tracks as the individualizing and interiorizing of television melodrama (even though many religious authorities preach against television). This is especially the case with the discipline of fasting, which she takes very seriously. She fasts all the days of Ramadan, like most Egyptian Muslims, making up later the days lost because of menstruation.[53] But she also fasts all the other possible and recommended days of the Muslim calendar. One can also see this concern with the self in the way she constantly asks others to forgive her for the smallest things—like angering someone or even helping herself to a piece of cake from an employer's larder. Her references to her sinfulness and the need to cleanse it with fasting, prayer, and asking forgiveness, were especially striking to me because her life was so moral and proper. This obsessive concern with the self is, it seems, strongly encouraged by the rhetoric of the lessons at the mosque.[54]

In a sense, television itself seems to be changing to accommodate (not to mention appropriate for its own legitimacy) this new intensity of religious practice and identity. There have long been religious television serials, historical costume dramas about the early history of Islam. These were often aired late at night and were not particularly popular. They, like all religious programming, were segregated from the popular evening serials, as if to compartmentalize religion. But in the last few years, major actors participated in the big-budget religious/historical serials broadcast during Ramadan, and major writers and directors were suddenly called upon to produce them. These serials were, it turned out, so popular that the newly appointed head of television production announced that they planned to do many more serials about "our Arab Islamic heritage," as he gingerly put it, over the next few years.

The serialization of the Hilali epic broadcast during Ramadan in the early slot that children are sure to be watching is part of this effort. Although not strictly speaking a religious serial, it gave a prominent place to discourse about God, as does the oral performed epic, since that is recited by and for people for whom being Muslim was an important identity. Yet there is a striking difference in the forms religiosity takes in the television version and the oral epic as performed by traditional poets. This suggests how television religion, much like Amira's, may be part of a new individualizing of religion.

In the epic, as performed in Egypt, God's power is a constant theme. All great deeds and miraculous happenings, like the birth of the hero Abu Zayd, are attributed to it. Poets always open their performances with a praise poem to the Prophet. This praise poetry introduces the themes of the segments to be recited but also, as Slyomovics argues, has the rhetorical effect of praising the poet himself by linking his poetic abilities and his status to that of the Prophet, whose divine words were miraculous, as well as praising the audience for being part of the community of Muslims.[55]

The television serial also represented God's miraculous power—in computer-generated special effects like the strong bird whose likeness Khadra's prays for in a son. But mostly religion figures as the emotionalized attitudes of characters—their supplication, their awe, and their gratitude. We saw this clearly when Rizq, the hero's father, waits anxiously while his wife is in labor. There is a cut to a scene (perhaps at sunrise of the same day) where he is standing by his horse, watching the sun, his hands held up in the position of prayer. Back home, his hands are clasped, and he asks God to keep his wife safe. When he is told the news that he has a son, he repeats again and again, "A thousand praises and thanks to you, O Lord." He faces different parts of the room, arms up toward Heaven, thanking Bountiful God for having generously given him a son after all these years, and for ending his sorrows and enabling him to face the men and know that his name would remain. He then drops to his knees, thanking God again. Later, his wife will say she accepts her son as a gift from God. In these scenes, it is the personal faith, rather than the power of God, that is stressed. Piety has been made into a characteristic of the self.

Thirty years ago, the anthropologist James Peacock wrote a book about a form of proletarian drama in Indonesia that he argued was a "rite of modernization": it helped its participants desire and feel comfortable with modern actions (linear, coming to a climax) and goals (individual achievement and nuclear families). Although his analysis was sophisticated, he shared the confident assumptions of modernization theorists of the time. Indonesia, like every other country, was on a path to modernity; modernity was a singular condition whose features could be easily outlined (rationalization, universalization, bureacratization, centralization, specialization, monetization, conjugalization); and finally, modernity was an unalloyed good, its individualism, for example, being a mark of increasing freedom, with no element of subjection (as Foucault later cautioned).[56]

My argument is different. A few years ago, in a popular Egyptian women's magazine, Muna Hilmi, daughter of Nawal El-Saadawi, the Egyptian feminist writer so well known in the West, wrote a paean to the American daytime soap opera *The Bold and the Beautiful,* then being broadcast on Egyptian television.[57] In an unusually sympathetic review of a serial widely condemned by the intelligentsia, she contrasted it to Egyptian serials, which she disparaged for their remorseless attention to social and political problems. She lauded the American soap opera for its feminism (in that it had strong women characters who were determined to achieve what they wanted in their careers and their lives) but most of all for its subtle exploration of the human psyche. She could have, but did not, mention the elite's disdain for the emotional hyperbole of Egyptian melodrama—the disdain so clearly reflected in the satire I described at the start of this chapter.

What I have tried to show here, though, is that the emotionality of Egyptian melodramas and the way they thus construct individuals in terms of vivid interior lives is the result of a local effort, developed in the context of Egyptian genres and social circumstances, that is part of the process of trying to produce those individual human psyches that this educated cosmopolitan writer extols. But there is a difference. Instead of constructing these human psyches in a generalized contentless context, as does an American soap opera like *The Bold and the Beautiful* (a lack of political context that initially rendered the serial harmless in the eyes of the Egyptian censors), producers working in a government-controlled medium and imbued with an ideology of national development and the legacy of Arab socialist ideals insist on placing them squarely within the social and moral national nexus. And because of the increasing hegemony of an assertive religious identity in a society in which most people had never accepted the principle that religious practice and morality were not part of modern everyday life—something of which Muna Hilmi most likely disapproves—the vectors of modernity crisscross. Melodrama, and to some extent what I would argue to be a new focus on the self in religious practice, may be encouraging the kinds of selves a sophisticated modernist secularist like Hilmi wants. But the enduring ties of kinship and the appealing—and modern—identity politics of Islam pull such selves in a different direction: into communities and subject to other authorities and disciplines. The trajectory of modernity in Egypt, in other words, is not predictable from the historically specific narratives of modernity in Europe, and the trajectory of selfhood, though related through melodrama, cannot be told in the same terms.

Notes

For contributions to the research on which this paper depends, I am especially grateful to Reem Saad, Omnia Shakry, Samira Muhammad, and many friends who watched television with me and shared their insights and reactions. Fieldwork in Egypt was supported by fellowships from the American Research Center in Egypt, the ACLS/SSRC Joint Committee on the Near and Middle East, the National Endowment for the Humanities, and New York University. The paper was sharpened by questions from Talal Asad, Nicholas Dirks, Timothy Mitchell, Gyan Prakash, Lisa Wideen, and other participants in the "Questions of Modernity" conference at New York University; Dwight Reynolds, Susan Slyomovics, Ted Swedenburg, and an anonymous reviewer for the University of Minnesota Press; and audiences at the College of St. Catherine, Smith

College, Princeton University, and the Institute for the Humanities at the University of Michigan. A John Simon Guggenheim Fellowship gave me precious time to rework it.

1. Peter Brooks, *The Melodramatic Imagination* (New Haven: Yale University Press, 1976).

2. Ibid., 15.

3. Ibid., 21.

4. Lila Abu-Lughod, "The Objects of Soap Opera," in *Worlds Apart: Modernity through the Prism of the Local*, ed. Daniel Miller (London: Routledge, 1995), 190–210; Veena Das, "Soap Opera: What Kind of Object Is It?" ibid., 169–89; Ranggasamy Karthigesu, "Television as a Tool for Nation-Building in the Third World," in *Television and Its Audience*, ed. P. Drummond and R. Paterson (London: British Film Institute, 1988), 306–26; Purnima Mankekar, "National Texts and Gendered Lives," *American Ethnologist* 20, no. 3 (1993): 543–63; and "Television Tales and a Woman's Rage," *Public Culture* 5, no. 3 (1993): 469–92.

5. Russell Merritt, "Melodrama: Postmortem for a Phantom Genre," *Wide Angle* 5, no. 3 (1983): 25–31. See also Christine Gledhill, ed., *Melodrama: Stage, Picture, Screen* (London: British Film Institute, 1994).

6. Robert C. Allen, ed., *To Be Continued . . . : Soap Operas around the World* (New York: Routledge, 1995), 21.

7. Ana Lopez, in "Our Welcomed Guests: Telenovelas in Latin America," ibid., 261, notes that the Mexican telenovelas are stereotypically more weepy. Clearly, the Egyptian serials are less sophisticated, glossy, and sexually charged than the Brazilian telenovelas, but even these have something in common: in Egypt, as in Brazil, many television writers are serious and progressive. For Brazil, see Alma Guillermoprieto, "Letter from Brazil: Obsessed in Rio," *The New Yorker*, August 16, 1993, 44–55.

8. See Talal Asad, *Genealogies of Religion* (Baltimore: The John Hopkins University Press, 1993), for a discussion of the idea that secularism and the notion of religion it implies is a concept that developed as part of the history of Christianity in the West.

9. Lila Abu-Lughod, "Finding a Place for Islam," *Public Culture* 5, no. 3 (1993): 493–513; Abu-Lughod, "The Objects of Soap Opera."

10. Michel Foucault, "Technologies of the Self," in *Technologies of the Self*, ed. L. Martin, H. Gutman, and P. Hutton (Amherst: University of Massachusetts Press, 1988), 16–49, and "About the Beginning of the Hermeneutics of the Self," *Political Theory* 21, no. 2 (1993): 198–227.

11. See Toby Miller, *The Well-Tempered Self* (Baltimore: The Johns Hopkins University Press, 1993), for an analysis that links modern forms of subjectivity—the individual as consumer and as citizen—to mass-mediated cultural forms.

12. Veena Das, "The Making of Modernity: Gender and Time in Indian Cinema," this volume, ch. 7.

13. Sheila Petty, "Miseria: The Evolution of a Unique Melodramatic Form," *Passages: A Chronicle of the Humanities* 8 (1994): 19–20; Paul Willemen, "Negotiating the Transition to Capitalism: The Case of Andaz," in *Melodrama and Asian Cinema*, ed. Wimal Dissanayake (Cambridge: Cambridge University Press, 1993), 179–88.

14. While no television serial can simply be attributed to the writer, as author, since it involves so many stages and so many personnel—from those in the television administration, including the censors, to those directly involved in production, including the director, other scriptwriters, and the actors—there is in Egypt a certain integrity to the texts of well-known writers. When they feel excessive censorship or radical changes endanger their text, they protest publicly and sometimes even withdraw their texts. The most respected writers, like 'Ukasha, are closely involved in all aspects of production.

Writers with less clout and standing lose control to the director and others. In most cases, though, the germ of the plot and the themes are retained, and so I will, in the discussion that follows, treat the serials as if they were the works of authors. On a comparative note, Guillermoprieto, "Letter from Brazil," 49, notes that in Brazil, authors are believed to be "the soul and essence of a *telenovela*," and Lopez, "Our Welcomed Guests," 60–61 extends this to all Latin American contexts.

15. Interview with the author, June 25, 1993.

16. Interview with the author, June 17, 1993.

17. The differences are reflected even in the aesthetics or styles of the melodramas. 'Ukasha's serials, like those of Kheiry and many other progressive writers, strive for realism, a style associated with socialism or the socially concerned. The moral universe, they suggest, lies within the lives of ordinary people. Some of Abaza's serials are striking for their exaggerated tones and lack of naturalism.

18. The secularity of the state is a complex question, of course. I say "ambivalently secular" because Islam and Christianity are still considered valid and important aspects of personal life and identity, even of public officials, and even beyond. Although the relevance of religion to state policy and law may have been minimized in this century, especially since independence, it is still given a role to play. For example, part of the religious establishment ratifies government policies and others can make trouble, and family law continues to be Islamic. See Partha Chatterjee, "Religious Minorities and the Secular State: Reflections on an Indian Impasse," *Public Culture* 8, no. 1 (1995): 11–39, for an argument that secularism is a Western concept that sits uneasily in other places, like India. On the exclusion of Islamists from Egyptian television, see Lila Abu-Lughod, "Finding a Place for Islam," and "Dramatic Reversals," in *Political Islam,* ed. Joel Beinin and Joe Stork (Berkeley: University of California Press, 1996), 269–82.

19. See Abu-Lughod, "The Objects of Soap Opera," for a discussion of the impediments nationalist programs confront in reaching subaltern audiences.

20. Jane Feuer, "Melodrama, Serial Form and Television Today," *Screen* 25, no. 1 (1984): 4–16.

21. Brooks, *The Melodramatic Imagination.*

22. Ien Ang, "Melodramatic Identifications: Television Fiction and Women's Fantasy," in *Television and Women's Culture,* ed. Mary Ellen Brown (London: Sage, 1990), 75–88, quotation at 81.

23. My hunch is that they do offer alternative models of the acceptability of emotional expression—especially of sadness or misery—to women and men like those I knew in the Awlad 'Ali community, for whom public expression of these was culturally restricted. See Lila Abu-Lughod, *Veiled Sentiments: Honor and Poetry in a Bedouin Society* (Berkeley: University of California Press, 1986).

24. Feminist critics have done for television soap opera what Brooks did for literary melodrama—forced a reevaluation of a genre dismissed as pap—as well as develop some critical ideas about female pleasure through its serious analysis. The feminist literature on soap opera is extensive and much of it quite good. Some key texts are Robert C. Allen, *Speaking of Soap Opera* (Chapel Hill: University of North Carolina Press, 1985); Ien Ang, *Watching Dallas: Soap Opera and the Melodramatic Imagination* (New York: Methuen, 1985), and "Melodramatic Identifications"; Mary Ellen Brown, ed., *Television and Women's Culture* (London: Sage, 1990); Charlotte Brunsdon, "The Role of Soap Opera in the Development of Feminist Television Scholarship," in *To Be Continued . . . ,* ed. Allen, 49–55; Feuer, "Melodrama, Serial Form and Television Today"; Christine Geraghty, *Women and Soap Opera: A Study of Prime-Time Soaps* (Cambridge, Eng.: Polity Press, 1991); Lynne Joyrich, "All That Television Allows: TV Melodrama,

Postmodernism, and Consumer Culture," in *Private Screenings*, ed. Lynn Spiegel and Denise Mann (Minneapolis: University of Minnesota Press, 1992), 227–51; Tanya Modleski, *Loving with a Vengeance: Mass-Produced Fantasies for Women* (Hamden, Conn.: Archon Books, 1982); Laura Mulvey, "Melodrama In and Out of the Home," in *High Theory/Low Culture,* ed. Colin McCabe (Manchester: Manchester University Press, 1986), 80–100; Laura Stempel Mumford, *Love and Ideology in the Afternoon* (Bloomington: Indiana University Press, 1995); Ellen Seiter et al., *Remote Control: Television, Audiences, and Cultural Power* (London: Routledge, 1989). Robert Allen's recent edited collection on the global reception of soap opera, *To Be Continued . . . ,* is also an excellent resource.

25. See Catherine Lutz, "Emotion, Thought, and Estrangement: Emotion as a Cultural Category," *Cultural Anthropology* 1, no. 4 (1986): 405–36.

26. Tanya Modleski, "The Rhythms of Reception: Daytime Television and Women's Work," in *Regarding Television,* ed. E. Ann Kaplan, American Film Institute Monograph (Frederick, Md.: University Publications of America, 1983), 67–75.

27. Raymond Williams, "Drama in a Dramatised Society," in *Raymond Williams and Television,* ed. A. O'Connor (London: Routledge, 1989), 3–13.

28. For critiques along these lines, see Lila Abu-Lughod, "Shifting Politics in Bedouin Love Poetry," in *Language and the Politics of Emotion* (Cambridge: Cambridge University Press, 1990), 24–45, and Abu-Lughod and Catherine Lutz, "Introduction: Emotion, Discourse, and the Politics of Everyday Life," ibid., 1–23.

29. See Dipesh Chakrabarty, "Witness to Suffering: Domestic Cruelty and the Birth of the Modern Subject in Bengal," this volume, ch. 3.

30. Michel Foucault, *History of Sexuality,* trans. R. Hurley, vol. 2: *The Use of Pleasure* (New York: Random House, 1985); also, "Technologies of the Self" and "About the Beginning of the Hermeneutics of the Self."

31. Abu-Lughod, "Shifting Politics in Bedouin Love Poetry."

32. Ann Cvetkovich, *Mixed Feelings: Feminism, Mass Culture, and Victorian Sensationalism* (New Brunswick: Rutgers University Press, 1992), 6.

33. Walter Armbrust's *Mass Culture and Modernism in Egypt* (Cambridge: Cambridge University Press, 1996) is a serious contribution to our understanding of modernist cinema. Lizbeth Malkmus and Roy Armes, in *Arab and African Cinema* (1991), also give some background. The background of Muhammad Fadil, Egypt's preeminent television director, hints at the kinds of influences on those in mass media. He describes having been exposed to theater in university and having pursued his interests through wide reading not only at the public library in Alexandria but at the U.S. Information Library (interview June 17, 1993). Many television writers have backgrounds in literature. For general background on radio and television in Egypt, see *Anciens et nouveaux medias en Egypte: Radio, television, cinema, video, Bulletin de CEDEJ* 21, première semestre (1989).

34. Dwight Reynolds, *Heroic Poets, Poetic Heroes: The Ethnography of Performance in an Arabic Oral Epic Tradition* (Ithaca: Cornell University Press, 1995); Susan Slyomovics, *The Merchant of Art* (Berkeley: University of California Press, 1986). My experience has been that many men and women in their sixties, at least in the Awlad 'Ali Bedouin community in Egypt's Western Desert, where I have spent the most time, can recite verses. Men of the next generation who grew up in cities around the Arab world have boyhood memories of listening to traveling poets reciting the tale in the coffee shops.

35. Susan Slyomovics, "Praise of God, Praise of Self, Praise of the Islamic People: Arab Epic Narrative in Performance," in *Classical and Popular Medieval Arabic*

Literature: A Marriage of Convenience, ed. Jareer Abu-Haidar and Farida Abu-Haidar (London: Curzon Press, in press).

36. Susan Slyomovics, "The Death-Song of ʿAmir Khafaji: Puns in an Oral and Printed Episode of *Sirat Bani Hilal*," *Journal of Arabic Literature* 18 (1987): 62–78. Dwight Reynolds argues that punning is actually quite rare in most Egyptian poets' recitations of the epic (personal communication).

37. See Reynolds, *Heroic Poets, Poetic Heroes,* 180–83.

38. All translations from Susan Slyomovics, "The Epic of the Bani Hilal: The Birth of Abu Zayd: II (Southern Egypt)," in *Oral Epics from Africa: Vibrant Voices from a Vast Continent,* ed. John William Johnson, Thomas A. Hale, and Stephen Belcher (Bloomington: Indiana University Press, 1997), 240–51.

39. *The Epic of the Bani Hilal,* trans. Dwight F. Reynolds (forthcoming).

40. Ibid.

41. As Foucault puts it, "The disciplines mark the moment when the reversal of the political axis of individualization—as one might call it—takes place. In certain societies . . . it may be said that individualization is greatest where sovereignty is exercised and in the highest echelons of power. The more one possesses power or privilege, the more one is marked as an individual, by rituals, written accounts or visual reproductions. The 'name' and the genealogy that situate one within a kinship group, the performance of deeds that demonstrate superior strength and which are immortalized in literary accounts. . . . All these are procedures of an 'ascending' individualization. In a disciplinary regime, on the other hand, individualization is 'descending': as power becomes more anonymous and more functional, those on whom it is exercised tend to be more strongly individualized" (Michel Foucault, *Discipline and Punish,* trans. Alan Sheridan [New York: Random House, 1978], 192–93).

42. It could be argued that the interiority of the domestic scenes of soap opera are metaphors of the inner life of the persons around which their plots revolve. Elsaesser, in his classic article on cinematic melodrama has suggested, in fact, that "the space of the home" does relate "to the inside space of human interiority, emotions, and the unconscious" (cited in Mulvey, "Melodrama In and Out of the Home," 95).

43. Abu-Lughod, *Veiled Sentiments.*

44. See Lila Abu-Lughod, "Islam and the Gendered Discourses of Death," *International Journal of Middle East Studies* 25 (1993): 187–205, for a discussion of some of the literature on lamentation.

45. Elizabeth Wickett, "'For Our Destinies': The Funerary Lament of Upper Egypt," Ph.D. diss., University of Pennsylvania, 1993, 166.

46. The televised version of the Hilali epic was preceded by a revival through commercial audiocassette for mass consumption. Listened to in Cairo as well as back in the Upper Egyptian villages where people had enjoyed poets' performances at weddings, it has taken on a new and different life, entering a cultural field where it can be deployed as a marker of the Egyptian "heritage" as well as a source of regional pride. Similarly, in the Western Desert, the Awlad ʿAli *ghinnaawa* has moved out of its context of the wedding and the oral recitation onto the commercial cassette, in the process excluding women reciters and being turned into a nostalgic form that marks regional or ethnic identity and an acceptable medium for the rebellion of young men against their elders (see Lila Abu-Lughod, "The Shifting Politics of Bedouin Love Poetry").

47. My fieldwork in Egypt, since 1990, has been carried out in two sites: Cairo, where I have interviewed producers of television and worked with domestic servants as television viewers, and a village in Upper Egypt. For more on rural responses to television, see Lila Abu-Lughod, "The Interpretation of Culture(s) after Television,"

Representations 59 (1997): 109–34, and "Television and the Virtues of Education: Upper Egyptian Encounters with State Culture," in *Directions of Change in Rural Egypt,* ed. Nicholas Hopkins and Kirsten Westergaard (Cairo: American University in Cairo Press, 1998), 147–65. For more on domestic servants, see Lila Abu-Lughod, "The Ambivalence of Authenticity: Making Cultural Identity on Egyptian Television in a Transnational Age," unpublished ms.

48. Ruth Behar, "Rage and Redemption: Reading the Life Story of a Mexican Marketing Woman," *Feminist Studies* 16 (1990): 223–58; Laurel Kendall, *The Life and Hard Times of a Korean Shaman* (Honolulu: University of Hawaii Press, 1988).

49. One could, of course, ask what the social effects of this discursive self-presentation were intended to be—especially for a poor domestic worker telling the tale to a wealthier foreigner. Certainly, Amira wanted sympathy and might have wanted to present herself as wronged and in need of support. The story, as I noted above, flowed easily and sounded well rehearsed, as are many of the stories people tell about themselves and others in cultures where storytelling is so important. And one could also ask about the personal or psychological functions, for the socially marginal Amira, of telling her own story in this melodramatic form—a form that, I have suggested, owes so much to television and radio, with their stars and glamor.

50. I discuss these domestic servants' stories in "Third Television: Marginal Women and the Eroding Hegemony of Development," unpublished manuscript.

51. See Dipesh Chakrabarty, "Witness to Suffering," and "The Difference-Deferral of a Colonial Modernity: Public Debates on Domesticity in British Bengal," in *Subaltern Studies VIII,* ed. David Arnold and David Hardiman (Delhi: Oxford University Press, 1994), 50–88, reprinted in *Tensions of Empire: Colonial Cultures in a Bourgeois World,* ed. Frederick Cooper and Ann Laura Stoler (Berkeley: University of California Press, 1997), 373–405. For other ways of thinking about alternative modernities, see Arjun Appadurai, *Modernity at Large* (Minneapolis: University of Minnesota Press, 1996).

52. For the opposition between television and religion, see my "Dramatic Reversals" and "Finding a Place for Islam."

53. Women cannot pray or fast while menstruating because they are not in a state of purity.

54. For an excellent analysis of the self-cultivation encouraged in women in the piety movement in Egypt, see Saba Mahmood, "Women's Piety and Embodied Discipline: The Islamic Resurgence in Contemporary Egypt," Ph.D. diss., Stanford University, 1998.

55. Slyomovics, "Praise of God, Praise of Self, Praise of the Islamic People."

56. James Peacock, *The Rites of Modernization* (Chicago: University of Chicago Press, 1966). The weakest chapter is the one in which he examines *ludruk* (the form of drama) in terms of Marion Levy, Jr.'s *Modernization and the Structure of Societies* (Princeton: Princeton University Press, 1966).

57. Muna Hilmi, "*Al-jari' wa-l-jamila*: Musalsal bi-dûn 'uqad dhukuriya" (*The Bold and the Beautiful*: A Serial without Male Complexes), *Sabah al-Khayr,* February 11, 1993, 59.

Five

The Thin Line of Modernity: Some Moroccan Debates on Subjectivity

Stefania Pandolfo

In epigraph, two unresolved stories of illness:

In March 1991 I traveled to the small community in southern Morocco where I had lived and conducted research for a number of years, with a young woman who was making this journey instead of visiting a psychiatric institution. Su'ad had been an inpatient at a Moroccan hospital once already in the past, and in moments of sudden lucidity—fragments of presence snatched from the other world into which she lapsed—was aware that she might end up there again.

Her relapse had shattered the fragile balance in her family, unleashed fears, and become intolerable. Fearing that a second hospitalization would impose on her a permanent seal of insanity, her mother was determined to prevent it. The mother knew that I kept in touch with a fqih, *a Quranic teacher and healer, in a region of the south and asked me to accompany them to visit him. The space of our journey was a detour of waiting, a postponed verdict, the hiatus of a dream. This was the first time Su'ad had traveled south. From the point of view of the middle-class urban neighborhood where she had been raised, the south was almost another world. (Much later, we recall that journey together. She explains to me what I did not understand then, what she thought I understood, and tells me about the* 'alam akhur, *the "other world" of her illness.)*

When we arrived at the fqih's *house, Su'ad was out of reach. For a long time the* fqih *sat there silently, as though aware that with her his customary ritual acts would not work. Finally he asked a question. She turned to him as if seeing him for the first time, and started to tell—stories of losses and feelings and dreams. A* fqih's *ritual economy is parsimonious with words and time. I wondered how he would take her urgent request, expressed in such a different style. He listened, asked questions, offered advice. I felt I had no right to be there, and left. When I returned, he was giving her his prescription—a fragment of Quranic writing to dilute in water and drink, another to burn.*

Su'ad tried to follow his prescription, but failed. Later, the fqih *expressed his sense of deception at the failure to help her with his methods. She did not return to see him. Yet something had happened, both to him and to her. She had not found a cure, a resolution, a deliverance, but, perhaps, for a moment, what in the language of psychoanalysis is called an* écoute—*an active listening, and a recognition. And he had found himself in a place that was novel for him, a place where the assumptions of his ritual acts were suspended.*

The second story travels in the opposite direction, from that southern village and healer, to the walls of the psychiatric ward at the Hospital Ibn Roshd in Casablanca. It concerns a young woman I knew well from the village, who for several years had suffered from intermittent seizures and absences that were attributed to the jinns through the intervention of sorcery. Fatna had recently given birth. Her husband telephoned from the village and asked me on her behalf to accompany them to the psychiatric hospital in Casablanca. She wanted to go to the hospital, talk with a psychiatrist, "sit" there.

When I met them at the bus station, Fatna did not recognize me. She seemed not to know her husband either, or their newborn daughter, whom he carried in distress. At the hospital we sat in the lobby, waiting to be received. She sat sunken in her state, rigid as a statue, elsewhere. A nurse came, took her by the arm, and led her into a room for a clinical interview. When she came back a little while later, as though by the effectiveness of a rite, she was back to presence as her usual self, without even a prescription for drugs. She took her daughter, gave her her breast, greeted me, and we walked back to the bus as if nothing had happened.

I wondered whether the fear of institutionalization fueled in her a desire to belong, to rejoin a community of speech. (I remembered the face of a woman, beating the glass surface of a closed door.) I posed the question to a psychoanalyst, the friend who had given me a letter of introduction for the hospital. "She needed to travel," he said, "to travel far, far from her village, and from the ties in which she was entangled; she needed une autre écoute, another listening." The walls of the hospital, paradoxically, had served her as the opening of another space—a space where voice could emerge and speech circulate again. At least for the interim of a moment.

Reflecting on his own clinical experience, and on the history of psychiatry in Morocco, Jalil Bennani, a Moroccan psychoanalyst, writes that since the establishment of the first psychiatric institutions during the colonial period, "the symptom has been increasingly addressed to the representatives of modern science, while people are increasingly alone with their suffering."[1] What colonial psychiatrists did not understand, however, and their Moroccan successors have trouble recognizing now, he says, is that the symptom has been also deeply entangled with an understanding of illness and its agents radically foreign to the discourse of that science.

The term "symptom" here refers not to that of psychiatry, or at least not just. It is not a psychopathological index to be read against the standard configuration of an illness—hysteria, melancholia, schizophrenia. It is a painful utterance, a glyph of desire; an unconscious production that may be addressed to an audience. "The symptom is itself structured as a language," Lacan writes. "It is a language whose speech is waiting to be delivered."[2] The interlocutor, Bennani says, is increasingly modern science. The patient's unconscious request, her speech of pain, is being expressed more and more within the medical psychiatric code and to an institutional representative of that code. Yet, at the same time, it digs its roots elsewhere, like a rhizome, in other ways of experiencing selfhood and madness.

As Moroccan psychiatrists themselves acknowledge, patients follow "traditional" and psychiatric cures side by side and are invested, if partially, in both. This raises two important sets of questions: the first concerns what happens to the symptom, to the perception and representation of illness, and to the position and speech of the subject, in moving from one institutional and symbolic set of references to the other. The second concerns the unequal power of the demonological and the medical discourses. What does it mean, for a man diagnosed as a schizophrenic, to spend his weekend "en permission" from the psychiatric hospital at the house of a traditional healer, performing the cures of the jinns? In what sense can the two institutional discourses, therapeutic techniques, and "experiences of madness" be said to be commensurable?[3] Or should the symptom itself be understood as a painful and unspeakable knot connecting discrepant and juxtaposed experiential registers? It is a suspended utterance that does not fit the customary interpretative frames and calls for theoretical reinvention: a bridge between worlds, simultaneously stating their contemporaneity and their distance, painfully telling the impossible.

This essay is a reflection on the possibility of speaking, listening, and dwelling on the boundary of Moroccan modernity, that intermediate zone where the two stories of illness belong. It sets as its limited aim to trace the implications of a specifically modernist Moroccan sense of temporality, the temporality of the "cut" or the "bridge," related to the drawing of a line that separates and joins worlds experienced as at once contiguous and remote.

Through the discussion of an experimental novel, an essay in the philosophy of alienation, and a psychiatric debate around the status of "traditional therapies," I consider three Moroccan modernist problematizations of the self and attempt to read them, as much as possible, in their own terms.[4] They are literary, philosophical, and therapeutical topoi, interpreting contemporary subjectivity within the visions of modernity they present. As I follow their different vocabularies, I raise the questions of subjectivity, emancipation, and time. What does it mean, within each view, to be a subject in postcolonial Morocco, to live and act in the present, to speak with one's contemporaries? What place is there, in these debates, for the unsettled speech, the questioning, and the unresolved therapeutical journeys of Suʿad and Fatna?

Incommensurable Past

In 1954, two years before the independence of Morocco, Driss Chraïbi published *Le passé simple,* a controversial novel that marked a generation of Moroccan intellectuals. Written in a dismembered narrative and temporal style, *The Simple Past* is the account of an epistemic break—a traumatic cut, which carved in the subject's history a discontinuity beyond return (the grammatical *passé simple,* the past historic tense alluded to in the title). It is a story of fractured identities and of impossible self-recognitions; and of betweenness and the practice of loss as possible emergent modes of subjectivity.[5] As such, the novel poetically raised a question that shaped Maghribi literature and post-colonial critique for the following three decades. In the words of Abdelkebir Khatibi, "Qui, nous-mêmes, dans la decolonisation," "Who, *ourselves*, in process of decolonization?"[6]

The cut, the trauma, is both the theme of the novel and the formal principle of its construction. Staged in the disintegration of the narrative body, in the fissure of the chronology, in the visual juxtaposition of scenes, it is the rift in the life of Driss Ferdi, caught in the interval between incommensurable worlds, unable to belong to either. "In the interval," he says, "I am at a standstill." The French *passé simple*, grammatically, is the tense of an impossible narration. Rarely used in the first person and almost untranslatable in English (*je fûs*, "I have been," but in a remote past, a past forever severed from myself), the *passé simple* conveys without mediation the uncanny temporality of a cut.[7] Both coeval and incommensurable, it is comparable to the "un-present" tense of a statement by Freud's hysteric patient Emmy Von N.: "I am a woman dating from the last century."[8]

In the interior monologue of a pseudo-autobiographical mode, *The Simple Past* narrates the ambiguous and conflictual relationship that Driss, the narrator (and author's name), entertains with his father, le Seigneur, in a wealthy traditionalist household in rapidly modernizing Casablanca. The Lord is a vivid allegory and incarnation of the Law, the law of God and of society, of its violence and paradoxes; such is the father as perceived by the son. The story also narrates the ambivalent exchanges Driss entertains with his milieu: his love-hatred for his Arabic-speaking home, full of Quranic quotations, moral precepts, and muffled tensions always about to explode, and his diffident attraction to his French-speaking friends and well-meaning teachers from the metropole, active promoters of the "universal" vocabulary of *liberté, egalité, fraternité*.[9]

Driss tells of the cleavage of his *langue fourchue*, his forked tongue,[10] split between Arabic and French, and his precarious existential stance, sitting on a jumpseat, he says, between Orient and Occident, between tradition and modernity, unable to identify with either; each concept gaining reality and substance from its reciprocal opposition to the other; suspended *f-l-baynat*, "in the betweens," as this condition is imaged in vernacular Moroccan Arabic. (He realizes, in the end, that both "our" tradition and "their" modernity exist only as powerful rhetorical tropes: that the Seigneur, embodiment of the principle of Islamic theocracy, is also a man tormented by doubt; and that the French teacher is a bearer of the value of *liberté* only to the extent of his bureaucratic office. It is then that, for the first time, he has a conversation with his father.)

Throughout the novel, Driss's predicament is expressed by a vision, a sensory hallucination, which, he says, "takes hold" of him and by which he "escapes"; he escapes to another scene. He calls this apparition "the Thin Line," *la Ligne Mince*: a boundary and a bar, a slash [/], a partition and a limit between opposed terms, but also an *entre-deux,* an interstitial zone, an emergent beyond, in between classificatory terms. She, the Thin Line, says to him:

> You were the issue of the Orient, and through your painful past, your imaginings, your education, you are going to triumph over the Orient. You have never believed in Allah. You know how to dissect the legends, you think in French, you are a reader of Voltaire and an admirer of Kant. And yet the Occidental world for which you are destined seems to you to be sewn with stupidities and ugliness, about the same ugliness and stupidities you are fleeing from. Moreover, you feel it is a hostile world. It is not going to accept you right away, and, at the point of exchanging the box seat you now occupy for a jumpseat, you have some setbacks. That is why I appear to you. Since the very first day I appeared to you, you are nothing but an open wound.[11]

He, Driss, the character and author, cries out for her: "*Thin Line, Thin Line,* I call out to you as a sleepless child calls a maternal lullaby. . . ."

> . . . It is the Thin Line by which I escape. It dropped into this room like a flash. . . . Like the thread of a spiderweb at first, so thin, so impalpable, that it is unreal. The thread is a letter, a cypher, or a broken line. It doesn't move, but I see it growing, Oh! So slowly, so softly, so imperceptibly at first. As it grows, as it specifies itself, the letter, the broken line, or the cypher acquires materiality, becomes concrete, and moves, swings and dances—faster and faster. And the Thin Line becomes as thick as a finger, larger than an arm, and takes on the look of an engine's piston, a plane's propeller, a rocket trajectory, it grows as huge as a mountain, always with its shape of a letter, a cypher, or a broken line.[12]

Letter, cypher, or broken line, the Thin Line materializes the fracture at the core of Driss's identity, the incision of the law, the exclusion. (You are, or you are not one of us, you are no longer part of our world, the Father says.) Broken line, *ligne brisée*: a visual translation of the Arabic term *musîba,* "disaster" or trauma; the passive participle of the verb *sâba,* to be right, to draw a straight line, from which the term *sawâb* derives, designating what is morally proper, ethics and just behavior; in its passive form, *usîba,* it means to be stricken, and connotes the interruption of the line, its fracture. The Line—so thin, so impalpable, that it is unreal—is the classificatory boundary between East and West, black and white, tradition and modernity; the unreal limit that constitutes their reality, the limit that should not be crossed. "You are about to cross the line; this is why I appear to you," she warns him.

It is the Line that cuts through Driss like a knife, that drops into his room like a flash, and produces phantasmagoric forms—dream images and hellish nightmares, born from the breach of the cut. Like a geological fault, a passage to the underground, the Thin Line is also a gate, from which spurt up mechanical monsters. Engine pistons, rocket trajectories, trains running, they are marvelous metamorphoses of the Thin Line itself. Reminiscent of Walter Benjamin's description of "Chthonic Paris," that mythological underworld of the modern, the Thin Line grows into a phantasmagoric topology, disclosing within itself a space of the archaic.[13]

Suggesting, perhaps, a mystical dimension of that modernist space (in the sense in which Michel de Certeau spoke of the enunciative space of seventeenth-century European mystics as modern),[14] the Thin Line is also a Quranic concept. It is the image of the *barzakh*—a partition, isthmus, limit, or barrier—which establishes a difference and which it is forbidden to pass (*Qur'an* 23:99–100). In its Sufi interpretation, and in the thought of Ibn 'Arabi in particular, the *barzakh* is a pivotal concept: a theory of the Intermediate World of absence-presence, region of the boundary and domain of the Imagination, in which contraries come together, bodies are spiritualized, and spirits become manifest in corporeal forms. Both a limit and an *entre-deux,* the entre-deux of the limit, the *barzakh* is a thin line. Pulsating and swinging, vertiginous and immobile, that interstitial zone is the enunciative boundary,[15] the emergent locus of subjectivity, of Chraïbi's book.

Modernity and Melancholia

With an existential questioning resonant of that of Driss, but in the language of philosophical historicism and with a normative perspective on the "stage of modernity," Abdallah Laroui raises the question of alienation and inauthenticity in the thought and intellectual productions of his Moroccan contemporaries. *L'idéologie arabe contemporaine,* published in Paris in 1967, thinks modernity as an imperative, a wound, and a lure. It considers the Arab predicament to be colored by a sense of despair.[16]

For Laroui there is no easy embracing of a modernist position. Modernity is inextricably bound with domination, and the desire for modernity, like the desire for tradition, is the insidious way in which domination works. Yet, he says, there is no other path. While approving of the nineteenth-century Muslim reformist Jamal ad-Dîn al-Afghâni (who saw the Orient's salvation in its reconciliation with reason and science), Laroui warns that Arab countries "only crossed the threshold of modern times in the pain of defeat and occupation" (31). That, he says, cannot be overlooked. Modernity is also that wound and that defeat, the inaugural defeat of the Arab self, the original loss, foreclosing the possibility of return. Any dream of returning to an authentic lost self only loses it further.

L'idéologie arabe contemporaine is the anguished attempt by a militant modernist to come to terms with this realization, by unraveling the symbolic structure of domination, which produces and reproduces subordination. It is an assessment of the imaginary servitude in which Arab consciousness is imprisoned without its knowing, and which makes impossible any autonomous definition of an Arab self. The task, difficult and uncertain, is to clear out a path toward emancipation.

In Laroui's view, the Arab servitude is twofold. On the one hand, it is the Arabs' alienating identification with their Other, the Occident. "It is in relation to the Other that the Arabs define themselves. The Other is the West. Hence to describe the Arabs' quest for self means to present, at the same time, a history of the notion of the Occident. . . . Having started from the question, 'Who are we?' we are facing another question, 'What is the Occident?'"[17] But servitude is also related to the affective tie the Arabs maintain with their past—a past long dead yet treated as present by the alienated self. Both the West and the Past are foreign voices that speak from the vacant place of the Arab self, determining the "retard culturel" of the Arabs and hindering the emergence of a modern self. It is in this sense, Laroui says, that the possibility of finding a voice, a voice that is one's own, can only be the outcome of a critical revision of "notre outillage mental," our mental tools:

Our world, social and mental, is steeped in influences. To think, we make use of concepts, images, and models that are entirely drawn from a reality other than our own. Without undertaking a rigorous analysis of our mental tools, we can never be certain that we are actually talking about ourselves; and the testimony we sign as our own will require interpretation by others (6).

Disavowal is the cause of alienation: a disavowal, in one sense, of the interpenetration of the Arab world and the West (for "one is in the other," Laroui says). Discourses of identity and cultural authenticity, such as orientalism and nationalism, obliterate the long history of exchanges and transformations in the shaping of those entities that are today called the Arab world and the West, and the fluctuation in what now appear as fixed identities. ("So many razed cities, poisoned wells, burned ships, before he could recognize himself in a[n Arab] Self that seemed at first for him unbearable and opaque" [84].)

But there is a more dangerous form of disavowal: that of the dependence of modern Arab forms of consciousness upon those of the West. It is at this imaginary level that domination holds its grip. As long as this is not subjected to critique, the history of exchanges can only remain disavowed. The three paradigmatic figures of Arab modernity—the Muslim reformist or "cleric," the political reformist, and the "technophile"—each make claims of authenticity and originality, and each is instead indebted to a borrowed European model. These models, as an ideological remote control or Laroui says, as "shadows," frame the discursive field within which Arab thinkers speak: "It is always the Other that poses the terms of the question, draws the boundaries of the field of research, and it is within this frame that contemporary Arab thought attempts to find its answers" (33).

Luring themselves to be modernity's agents, they mimic anachronistic forms of Western consciousness. And this is the core of Laroui's argument. Whether clerical, political, or technological, Arab modernists reproduce models that, in the West, are already obsolete. Arab consciousness is shaped by "superseded forms of Western consciousness," forms in which the West no longer recognizes itself. Having long ceased to be the expression of the real "productive core of Western society," these forms of consciousness are purely ideological (34). They are exported, Laroui says, "in their twilight form." Arab modernity is archaeological:

It is as if, in the effort to make sense of itself, the Orient turned into an archaeologist and rediscovered superseded forms of Western consciousness. In as much as each time it is the West that provides the elements of the discussion, one might be tempted to say that it confuses us on purpose, by artificially keeping alive a few of its older sloughs. This would be wrong, however, for it is clear that these two societies, slowly interpenetrating, can only dialogue in terms of religious consciousness at first, then political and finally technological consciousness. . . . Yet, because of the time-lag effect [décalage dans le temps], in contemporary Arab thought the phase of reality for each form of consciousness is already ideological. This explains, perhaps, the lack of freshness and the superficiality that many readers, familiar with European history, feel in reading modern Arab writings (37).

Despite the movement of interpenetration, the two societies cannot encounter each other. "Historical distance," Laroui says, makes recognition impossible: "contact between two societies can be inconsequential; for one society can simply *not see* the other" (40). Laroui calls this strategy of domination, based on reciprocal blinding and on the "time-lag effect," a *Machiavélisme objectif,* a Machiavellian strategy of power that has to do with the structure of the situation itself (39).

At the heart of Laroui's argument, again, there is time. Temporal *décalage,* or *déphasage,* an effect of delay in the structure of consciousness, and a "falling out of synchrony" that is also out of touch, are symptoms, and agents, of subjugation. Arab consciousness, he says, does not live in the present. It dwells in the ambiguous region of an anterior future, "a future already outlined elsewhere, which we are not free to reject."

Our consciousness, in Morocco, drifts between the determinations of the past and the call of the future. It dwells in the peculiar temporal category of an anterior future, which radically changes the meaning of all other temporal parameters: neither our present, nor our past, nor our future, are real, and can be lived as such (66).

Arab lives are determined elsewhere, where the balance of power lies, in the industrialized West; this is how "today's humanity is really partitioned." But, Laroui says, contemporary Arab consciousness cannot see this, for it dwells in "another world," an "unreal" world, populated by the ghostly presences of absent interlocutors. It is a world made of mythic forms, images, fetishes: "a condensed image of the past, [the Arab] language itself becomes a fetish" (96). They are ruins, the result of the trauma of loss—the self-defeat that is modernity itself. Born of a narcissistic wound, the Arab self is dupe.

Estranged from quotidian life, unable to participate in the present, the self is "elsewhere" *(ailleurs)*; it is "absent"—in Arabic, *gharîb*. *Gharîb*, or as a noun *al-gharîb*, is the absent and vanishing, the strange, the uncanny. As a classical literary figure, *al-gharîb* is the art of lexicographers, the poetic knowledge of lost worlds and words; a knowledge of "archaeological deposits," Laroui says.

To explain the archaeological predicament of modern Arab culture, he turns to the practice of *al-gharîb* and to the melancholic mood of classical Arab poetry. Ibn Shyhayd, a fifth-century Andalusian poet, lives in a sophisticated urban society, "yet his soul, exiled from the present, is elsewhere. . . . His soul does not see the stormy Andalusian skies; it is moved, instead, in a dream, by a sand storm in a remote world he never knew" (87). Refusing to see that exile as a rhetorical flight and a source of poetic inspiration, Laroui condemns it as a self-deceiving ruse, an escape from the responsibilities of real life into a delusional search for authenticity. Similarly self-deceptive, contemporary Arab culture is a "culture de la scission intérieure," where modern Arabs dwell "in an hypnotic state": "Internally cleavaged, nostalgic man is always elsewhere, faithful to the world of his dreams, of his myths, and his inner upheavals" (89).

Condemned to the fate of an ineluctable repetition, contemporary Arabs do not live, Laroui says: "They re-live in the mode of melancholy" (49). Melancholy: an excess of black bile in Arab medicine and Galenic humoral physiology, slowly sinking the complex body-soul into a state of paralysis and death; or the inability to mourn and the morbid attachment to the vanished object, which for Freud causes the self to consume and become that loss.[18] Consumed by a loss of which they remain unaware, modern Arabs are unable to mourn—to acquit themselves from the past and move on to new forms of expression. This, in Laroui's view, is the most insidious form of domination. Under the gaze of melancholy, historical consciousness comes to a halt, and history is "hypostatized," frozen in the "unpresent" tense. Only fragmented images remain: "images, veritable incarnations of a compressed history, are the center of gravity of the Arab soul" (81). Arab modernity is a space of disaster.

For Laroui this is the stage of despair: "Le mort saisit le vif" (the corpse seizes the living) (88). Anguished and enraged by what he sees as a predicament of subjugation and impasse, Laroui does not explore the revolutionary possibilities of the melancholic subject he describes: a subject born from the incorporation of loss, who creates and recreates new worlds in a space of unresolvable mourning.[19] Yet it is at this point that Laroui's theory of temporal disfunctions, unwittingly, and from the opposite perspective, meets Walter Benjamin's reflections on modernity, allegory, and mourning.

Laroui cannot pursue the path of melancholy, for in his view melancholy—the inability to complete the process of grieving—produces myth as a delusional formation and forecloses the possibility of emancipation. *L'idéologie arabe contemporaine* advocates emancipation as an overcoming, a detachment from the object of grieving and a sublimation of the loss in "expression." Expression, the antidote of myth, is for Laroui the direction of a possible agency: "Any work that does not address clearly the problem of expression, which does not aim, in other words, at sublimating our backwardness *[retard]* by way of the Word, is tainted with essential inferiority" (179).

"Folklore" is Laroui's name for myth. Classical Arab culture is folklore, for it draws its life from "the solidified expression of a defunct society." Contemporary oral culture and lived custom are folklore, no less than their colonial and bourgeois commodification; the nationalist search for culture is but "recuperated folklore." Like a deceiving echo, they celebrate the void of the Arab self. Lived custom, oral culture, and their colonial and bourgeois commodifications are "folklore" because their reality is a modern European production in its entirety. There has never been a living Arab culture. If today culture is a commodity offered to the European gaze, "beforehand it was only archaeological deposits of a petrified society [auparavant, il n'était que dépôts archéologiques d'une societé engourdie]" (175). *Auparavant,* "beforehand," is not a temporal adverb, denoting, for instance, precolonial times. It designates a past fallen out of reach, the other side of a chasm; any knowledge of it is either inauthentic (the kitsch of tourism, *artisanat, arts populaires,* etc.), or it has the uncanny status of a traumatic memory.

Distance, then, becomes incommensurable. Not just the "historical distance" between the Arab world and the West, but that between the critical historian and his society.[20]

The Old Cemetery, the I, and the Present

As in the case of Driss, the protagonist of *Le passé simple,* Laroui's questioning opens on the aftermath of a trauma, a rupture, which hurled a portion of the subject's history into an incommensurable past. In Chraïbi's terms, it is the past of an old Muslim cemetery:

> Coming here this morning, I met an American from the Military Police. He stopped his Jeep.
> —You French? he asked me.
> —No, I answered. Arab dressed in French.
> —*Then* . . . where are the Arabs dressed as Arabs, speaking as Arabs, and . . .
> I raised my hand in the direction of the old Muslim cemetery.
> —Over there.
> He set off.[21]

A product of the trauma of colonization (which for Driss is both a wound and a gift), the modern subject is "arabe habillé en français," Arab dressed in French. This is not to say that, for Chraïbi, the Arab self is disguised (or trapped) under the borrowed French attire but that ill-fitting identities are all that is left. Well-fitting cultural identities, Arabs dressed as Arabs, speaking as Arabs, are "over there" (gesture of the raised hand), in the old Muslim cemetery. They belong to a remote past, a past that is neither mine nor not mine.

The image of the old cemetery, a burial site no longer in use, is a charged one in the Maghribi popular imagination; realm of the "forgotten tomb" and site of magical operations, it designates a zone of opacity beyond memory, an alterity that can only be approached through myth. Such is the status of "our own culture," Driss says. *Unheimlisch* in the Freudian sense, culture becomes the elusive place of origin that can only be encountered in the phantasmagoric forms of myth. An origin that inhabits the present as phantasm.

In different ways, both *L'idéologie arabe contemporaine* and *Le passé simple* acknowledge and ponder this fact. It is in their views of the present, rather than of the past, that they most fundamentally diverge. Chraïbi's present is a state in the making, populated with mythological figures and yet compellingly real. It attempts to capture the experiential reality of the break, the shattering, through the experiment of a composite tense, the place of a fissure and of the contemporary encounter of discrepant temporalities. In that space the ventriloquist subject speaks in a multiplicity of voices.

Laroui's present is a normative state, a goal to achieve. It denotes a subjectivity (and a grammatical tense) Arabs do not have but must acquire to overcome their temporal disfunction, their *retard*, if they do not want to remain the parrots of European modernity. It is a punctual, one-dimensional tense, defined in opposition to the past as the self-mastery of historical consciousness. To be modern, for Laroui, is to possess the present, such a present; to be emancipated from myth, from mimetism, from the lingering weight of melancholic humors; to do away with voices that are not one's own. To possess the present, in the end, is to deal in universal values: cultural pluralism, he says, is the last imperial ruse of the West.

Laroui's conclusion is a plea for the resolution of all cultural ties, for the completion of mourning toward a new universal identity— the only true path, in his view, toward emancipation and agency: "Reconnaître l'universel, c'est en réalité se réconcilier avec soi-même" (recognizing universal values is the true way to be reconciled with oneself).[22]

Les Thérapies Traditionnelles

At the Conference on the Psychotherapy of the Maghribi Patient, held in Casablanca in April 1992, two days were dedicated to a debate on *les thérapies traditionnelles*. The term, which was quickly becoming a code, referred to the constellation of practices related to the care of the body-soul complex in the vernacular understanding of illness, with special reference to the therapies known as "cures of the jinn." The participants in the conference were clinical psychiatrists, psychoanalysts, psychologists, and psychotherapists from Morocco, Tunisia, Algeria, and France. A number of panelists practiced at neighborhood clinics in France and reported on cases of immigrant psychopathology; others worked in public hospitals or private practices in the Maghreb.

A central question, of technique but also of professional ethics, concerned the attitude Maghribi psychiatrists and psychoanalysts should assume toward their patients' persistent resort to the vocabulary of spirit possession, magic, and bewitchment, and their continuing recourse to the parallel attention of traditional healers. Should one refuse to listen, since any listening is a form of indirect validation, or instead attempt to hear what was said in the traditional idiom? Should one treat traditional practitioners as potential fellow psychotherapists, or dismiss them as charlatans whose activity reproduced false beliefs, contributing to the cultural *retard* of the country? Should a distinction be drawn between old traditional cures, grounded in religious faith, good intention, and a mystical knowledge of the cosmos, and the new speculative growth of false thaumaturgists, dealers in societal suffering, that proliferated in the Moroccan cities? Or should it simply be acknowledged that in formerly colonized countries like Morocco several medical systems operated at the same time, and a part of the population, only passively touched by the process of modernization, did not participate in and even resisted the discourse of individual agency and the project of a responsible subjectivity—a project that could be defined as psychiatry's and, to some extent, psychoanalysis's own?[23]

I participated in the conference from the floor, as an anthropologist interested in the terms of a possible conversation between the cures of the jinns and the psychoanalytic exploration of the unconscious. I had myself worked with traditional healers on the ontological dimension, the specificity and effectiveness, of their technique. I was conversant with Freudian and Lacanian psychoanalysis and I believed, at least in an abstract sense, in the ethical possibility of a dialogue between different approaches to subjectivity and alterity— different but, in my view, commensurable ways of raising the questions of self, voice, meaning, unmeaning, and death. Yet what the conference urgently made me realize was that the historicity of the different subjective positionings—my own included—could not be bracketed away. Commensurability was not just an epistemological question.[24] The conversation I sought was impossible, at least in the institutional sphere. Attempting to understand, and question, that impossibility meant to become attuned to a modernist passion, the desire for a new self, and a sense of break from the past, from "culture," understood both as a mode of colonial subjection and as the source of an identity that is no longer one's own. An identity that inhabits the present as phantasm.

It was in order to understand the stakes in this debate, the different subjective positionings, norms, desires, and impossibilities, that I sought an interpretative lead in the modernist visions of Driss Chraïbi and Abdallah Laroui, in their contrasting ways of thinking the Moroccan postcolonial self. For in the course of that conference and other conversations that followed, two things began to emerge with some clarity. First, unlike the case of the Brazilian Cuña in Lévi-Strauss's famous comparison of shamanic and psychoanalytic cures, in contemporary Morocco the relation between the two practices is a fact of life, rooted in the experience of suffering, in the speech and the therapeutic quest of countless individuals.[25] Second, in the current situation, any discussion of that relationship or any attempt at interpretation and translation situates the analyst in the midst of an ideological field, calling for his or her positioning vis-à-vis the predicaments of decolonization, emancipation, and the characterization of a "modern" subject.

The status of the "cultural factor" in the symptomatology, diagnosis, and care of mental illness is an important knot of the debate. Against the return of ethnopsychiatric theory and clinical practice in France in the context of immigrant psychotherapy,[26] several Moroccan psychiatrists point to the danger of the relativist position, arguing—in this sense like Laroui—for the irreducibility of the universal structure of the human psyche.

Variously argued in the Freudian and Lacanian vocabulary by psychoanalysts, or in the nosological idiom by clinical psychiatrists, the main objections to the possibility of engaging in a dialogue with traditional therapies are two. The first is the caveat against cultural relativism. Treating indigenous psychotherapies as a culturally specific form of healing, and an effective one, has the risk of replicating the colonial operation of circumscribing an indigenous mentality and pathology as something essentially specific to a dominated race, in this case "one's own." The racist approach of Antoine Porot and the Algiers School of Psychiatry, or the theory of a specifically North African psychosis christened "Paléophrénie réactionnelle," after the primitive (paleo) nature of the violent impulses it unleashed,[27] are the often-cited examples. The second and more crucial objection concerns the assessment of traditional therapies from the point of view of modernist norms of subjectivity. Predicated on projection, suggestion, mimicry, and the displacement of agency onto imaginary entities (the jinns, or other human persecutors), traditional therapies are viewed as reproducing and reinforcing an alienated structure of the self. I will consider both objections in some detail.

First, the question of culture. The signifier "culture" has a double place in this debate. On the one hand, it is blurred with what during the colonial period was called *la mentalité indigène* and as such becomes an emblem of what decolonization must reject. The study of culture in general, and of "traditional therapies" in particular, is viewed as carrying the legacy of a psychiatric rhetoric systematically seeking in the culture, and especially in the Islamic religion, the roots of North African psychopathology. On the other hand, in a less obvious but perhaps more crucial sense, the sense explored in different ways by the works of Chraïbi and Laroui and by a generation of Maghribi literary writers, "culture" summons mythological presences from a vanished world—archaeological deposits, old cemeteries.

La Psychopathologie Marocaine

"Nothing durable can be done in the field of public health if the dominant mentality does not evolve," the Director of Public Health and Hygiene in Morocco during the 1920s and 1930s, Dr. Jules Colombani, wrote in 1924. "We must take the pulse of its evolution every day. I will only cite, as an example, the many difficulties we have encountered in our attempts to transform the regime of insanity [régime des aliénés], difficulties we have hitherto been unable to overcome."[28]

Since the beginning of the century, French colonial health officers in North Africa had been confronted with the imperative of seizing the indigenous mentality, cognitive processes, and sense of self. The proclaimed task of the Algiers School of Psychiatry, founded by Antoine Porot in 1918 and inaugurated by his paper "Notes de psychiatrie musulmane," was to study "the indigenous mentality," to better understand its pathology and make it progress effectively.[29] The views of the School were inspired by a reductive reading of Levy-Bruhl's theory of "primitive mentality."[30] Porot borrowed from Levy-Bruhl the hypothesis of a pre-logical cognitive function characterized by a predominance of visual over conceptual representation, of allegorical memory over logical reasoning, and of temporal simultaneity over diachronic periodization. But Levy-Bruhl's phenomenological explorations were aimed at understanding other forms of cognition in their own terms and eventually led him to abandon the notion of a primitive mentality altogether to pursue the hypothesis of a pre-logical function in the philosophy of modern science. Porot's racist appropriation, instead, bent Levy-Bruhl's ideas toward the theory of a pathological mind. A *mentalité indigène prémorbide* was described in terms of lack of the concept of time, deficiency of the critical faculty, and inability to think conceptually, each related to a fundamental inability to symbolize and to an excessive development of the mimetic faculty. Arabs were prisoners of the image, Porot said, and this explained the diffusion of what he called *les troubles de la mimique,* mimeological disorders: contagious hysterical states, which often grew into collective hysteria.

Echoes of this approach are found in Carl Antoine Pierson's theory of "reactive paleophrenia," developed in the 1950s from the psychiatric evaluation of mentally ill patients who had committed murderous criminal acts. As one considers these crimes, Pierson writes, committed without a reason, under the influence of a sudden rage comparable to the impulsiveness of children, "le fond des tendances natives apparaît à nu, laissant voir une immédiate régression vers un primitivisme lointain, mal déguisé sous des attitudes collectives peu solides."[31] (When I first started conducting research at the Arrazi psychiatric hospital in Sale, the example of "reactive paleophrenia" was brought up, only half jokingly, to warn me against the methodological risks of an approach that pursued the cultural specificity of the expression of illness and healing. I studied Moroccan culture and was married to a Moroccan man. I should then be aware that there is a specifically Arab psychosis, paleophrenia. My husband could wake up one night and, seized by a raptus, murder me. How did that aberration affect my methodological approach? Underpinning this question is the position that psychiatry is a set of universal diagnostic and therapeutic techniques predicated on the assumption that, independent of culture—of the cultural differences in the perception and expression of illness—mental illness is the same everywhere, and can be detected and treated on the basis of standardized criteria of validity and reliability. This is the only insurance, the antidote, in fact, against the return of colonial aberrations.)

Toward the end of the colonial period, in the late 1940s and 1950s, a new approach was developed in Morocco against the racist orientation of the Algiers School. In an attempt to rethink the complex interpenetration of cultures issued from the colonial experience, and to understand the destabilizing psychosocial impact of modernization, the Groupe d'étude de psychologie de l'inconscient et de médecine psychosomatique (Research Group on the Psychology of the Unconscious and Psychosomatic Medicine) gathered in Casablanca several French psychiatrists and *médecins militaires* around the person of René Laforgue, an expatriate French psychoanalyst, former friend of Sigmund Freud, and former president of the Psychoanalytic Society of Paris.[32] The position of the group was elaborated in a series of articles published in the journal *Maroc médical*. The approach was empirical, research oriented, open to understanding cultural difference and change. The contributors reflected on the attitude that French mental health officers should assume toward indigenous medicine and age-old beliefs, and on the responsibilities of psychiatry toward the social traumas of modernization, urbanization, and increasing proletarization, "a true drama in the psycho-social evolution of a country whose traditional structures are shattered, and which does not seem prepared to quickly come up with novel institutions."[33]

A crucial feature was the focus on culture—the attempt to situate psychopathological affections within the sociocultural context in which they were produced. The task, in the wake of "the American school of cultural anthropology," was to formulate a theory of the Moroccan personality structure *(personalité marocaine de base)*. Partly conceived in the genuine appreciation of human difference, the emphasis on culture served at the same time the purpose of identifying the areas where sociocultural personality traits would be dysfunctional in the process of modernization.

Maurice Igert's "Introduction à la psychopathologie marocaine" (1955) is an articulate exposition of this approach. Opening with the notion that "an initiation to Moroccan psychopathology should be an invitation to journey," Igert—a military physician turned psychoanalyst—reflects on what it entails, for European health officers, "to establish a contact with human beings governed by internal laws other than our own," fundamentally different and yet so closely related in daily commerce. ("The contact between French and Moroccan people is no longer that of two cultures that exist as two independent realities, but that of two human societies that have a certain common history, common interests in partnership and, obviously, some areas of friction.")[34]

The idea is to identify "the cultural tensions generative of neuroses" specific to the Moroccan cultural milieu. Igert's text oscillates between the desire to "journey," listening to the speech of Moroccan patients, to the stories of possession and suffering he analyzes, often with remarkable insight, and the project to produce a chart of sociocultural features with pathological potential. The detailed observation of Bouzoukri, a soldier admitted as a patient to the Centre Neuro-Psychiatrique des Troupes du Maroc, includes long sections of the man's direct narration. It is a sensitive effort at listening to a subjectivity other than one's own and to the "mythical themes" of a delirium, which, Igert says, are "not so foreign to us after all."

But the task of mapping the configuration of Moroccan psychopathology prevails, leading Igert to diagnose the neurotic orientation of the culture as a whole. Moroccan personality is characterized by "mental plasticity," "suggestibility," and the collective alienation of a society that cannot sanction the insanity of the mentally ill but instead shares and validates their delusional tales of possession by the jinns. The real obstacle preventing the possibility of emancipation and cure is therefore, for Igert, the "unlimited tolerance of the Moroccan social milieu vis-à-vis mental disorders that draw their themes from the very sources of collective belief," for "as long as the individual remains faithful to this common source, he cannot be considered as insane [aliené]."[35] And for a cure to be possible, alienation must be recognized.

The cultural tensions in question are described as structurally conflictual features of the Moroccan patriarchal family, related to "the profound impregnation of Islam" in the culture. "Psychological plasticity" and the inability to take responsibility for one's acts are a consequence of what Igert sees as the cultural system established by Islam. A tyrannical cultural Super-Ego associated with the paternal configuration of father-sultan-God led to an excessive identification of the children with an all-powerful father. The impossibility of finding resort in a mother hierarchically inferior and culturally devalued, and the related inability to develop "an opposition to the father, a pivotal factor in the acquisition of individual autonomy in Europe," determined the imbalance of the "trio father-mother-child." This caused the absolute subordination to a despotic paternal authority, "condemned the son's aggressive impulses to a total repression," and in turn led to the conversion of those impulses into numerous neurotic symptoms. The submission made impossible the development of self-confidence and "individual sovereignty."[36]

Igert's conclusion was that "other than escaping into spirituality, an avenue which is indeed wide open in the cultural milieu, he [the son] will have the option only of bending. . . . Thus develops a remarkable mental plasticity. . . . In the eyes of the psychiatrist, this plasticity represents a simple defense mechanism encompassing a vast field of reactions, ranging, according to its modalities, from utilitarian and banal lying, to hysteria, passing through simulation and suggestibility. This cultural trait marks Moroccan mental pathology with certain typical features, particularly the manifestations of individual and collective hysteria."[37] Magical and religious practices, the belief in spirits (and particularly the role of "castrating female spirits" such as 'Aicha Qandisha, expressing the "occult revolt of Moroccan women"), indigenous healing, the place of saints in the society, and the many varieties of Sufi mysticism, were all, for Igert, coherent manifestations of this neurotic personality structure.

Cultural Uncanny

At the conference forty years later, the characterizations *medicine indigène* and *mentalité indigène* were updated by the qualifier *traditional*. For they now designated a domain of practice and belief specific to a society that was the therapists' own—that was, and yet was not, for its tense was an archaeological past, a *passé simple*. The domain had a name, *le magico-religieux*, a term recycled from colonial ethnological accounts to designate the realm of what was beyond the Line. Descriptions of trancing lent body and image to this space, evoking the slashing of Hamadsha devotees at the Festival of Sheikh al-Kâmal, or the chaining of the insane on the columns of Buya 'Omar's sanctuary. Most of the conference papers emphasized the need to study "traditional therapies"; some offered a classification of the range of practitioners (soothsayers or Quranic scholars, talisman writers or exorcists) and proposed a translation of traditional symptomatology into the Freudian vocabulary of psychoneuroses or in psychiatric nosological terms.

The ethnographic reference was to old French accounts, such as Edmond Doutté and Émile Dermenghem, at once criticized and invoked as a source of archival knowledge about the other.[38] In this manner, at least in one sense, postcolonial psychoanalysis could delimit "traditional therapies" as a field of normalizing knowledge about an Other. This was related to the development of medical structures throughout the country, and to the struggle for the control of the "regime of insanity" and the definition of subjectivity. There was an increasing awareness that the "modern" and the "traditional" approaches to health coexisted and were not incompatible in the eyes of many patients who made recourse to both; and that even though the psychiatric hospitals were full, patients held on to their own interpretations of illness.

Looked at from this angle, the situation bore a certain resemblance to the colonial project of seizing the *mentalité indigène,* all the while enforcing a policy of public health and hygiene. For the French Protectorate's attitude toward "indigenous medicine" had itself had many faces. The French fascination with the realm of the *magico-religieux* (Durkheim's *sacrée*) had inspired monumental works such as Edmond Doutté's *Magie et Religion dans l'Afrique du Nord,* a survey of magico-medical beliefs and techniques based on a detailed study of classical and vernacular Arab treatises of magical and prophetic medicine. By systematizing and classifying indigenous medical knowledge, works such as *Magie et Religion* gathered a dispersion of practices and techniques into an encompassing field, creating the possibility of indigenous medicine as a modern object of study. Yet this attitude went hand in hand with a ban on the practice of indigenous medicine and the militarized enforcement of what Dr. Colombani called "la dictature sanitaire," the Dictatorship of Health.[39]

Yet, beyond superficial parallels with the colonial policy of health, what emerged from the Casablanca conference, from the silences, the imprecisions, and the omissions in the characterization of the "traditional" realm, was a sense of malaise, an embarrassment with the object of knowledge that is absent in the colonial discourse. The fact of raising the subject was in itself important. It indicated a desire to move beyond the inscription, in the patient's clinical file, of the diagnostic notation "delire à thème magico-religieux," "de sorcellerie," "de persecution par les jinns"; to move beyond the clinical practice of listening, in the patient's speech, for the manifestation of the psychopathological symptom against a background of culturally coded material. It indicated an interest in approaching the "other life" of patients, outside the frame of the psychiatric encounter, when they sought the help of a fqih, visited a sanctuary, or expressed their suffering in different words. Yet, paradoxically, that opening had the effect of a closure. It was an assignment of places that left no space for the unsettled and destabilizing utterances of patients. *Les thérapies traditionnelles* were folklore, in Laroui's sharply critical sense: an object ready-made, to be consumed by the medical gaze. Or they remained inaccessible, vestiges from an incommensurable past. Hence no serious comparative discussion of technique seemed possible. For an encounter to be possible, there must be a sense of coevalness—the sense of sharing within a common, if discrepant, present.

The issue was troubling, involving the subjectivity of the psychiatrists themselves. Strategic in a different sense, the psychiatric subjective positioning vis-à-vis *les thérapies traditionnelles* was structured by a claim of incommensurability,[40] pertaining, rather, to a register Freud designates as "the uncanny."[41] The disquieting unfamiliar-familiarity of what has fallen beyond the Line, and returns as an urgent questioning from an archaeological beforehand: that of the fissure of one's own/other history.

Cures of the Jinns, Mimetic Speech, and Hysteria

Beyond the issue of culture, however, the fundamental objection to the possibility of engaging in a conversation with the "cures of the jinn" has to do with modernist norms of subjectivity. At stake, according to the clinical psychiatrists with whom I spoke, is the issue of personal responsibility: responsibility for one's own acts and speech, a sense of guilt, a sense of loss. For the psychoanalysts with whom I raised the question, what is at stake, beyond the issue of responsibility, is the possibility of the truth of the subject.[42]

To state that one is bewitched *(mshur)*, as patients often declare in the psychiatric consulting room, amounts to saying "it is not me"; my suffering comes from elsewhere, others are the cause of the harm. To say one is possessed *(majnun, mskun, mshiyyer)*—a statement seldom uttered in the first person, because it is an enunciative prerogative of the fqih and because, in a fundamental sense, it pertains to the unutterable of the psychiatric encounter—is to be unable to assume one's own suffering and desire, to push agency outside of the Ego. It means to be neurotic,[43] possibly schizophrenic—and, in all cases, fundamentally alienated. Rather than challenging that alienation, traditional therapists operate from within it and put it to work.

In its systematic form, the discourse of contemporary Moroccan psychiatry and psychoanalysis about its Other is one of emancipation not unlike that of Laroui's modernism. It revolves around the themes of suggestion, mimetism, and hysteria, and the alienating status of the subject's "other voice." I will outline the psychoanalytic position on traditional therapies on the basis of conversations I had with Moroccan psychoanalysts. These took place in the margin of ethnographic work with "traditional therapists" *(tâleb, fqih)*, centering on the vocabulary, the religious and philosophical horizon, and the technique of a diverse range of cures understood as 'ailâj al-jinn, "therapies of the jinn," in Arabic manuals of medicine and magic.[44] I was induced into a debate with psychoanalysts both by my own interest in the Freudian and Lacanian theories of the unconscious and because of the realization that in contemporary Morocco, an anthropological study of the therapies of the jinns that does not take into account—theoretically as well—their dialogical implications with the technique and discourse of psychoanalysis and psychiatry is fated to follow the steps of the colonial studies of indigenous mentality.

In the eyes of the healers, two techniques are particularly significant: the technique of as-srâ', which can be translated as "eclipse," or "annihilation," and that of al-istinzâl, meaning "descent," or "apparition."[45] (They are significant, too, in terms of their diffusion and growing practice, increasingly taking root in the ever-expanding hinterlands of the large cities, where the bidonvilles of the 1970s have been replaced by underserviced sprawls of illegal housing.) They are techniques for "making appear," "making speak," and "bringing to trial" the jinns, in an "other scene" where a renegotiation of the symbolic tenets of reality becomes possible. The srâ' makes the demonic voice speak through the body of the patient fallen into a deathlike "state of absence" (one of the senses of the verb insra'); the istinzâl makes the jinns appear on the palm of a medium's hand, producing a theater that renders the represented real. They are techniques of the self as another where the self is that other, without symbolic mediation. In relation to the technique of psychoanalysis, Lacanian psychoanalysis in particular, they raise a question concerning the status and the modality of the position of subject. What does it mean to assume a subject position in the context of the "therapies of the jinns"?

I posed this question to a number of psychoanalysts. The answer was peremptory: from within the therapies of the jinns there can be no access to subjectivity—to a subject position in the Lacanian sense. For the "cures of the jinns" are predicated on imitation and identification, and allow no responsible engagement of the subject of speech. They are comparable to the hypnotic treatment of hysteria in the prehistory of psychoanalysis; it is on hysterical symptoms that they are most (indeed solely) effective.[46]

As in the dédoublements of Anna O. (Josef Breuer's famous patient), who split into different personages that spoke languages other than her own, the jinns speak through the person.[47] Or they make the person speak, as in the case of the Rat Man studied by Freud, who is afflicted by voices that tell him things he cannot recognize as his own. But unlike psychoanalysis, which is interpretative, the cures of the jinns operate through "suggestion" and the displacement of agency onto imaginary entities. Freud abandoned therapy through hypnosis and developed psychoanalysis instead, because suggestion can temporarily eliminate the symptom but cannot cure. "There is the greatest possible antithesis between suggestive and analytic technique," Freud wrote, for one works by veiling, the other by unveiling.[48] One works by producing illusions and adds alienation to the alienation of the illness; the other uncovers the truth of the subject.

This is essentially why contemporary Moroccan psychoanalysts, who reformulate the problem within a Lacanian vocabulary, say that traditional therapies remove the symptom by adding alienation to the alienation of the illness. The therapies mimic the ailment they are presumed to heal; the self becomes the passive recipient of demonic action, and the "I" is lost, never to be recovered, in the lure of its identifications. The patient never manages to take responsibility for his or her own speech and can never rise to the position of subject. Like a trompe-d'oeil, traditional cures operate exclusively in the register of the Imaginary, without ever reaching the dimension of the Symbolic—the order of responsibility and assumed subjectivity. And since the Imaginary is the register of alienation and *méconnaissance,* these therapies are said to be unable to cure—that is, to free the "true speech" of the subject and emancipate the "I" from the capture of its identifications.

In this strategic adaptation of Lacanian concepts to a local ideological struggle, the supremacy of the Imaginary over the Symbolic is understood as the mode of "tradition," phantasmatic imprisonment, and the world of the *magico-religieux,* while the possibility of reason under the rule of the Symbolic is associated with the technique of psychoanalysis, the self-recollection of responsible subjects, and, implicitly, with modernity itself. The Moroccan psychoanalytic assessment of "traditional therapies" echoes Laroui's dis-alienating project. But what does it mean to become *independent,* for a country and for a person?

Between Dispossession and Belonging

". . . making the world into the place, never still, always perpetually reopened, of its own contradiction."[49]

"Je n'aime pas cette ville. Elle est mon passé et je n'aime pas mon passé. J'ai grandi, me suis émondé. Fés s'est ratatinée, tout simplement. Pourtant, je sais qu'à mesure que je m'y enfonce elle m'epoigne et me fait entité, quanta, brique d'entre les briques, lézard, poussière—et sans que j'ai besoin d'en être conscient."[50]

Two years after writing a first version of this essay I am doing fieldwork at a Moroccan psychiatric hospital.[51] A university hospital, site of suffering and care, site of learning, where a scientific tradition is produced and reproduced in the form of psychiatric training; but also a site of opening, contradiction, and questioning, in an encounter with madness that, for each party involved, raises unsettling questions. I was led to the hospital, in part, by a desire to understand the stories of Su'ad and Fatna, with whom I began this essay: their quest, the non-resolution, and the way in which their journeys open and reopen a world. The question of whether and in what sense the hospital can be a site of speech, a boundary zone where something else, something new, is created, shapes conversations with psychiatrists and patients. What are the stakes in being called to reply to the therapeutic demand of women and men for whom the hospital is a last resort, and yet a foreign and a violent one?

For in coming to the hospital, patients and their families hand their suffering and their story to the institution of modern science— modern science as a practice and as a symbolic position. They hand it to a psychiatrist, the embodiment and representative of modern science, in the presence of whom that painful utterance is at once silenced and made possible. The psychiatrist listens, receives that gift of pain, and attempts to identify a symptom that corresponds to a psychopathological tableau. A diagnosis is made, a psychotropic treatment and sometimes hospitalization are prescribed. And yet, as it offers itself, as it molds itself metamorphically to address the institution of science, that speech of pain steals itself away, reaching out for other ways of being, speaking, imagining—ways that are foreign to the discourse of psychiatry but remain audible in watermark. It is that complex texturing of the voice between different sites of experience that, in the cloistered area of the hospital and in the transitional space of a transference, can be productive of subjective speech.

In the grassy area outside the Urgent Care building, people are sitting under a tree; a woman nursing a child, men talking, children playing. For patients, the *urgences* are the first exposure to the hospital, an interface between the inside and the outside, between the hospital and the world. The building itself is located at the edge, by the wall, the wall on the other side of which, until not long ago, traditional therapists used to sit and draw magic squares with their patients, the hospital's patients.

Inside the building patients wait their turn. The attendance is mixed, as at any public hospital; for the most part men and women from the lower urban strata, sometimes from nearby rural areas. Patients are accompanied by members of their family. The language spoken is Arabic. The language of patient files and other written records is French. It becomes clear, after witnessing a few clinical interviews, that the psychiatric consultation is the last step in a therapeutical quest that began with the visit to a *fqih* and the journey to a sanctuary. Sometimes it is a fqih who directed the patient to the hospital; the cause of illness is l-'asab, he said, the nerves, and not the jinns. Sometimes, after visiting the hospital, the patient returns to the fqih and follows both therapeutical paths.

What does it mean, for patients, to bring to the consulting room, concealed or only partly disclosed, their baggage of language and thought, their own understanding of illness, their story, and to have that cast into the foreign language of science? And what does it mean for a psychiatrist to listen to a speech that is both familiar and foreign, distant and secretly close, and to draw a diagnosis on the basis of those utterances? What is the place of culture? For "culture" only manifests itself as such as an absence, as the result of a loss, a severing, a *coupure*. Situating oneself *dans la coupure*, as a psychiatrist phrased it, "in a position of break," but also, and more interestingly, "in the space of that rift." Between dispossession and belonging. In the rift there are possible worlds, and, perhaps, the *lieu* of an encounter. What is the work of a subjectivity in the making?

Speaking of *les therapies traditionnelles, les marabouts, la possession,* as traits of folklore circumscribing the place of the other, is a way to deflect the unsettling force of these questions. Yet, in the daily confrontation with suffering and madness, abstract positions come undone. Efforts to systematize and explain, even this particular one, fail to appreciate the creative force of that undoing. The space of practice is one of epistemological instability. Asked about therapeutical sites of speech, productive of subjective truths in Morocco today, a psycho-analyst with whom I had debated the issue of suggestion in the cures of the jinn (and whose views had shaped the interpretation I provide in this essay), surprised me with an unexpected answer. If the alterna-tive is a strictly nosographic approach, he said, for which the illness and not the subject counts, then one should recognize that *la parole vraie*, "true speech," a speech that tells the truth of the subject, is ut-tered mostly, if not solely, in the presence of a fqih.

In the multiple and contradictory worlds of Moroccan modernity, subjectivity is constructed in between sites. It is born from the incor-poration of loss, a loss that makes the subject but that can only be en-countered in the metamorphic forms of myth. The epistemological "cut"—the severing that defines a modernist position—is at the origin of a double exclusion: the exclusion from "culture," and from the sense of community associated with it, of those who have consumed the break and situate themselves outside; and the exclusion from the "present" of those who have not experienced that break or have expe-rienced it in a different way.

Seeking allegorical insight I return to the works of Chraïbi and Laroui. Their different modernist styles exemplify for me two op-posed, if related, ways of experiencing the space of the rift. What of the possibility of emancipation and encounter? For Laroui there is no possible encounter. His modernist position stresses the present as a punctual singularity; it is the tense modern Arabs must acquire. Emancipation is the process of freeing the speech of the subject from all prior and external determinations, alien voices within, to which the self is subjected. It is the severing of all ties toward a new universal identity, to establish the possibility of thinking a "here" and a "now." Laroui sees it as an emancipation from the image of the West within, from the melancholic attachment to a vanished Arab past, from cul-ture, always already lost, from phantasmatic desire, from a lingering sense of loss. Only those who have accomplished the path of emanci-pation are entitled to speak, have a voice in the present. All others dwell in an incommensurable past. The patient's speech, if one were to extrapolate from Laroui, can never be encountered in the present. It is already, and by definition, "folklore"; it belongs to a remote past, the archaeological past of cemeteries.

Chraïbi's text, in contrast, is a narrative of encounter. It stages a multidimensional present where in spite of the "cut," and in fact precisely in its place, an encounter becomes possible. A visionary materialization of the rift, the Thin Line is a space of a subjectivity. Driss Ferdi, protagonist of *Le passé simple,* lives his relationship with the world *dans la cassure.* It is a breaking that breaks him, a source of unbearable suffering that inaugurates for him the possibility of speech. *Ntqta',* "I am tearing," "I am being torn," a youth at the hospital explains to me, is the street term for suffering, *kansufrir.* The word tells of the laceration, *le manque,* "the lack," the anguish of separation, the painful sense of loss and fragmentation; it tells of the incorporation of loss, which is also a modality of the subject.

Modernity, for Driss, is a space of unresolvable mourning. The loss, which is modernity itself, cannot be overcome and returns as a phantasm. And the subject, "wrenched" and "torn" in every direction, discovers in this non-resolution the possibility of speech and perhaps the path of another emancipation.

Notes

I would like to thank the participants in the symposium Questions of Modernity, and in particular Tim Mitchell, Talal Asad, Gyan Prakash, and Veena Das. I am also grateful to the staff of the psychiatric hospital Arrazi in Sale. Drs. M. Paes, J. E. Ktiouet, J. Toufic, M. Laymani, M. Zenati, and F. Benchekroun, shared with me their reflections on madness, psychiatry, and their clinical work in Morocco. Hakima Lebbar shared an interest in "traditional therapies" from the standpoint of her clinical work. This essay, which is but the prolegomenon to a book still in the making, could not have been written without their help. My thanks to Abdallah Laroui, for our discussions of his work, in Berkeley in 1994. Earlier versions of this chapter were presented at the Department of Anthropology, University of California, San Diego, and at Berkeley. Thanks to Tanya Lurhman, Michael Meeker, Luce Giard, Laura Nader, and Paul Rabinow, for helpful critical comments on earlier versions. Luca D'Isanto read many versions of this paper and was a crucial critical interlocutor. Research in Morocco in 1995–96 was funded by the Social Science Research Council.

1. Jalil Bennani, *La Psychanalyse au pays des saints* (Casablanca: Le Fennec, 1995), 113.
2. Jacques Lacan, "Fonction et champ de la parole et du langage," *Ecrits* (Paris: Seuil, 1966), 147, my translation.
3. The expression "experience of madness" is Michel Foucault's, in *Histoire de la folie* (Paris: Gallimard, 1972).
4. On the notion of problematization of the self, see Michel Foucault, *Histoire de la sexualité,* vol. 2: *L'usage des plaisirs* (Paris: Gallimard, 1983), English trans., *History of Sexuality,* trans. R. Hurley, vol. 2: *The Use of Pleasure* (New York: Vintage, 1986).
5. Driss Chraïbi, *Le passé simple* (Paris: Denoel, 1954), English trans. *The Simple Past,* trans. Hugh A. Harter (Washington D.C.: Three Continents Press, 1990). Translations from *The Simple Past* are modified. All other translations from the French are my own, except where noted.

6. Abdelkebir Khatibi, "Pensée autre," in *Maghreb Pluriel* (Paris: Denoel, 1983), 5.

7. It should be noted that the tense called "preterit," or literary preterit, in English is in fact a literary and narrative tense, which does not convey the sense of separation and fracture of the French *passé simple*. The French "simple past" is the tense of an impossible narration, and this is why it is never used in the first person. When in historical writing the "je" intervenes, the grammatical tense switches to the *passé composé*.

8. Josef Breuer and Sigmund Freud, *Studies on Hysteria* [1895], ed. and trans. James Strachey (London: Hogarth Press, 1956), 52.

9. Chraïbi, *Le passé simple*, 208. But the book also says on the same page: "We, the French, are civilizing you; you, the Arabs. Badly, in bad faith and without any pleasure from this. Because if by chance you were to become our equals, I'm asking you: in relation to whom or to what would we be civilized, we ourselves?"

10. The expression is from Abdelfattah Kilito, in "La langue fourchue," RE.M.M.M. 70, 1993/4, *Proceedings of the Conference "Maghreb-Europe,"* Madrid, June 1992, pp. 72–75.

11. Chraïbi, *The Simple Past*, 56, translation modified; idem, *Le passé simple*, 106.

12. Chraïbi, *Le passé simple*, 63, 64, translation modified.

13. Cf. Susan Buck-Morrs, *The Dialectics of Seeing: Walter Benjamin and the Arcades Project* (Cambridge: MIT Press, 1989). "The metro, where evenings the lights glow red [. . .] shows the way down into the Hades of names: Combat, Elysée, Georges V, Etienne Marcel, Solferino, Invalides, Vaugirard have thrown off the tasteful chain of streets and squares, and, here in the lightening-pierced, whistle-pierced darkness, have become misshapened sewer gods, catacomb fairies. This labyrinth conceals in its innards not just one, but dozens of blind, rushing bulls, into whose jaws not once a year one Theban virgin, but every morning thousands of anemic young cleaning women and still sleepy salesman are forced to hurl themselves" (Walter Benjamin, *Passagen-Werk*, cited ibid., 102).

14. I am thinking here, specifically, of the work of Michel de Certeau on the seventeenth-century European mystics as "moderns" and, in general, of his exploration of the Baroque side of Western modernity, the side of movement and metamorphosis, alteration and alterity (*La fable mystique* [Paris: Gallimard, 1982]; *La possession de Loudun* [Paris: Gallimard, 1980]). In the Moroccan context, see the work of Abdelkebir Khatibi, particularly *Maghreb pluriel* (Paris: Denoel, 1983); *Le livre du sang* (Paris: Gallimard, 1979), and *Amour bilingue* (Paris: Fata Morgana, 1982).

15. Cf. Homi Bhabha, *The Location of Culture* (New York: Routledge, 1994).

16. Abdallah Laroui, *L'idéologie arabe contemporaine: Essai critique* (Paris: Maspero, 1982 [1967]). Subsequent references to this work are given in the text.

17. Laroui, *L'idéologie arabe contemporaine*, 4, 42. The passage on page 42 continues: "This distancing was a necessary one—this impossibility to find ourselves through the other—for the empty self to be filled with bitterness and anger, and gain the front of the stage. The place of this exhibition will be, of course, the Nation-State."

18. Sigmund Freud, "Mourning and Melancholia" [1917], in *General Psychological Theory: Papers on Metapsychology* (New York: Macmillan, 1963).

19. Besides the work of Walter Benjamin, toward the theory of a melancholic subjectivity see Giorgio Agamben, *Stanze* (Turin: Einaudi, 1977); Stefania Pandolfo, *Impasse of the Angels: Scenes from a Moroccan Space of Memory* (Chicago: University of Chicago Press, 1997); Philippe Lacoue-Labarthe and Jean-Luc Nancy, *Retreating the Political* (New York: Routledge, 1997); Judith Butler, *The Psychic Life of Power* (Stanford: Stanford University Press, 1997).

20. It is perhaps the solitude issued from the structure of this predicament that in

later writings led Laroui's thought away from the concept of reason and toward a theory of the strong state. In his book *Mafhûm al-idyûlûjiyya* (The Concept of Ideology) (1984), Laroui describes the evolution of al-Ghazzali's political thought, the philosopher's mistrust of the logical truth of ideas, and his advocacy of their enforcement by power. He concludes: "Al-Ghazzali had lost faith in the possibility of convincing the beholder of wrong ideas, and advocated a recourse to physical force to compel him to submit to the Law, for he related the belief in wrong ideas to a cosmic conspiracy fomented by Satan" (cited by Driss Mansouri, "A. Laroui, ou l'obsession de la modernité," in *Penseurs maghrébins contemporains* [Casablanca: Eddif, 1993], 224).

21. Chraïbi, *Le passé simple*, 208, translation modified. The original French text reads:

Ce matin, en me rendant ici, j'ai rencontre un Americain de la Military Police. Il arrêta sa Jeep.

—Toi Français? Me demanda-t-il.

—Non, répondis-je. Arabe habillé en Français.

—Then . . . où sont Arabes habillés en Arabes, parlant Arabe et . . .

—J'étendis la main en direction du vieux cimetière musulman.

—Par là.

—Il embraya.

22. Laroui, *L'idéologie arabe contemporaine,* 169.

23. Franz Fanon, himself a practicing psychiatrist in Algeria, had stressed that under colonial conditions indigenous medical practices became the locus of anti-colonial resistance and the bodies of patients "the battleground for different and opposed forces" (Franz Fanon, *L'an cinq, de la revolution algerienne* [Paris: Maspero, 1959], English trans., *A Dying Colonialism* [New York: Grove Press, 1967], 131).

24. For a discussion of the historical production of incommensurability (and commensurability) in the history of science, see M. Biagioli, "The Anthropology of Incommensurability," in *Studies in the History of Philosophical Sciences* 21, no. 2 (1990): 183–209. For an interesting but ahistorical textual attempt to explore the commensurability of Hindu notions of consciousness, reality, and illusion with Freudian concepts and concepts in the philosophy of science, see W. Doniger O'Flaherty, *Dreams, Illusions and Other Realities* (Chicago: University of Chicago Press, 1984). In a previous work I have myself attempted to establish the terms of a dialogue between the phenomenology of dreaming in the understanding of a Moroccan fqih and the Lacanian theory of the subject as founded in the unconscious (Pandolfo, *Impasse of the Angels*).

25. Claude Lévi-Strauss, "L'efficacité symbolique," *Anthropologie structurale,* vol. 1 (Paris: Plon, 1957).

26. See the writings and the ethnopsychiatric clinical practice of Tobie Nathan, for example, *Le sperme du diable* (Paris: PUF, Les Champs de la Santé, 1988); *La folie des autres: Traité d'ethnopsychiatrie clinique* (Paris: Dunod, 1986).

27. Carl Antoine Pierson, "Paléophénie réactionnelle: Psycho-pathologie de l'impulsion morbide en milieu Nord-Africain," *Maroc Médical* (April 1954): 642–47.

28. "Rien à faire de durable, en matière d'assistance publique si la mentalité ambiante n'évolue pas, et c'est cette évolution dont il faut ausculter le degré tous les jours. Je ne citerai, pour exemple, que les difficultés multiples auxquelles nous nous sommes heurtés pour transformer le régime des aliénés, difficultés non encore résolues" (Dr. Jules Colombani, *Le ministère de la Santé et de l'Hygiène Publique au Maroc* [1924], 19).

29. A. Porot, "Notes de psychiatrie musulmane," *Annales Médico-psychologiques* 9

(May 1918): 377–84; see also R. Berthelier, *L'Homme maghrébin dans la littérature psychiatrique* (Paris: L'Harmattan, 1994); Bennani, *La Psychanalyse au pays des saints*; Françoise Vergès, "Monsters and Revolutionaries: The Colonial Family Romance at Reunion Island," Ph.D. diss., Department of Political Science, University of California, Berkeley.

30. Lucien Levy-Bruhl, *Les fonctions mentales dans les societés inférieures* (Paris: Alcan, 1910).

31. "The deepest nature of the native's inclinations becomes visible in its bare form, showing a sudden regression towards a distant primitivism, badly disguised under a clothing of fragile collective attitudes" (Pierson, "Paléoprénie réactionnelle," 643).

32. In much of *La psychanalyse au pays des saints,* Jalil Bennani analyzes the history and legacy of René Laforgue's Casablanca group (Groupe d'étude de psychologie de l'inconscient et de médecine psychosomatique). Although my discussion relies directly on articles from *Maroc Médical,* I am indebted to Bennani's work for realizing the importance of this work.

33. Maurice Igert, "Introduction à la psychopathologie marocaine," *Maroc Médical,* no. 360 (1955): 1324.

34. Ibid., 1331, 1323.

35. Ibid., 1329.

36. Ibid., 1329, 1319, 1320.

37. Ibid., 1319, 1320, 1321.

38. Edmond Doutté, *Magie et religion dans l'Afrique du Nord* (Algiers: Jourdan, 1908); Émile Dermenghem, *Le culte des saints dans l'Islam maghrébin* (Paris: Gallimard, 1954).

39. Dr. Jules Colombani, *Le Ministère de la Santé et de l'Hygiène Publique au Maroc* (Rabat: Blanc & Gauthier, 1924); *La Protection Sanitaire de l'Indigène au Maroc,* Conférence faite aux Journées Médicales Coloniales de Paris, 1931 (Rabat: Blanc & Gauthier, 1932). This is how Dr. Colombani defined the "Dictatorship of Health": "Civil and military personnel, civil and military equipment, are in the same hands; the entire organization of health obeys a single directing mind, all the beams of the medical network, whose lines extend to cover Morocco in its entirety, are oriented towards a single optical center" (*Le Ministère de la Santé,* 16). The aims of this all-seeing health dictatorship are, according to Dr. Colombani, to "recognize the pathological dangers," establish a "medical topography" through a systematic work of "reconnaissance médicale" performed by the Groupe Sanitaire Mobile, and above all, keep watch over the movements of population from the *bled,* the back country, and develop what he called "dispositifs de désinfection," disinfection devices, both mobile and stationed at neuralgic geographical junctures, in order to "neutralize all the carriers of errant germs, half-starved, jobless; assemble these crowds outside the city limits, and send them back in small groups to their respective home regions" (32). While in Dr. Colombani's view, "the stage of defense" must precede in the colonies that of *pitié humaine,* the issue of indigenous mentality is central: "Our administrators must have the better of fatalism, smiling or melancholic, both indomitable, they must have the better of an ancient milieu, older and more crystallized in its ancient forms than our own" (32).

40. I use the notion of incommensurability as it is used in the history of sciences. Cf. Biagioli, "The Anthropology of Incommensurability."

41. Sigmund Freud, "The Uncanny" (1919), in *The Standard Edition of the Complete Psychological Works of Sigmund Freud,* ed. and trans. James Strachey (London: Hogarth Press, 1955), vol. 17.

42. It should be noticed that unlike the American vernacular use according to which the terms "psychiatrist" and "psychoanalyst" are interchangeable, in the Moroccan use, consistent with the French and in general European use, the terms refer to very different therapeutical practices and bodies of knowledge. Psychiatrists are above all medical practitioners, diagnosing and treating mental illness as illness—an objective reality that manifests itself through psychopathological symptoms that largely correspond to the symptomatic tableau of standard illnesses. In the psychiatric style of treatment the use of psychotropic drugs is routine, even though most practitioners recognize that it is only an aid, a therapeutic support, in which the therapeutic effort must intervene. Psychoanalysts (who often have a medical psychiatric background, and, in Morocco, a Freudian-Lacanian analytical orientation) define their therapeutical practice as a transferential process of intersubjective communication, a performative act of speech, in the course of which the patient recovers subjectivity through speech.

43. The diagnosis of hysteria is still very much in use in Morocco, where French psychiatric classifications are followed along with the American DSM IV *(Diagnostic and Statistical Manual of Mental Disorders).* One of the objections raised by Moroccan psychiatrists against the adoption of the DSM approach is the disappearance of hysteria.

44. These manuals are part of the therapeutic panoply of healers, fqihs. Printed for popular consumption and sold at the entrances of mosques, these texts are also rooted in the Sufi classical tradition. Their informal distribution and affordable price make this literature the pillar of a parallel system of knowledge accessible to large sectors of the population—a knowledge that eludes, to a large extent, institutional and educational control.

45. A detailed theoretical discussion of these techniques, the only avenue toward a possible dialogue with psychoanalysis, is beyond the scope of this paper. For an analytic and theoretical discussion of the technique of *sra'*, I refer to my article "Rapt de Voix" [The Theft/Rapture of the Voice], in *Awal: Revue d'Etudes Berbères* (Paris), no. 15 (April 1997): 31–50. An ethnographic discussion of the technique of the *istinzal* is found in my book, *Impasse of the Angels.*

46. The diagnosis of hysteria is still current in French psychiatry. Even though Moroccan psychiatrists are increasingly conversant with the American system and with the series of DSM diagnostic manuals, the important difference with the U.S. system is the centrality of the category of hysteria.

47. Breuer and Freud, *Studies on Hysteria.*

48. Suggestion works *per via di porre,* as Leonardo said of painting, but analysis *per via di levare,* like sculpture, for, says Freud, "it takes away from the rough stone all that hides the statue contained in it" (Sigmund Freud, "On Psychotherapy" [1904], in *Therapy and Technique* [New York: Macmillan, 1963], 67).

49. Lacoue-Labarthe and Nancy, *Retreating the Political,* 158.

50. Chraïbi, *Le passé simple,* 74.

51. A first version of this essay was presented on April 19, 1996, at New York University at the plenary session of the symposium "Questions of Modernity." During the debate that followed, and particularly the discussion by Talal Asad, a question was raised about the issue of emancipation. That question, which I could not answer at the time, led me to a reconsideration of my argument, to a second reading of Laroui's work, and in general to an opening as to the multiple possibilities and impossibilities of a modernist subjectivity; to questions, my questions as well, that can find no univocal answer, about the contradictory nature of experience, about desire, and about the experience of suffering. I have tried in the rewriting of the paper to convey, if partially, some of this.

Six

The Sovereignty of History:
Culture and Modernity in the
Cinema of Satyajit Ray

Nicholas B. Dirks

After the opening credits, which flash against a glorious chandelier that will carry the symbolic burden of the fortunes of a palace and its royal family in modern rural Bengal, *The Music Room* (*Jalsaghar*, 1958) opens with the face of a turbaned man who, it soon becomes clear, is a zamindar, or landlord. As the camera pans back, the image is uncannily still, until we realize that we are looking at a photograph, at a face frozen on paper. The scene then changes to a palace, where we see, from behind, an old feudal retainer bringing a hookah to the shapeless and, once again, still figure reclining in a chair. Only after what seems an interminable time, the shape moves, the left hand reaching out listlessly for the hookah, the figure acting out as if by primordial habit a desire for some residual consumption of pleasure in life. As the retainer retires, the zamindar suddenly calls out, asking what month it is. The zamindar is still etched as if in a timeless, now somewhat frayed, photograph, in a space both outside and after history.

History, and memory, enter with the sound of a *shehnai*, bringing a look of distress to the otherwise immobile features of the zamindar. The retainer tells the zamindar that the music is in celebration of the coming-of-age ceremony of the neighbor's son. We can already sense that this neighbor, a moneylender and business man, has somehow displaced the zamindar, producing the occasion for music that once upon a time would only echo forth from the main palace, the sign of the zamindar's cultural authority and ritual centrality. Now he sits bereft in a palace, slowly revealed by the camera as decayed and empty, listening to the sounds of a new time, a time that has shunted his own critical role in history and culture aside. But memories of other times come flooding back, and we are transported through flashback to a time before, when the zamindar held the coming-of-age ceremony for his own son, with the pomp, circumstance, and music of a genuinely noble age. The film, by bringing us up to the present, will allow memory to overtake history, in order both to fill us in on the past, and to narrate the forces with which history has now worked to obliterate memory itself.

At one level, it is a familiar story. A prominent Bengali landlord, beneficiary of Lord Cornwallis's preposterous idea that a permanent settlement[1] with the feudal remnants of old India would introduce a new managerial landed elite to the Indian countryside, an entrepreneurial gentry that would both replicate the best of English history and combine stable property rights, a secure tax base, and a sedentary lifestyle with the entrepreneurial spirit of world capitalism, undergoes a tragic fall due to the relentless hold of the feudal past. Instead of managing his lands, controlling the river that slowly though steadily eats up the soil of this once-fertile deltaic region, the zamindar holds one musical soirée after the next to satisfy his highly cultivated aesthetic, gives lavish gifts to his favorite musicians and dancers, and feasts both the small number of local notables who attend his concerts and large crowds of villagers who must still look up to him as the bountiful king of a more glorious past. Taste seems inextricably tied up with prestige, for while the zamindar is clearly obsessed by the pleasure of his music room, he is also unwilling to accept that the pleasure of music could be produced by any other place. For him to experience the aesthetic of cultural performance, he has to be in a position to give the first gift, as the great benefactor, the primary mediation of all cultural possibility. But of course this means that he neither pays attention to the sources of wealth that make his benefaction possible nor concerns himself with the obvious fact that he is squandering away his fortune and his inheritance. The story we see is one of sad ruin, in which old India is unable to adjust to the demands as well as the opportunities of the new world.

In large part, this is one of the master narratives of colonial rule in

India. How often have we read colonial accounts of the sad betrayal of the hopes of a once-liberal imperialism, introducing the best of the West only to run aground against the monumental and immobile bedrock of tradition. Even when these stories are modulated by condemnations of the pathological moment of late Victorian imperialism, the primary responsibility for India's political immaturity and economic untenability is vested in something essential to India, before the British got there: institutions like caste, preoccupations like prestige, histories characterized by cyclic alternations between oriental despotisms and village republics. The British maintained lavish museums of old India, in the great zamindaries of places like Bengal and in the princely states of Rajasthan and Central India, that facilitated conquest at the same time they were constant reminders of the justifications of British rule. India had been unable to rule itself because its political system, commanded by grand but quarreling kings who would shamelessly exploit their subjects in order to accumulate unlimited wealth and prestige, had neither attended to basic principles of justice nor concerned itself with the formation of organized administration and stable, centralized power. First, the British walked into a vacuum, conquering India, as the Cambridge imperial historian John Seeley said, "in a fit of absence of mind"; then the British ruled India for the sake of its own subjects rather than for any gain of its own.

These colonial narratives seemed exemplified by case after case in which landlords and princes would fail to exploit the opportunities afforded by permanent settlement and indirect rule; theater states grew up all over India in which issues of ceremony and prestige, hierarchy and protocol, accumulation and expenditure, seemed of far greater moment than either sound management or popular representation.[2] A kind of embarrassment set in, I would suggest, in which it became difficult to point to recent history, and the vast estates and quasi-autonomous tracts under royal control, as arguments for national self-confidence, let alone self-rule. In cities like Calcutta, where the elite was in large part supported by the profits that came from landlord rights to these same rural estates, the recognition of the power of the West became the basis both for colonial mimicry in areas ranging from political theory to cultural production and for the development of forms of resistance that justified itself by the glorious past record of India's civilizational achievement. A new vision celebrated the civilizational and spiritual achievements of old India, not the political history of precolonial times, in what was a conspicuous silence around the material basis of its own conditions of possibility. Partha Chatterjee has recently argued that the inner domain of sovereignty in colonial India, the sphere that shielded itself from the colonial gaze and provided a certain kind of space for autonomy under and away from the weight of cultural domination, was constructed around conceptions concerning religion, spirituality, tradition, femininity, and the home.[3] India's strength was seen to be in areas untouched by colonial rule and unaffected by the mimetic deployment of Western nationalist rhetorics and politics as the necessarily derivative basis for colonial nationalism.

Chatterjee's argument seems clearly to accept the extent to which an Oriental construction of India set the terms for what he sees as its own colonial autonomy—terms I have argued elsewhere were critiqued and challenged in important ways by both Tagore and Ray.[4] At the same time, Chatterjee at some level concedes the colonial narrative of the Indian political, in which the king, or the prince, or the zamindar became symbols of colonial embarrassment for Indian nationalism. So also, it would seem, does Ray, for *The Music Room* shows us in dramatic fashion all the many reasons that seemingly old forms of political order and obsession would die out in the face of the forces of the new colonial and capitalist order. The zamindar of the film is willing to spend his last resources, even pawn his wife's inherited jewelry, to stage one last *jalsa*, or concert. His proud refusal to accept the local moneylender/businessman's right to host musical concerts in his estate led to the precipitate decision to stage an event that brought the tragic deaths of his wife and son—hurriedly called back for the concert in the middle of a thunderous monsoon storm. The death of his family by drowning in the river adjoining his estate becomes but an extension of the swallowing up of his estate by the same river he is unable to manage and control. The zamindar loses his furniture and possessions and, by the end of the film, when the flashback begins, has nothing but the shell of his old palace to remind him, and us, of his former regal glory. But the story has made it clear that the reason for this is his stubborn and narcissistic pride, his complete inattention to the political and material responsibilities of his position. His obsession with musical performance may suggest a devotion to culture, even a kind of purity of mind, but we now know that he is the agent of his own tragedy, gambling away his kingdom for a few nights of glory. History might have left him behind but that is because he refused the lessons, and burdens, of history itself.

And so we return to the beginning of the film, when the zamindar is reminded of time by the sound of the *shehnai* drifting across his rooftop from the house of Mr. Ganguli. Coming to his senses, he decides to spend his yearly temple fund to stage one last concert, hiring the musicians and dancer who had come to town to perform in the moneylender's house. He opens the music room, to the dismay of his manager, who knows that this final extravagance will consign even the shell of the palace to bankruptcy, but to the almost delirious delight of the retainer, who cleans the room and polishes the mirrors and lamps as if the clarity of his memory for the past—and of the newly swabbed glass of the chandelier—will somehow bring back those times of old.

Alas, the concert betrays the hollowness of royal conceit, the extent to which the position of the king had been evacuated by his weakened circumstance and the accompanying rise in the position of the merchant, the new colonial compradore. Ganguli swaggers into the palace, very different in demeanor from the first time he came for a concert, delighted then just to be included in the noble affair and so decidedly ignorant about music, despite his professions of interest, that his efforts to display his appreciation are shown by the camera as both parodic and vulgar. Now Ganguli virtually usurps the zamindar's position, though when he tries to throw a bag of money, offering the first gift to the musicians, he is restrained by the zamindar's cane, and reminded that it is the perquisite of the patron to offer the first gift. And so, what is clearly the last sack of coins in the zamindar's possession is spent in this final gesture of mock authority. Later that night, after the guests and musicians have departed, the zamindar staggers around the music room, drinking glass after glass of whiskey, deliriously happy at his victory. Talking to his palace retainer, who follows him around desperately trying to keep his glass full, he says, "Do you know why he failed," himself supplying the answer: "blood." He then translates the Bengali word *rakto*, and says, in English: "blood . . . ," continuing in English to say, "The blood in my veins." He looks at himself in the full-length mirror and at the many portraits of his ancestors hanging on the music room's walls. He toasts the portraits and says, again in English, "To you my noble ancestors," though no sooner than he tries to drink he sees, on the portrait of his dead son, a black spider. In a gesture like that with which he subdued Ganguli, he takes his cane to brush the spider aside, but this momentary victory is followed by darkness. The lights in the chandelier begin to go out, one by one, and soon all the lights in the palace are extinguished. He calls his servant, who enters the completely still and darkened scene as a moving reflection in the mirror, as if he appears through the looking glass of memory and time, to remind his master that "lights do go out."

This penultimate scene leads directly to the denouement, when the zamindar hears his horse neighing at the dawn and orders his riding gear for a morning ride. But by now he is blind drunk and is thrown from the horse as it gallops toward the bank of the river. As the retainer comes close to the fallen body of the zamindar, he reaches down and cries out a single word: "blood." The camera sweeps away, finally dissolving into a final scene of the swinging chandelier, in the blackness that is the end of the story of this noble tradition, this royal family.

It has often been said that Ray betrays his political conservatism by participating in the nostalgia of the feudal lord for a past in which palaces patronized learning and the arts. There is a sense of tragedy in this film, which even as it appears to be brought on directly by the landlord, has as its counterpart the sense we get of the loss of culture and refinement. The zamindar may be a self-absorbed fool, but he does genuinely love music and dance, in marked contrast to Ganguli, who is depicted with palpable disdain for the new moneyed classes in India, vulgar and uncultured. At the same time, however, the zamindar is so clearly and so completely narcissistic and irresponsible that we feel nostalgia much less for him—whose death comes at the end almost as a relief—than for the ideal of learning and culture that he seems to have abandoned as readily as his managerial relationship to the estate that provided the resources for cultural capital. And yet, as I mentioned before, this nostalgia or sense of pathos is itself modulated by the clear message of the film that the exquisite aesthetic of the zamindar is deeply compromised by the performative politics with which it seems essentially linked. After all, our zamindar could only enjoy culture when he staged it, when performance was an expression of power, an adornment of the crown.

For Ray, the old regime seems necessarily viewed through a lens of pathos and pathology, with the embarrassment that great cultural achievement has been produced by structures of domination—that, to paraphrase Benjamin, all civilization is a sign of barbarity. Nevertheless, it is significant that Ray chooses to focus on the precise relationship between creativity and corruption, rather than depicting zamindars, as has been done in countless New Wave films, as simply exploitative figures with no mitigating circumstances, no complicating conjunctures. Ray seems intent on using this story as an allegorical vehicle for negotiating both the contradictory relationship between tradition and modernity, and between culture and production. Given Ray's own difficult financial circumstances in making his films, we would be justified in thinking that Ray is also making a rather personal statement about the problems he faced in funding his own cultural work. *The Music Room* was made after the box-office failure of *Aparajito* (1956), and the use of a story in which music and dance would figure prominently played an important role in his choice of this story. But Ray is, no doubt, generalizing his predicament to question the conditions under which culture can be subsidized and supported, and the evident costs to his own modernist aesthetic ambition when the film world was so pervasively driven by the relationship between mass popularity and profit. In the modern age, how would specialized, exquisite, elite forms of art survive, even if this question for Ray was asked in full recognition of the serious deficiencies of the past.

So if the figure of the king, for all its perversions, nevertheless recalled a past in which the arts could be patronized outside the growing corruption and vulgarization of capitalism (and remember here that Ray worked in advertising before he made films), what went so very wrong, and how does Ray address this principal question in this work? As noted above, Ray was sharply critical both of the particularity of this zamindar and the more general system of feudal rule that had been maintained under British colonialism. Nevertheless, Ray wished to complicate the critique of feudalism—and here he does not, like so many others, take embarrassment as the occasion for silence about kings. *The Music Room* suggests that the standard critique has to be set alongside a similarly critical examination of the institutions and values that were coming to replace it. Of course, the most vehement dismissals of Ray have come from those who knew he had no utopian socialist vision that could ultimately transform the historical encounter between feudalism and capitalism; Ray, like Tagore before him, was no revolutionary idealist. Rather, Ray wished to disturb the stability of the categories that were used to think about feudalism and capitalism, tradition and modernity, colonialism and postcolonialism. In *The Music Room,* Ganguli serves only as a foil for a certain kind of capitalist excess; in many other films, Ray takes both the growth of capital and the rise of modernity as his fundamental theme.[5] Here, Ray focuses, as he does in *The Chess Players* (and, from a different perspective, in *Devi*), on tradition, and he makes it clear that for all the glories of the past, so palpably captured in the wonderful music and dance of those long evenings in the music rooms of old India, the past must be left behind.

For all the recent writing about tradition, as I mentioned at the outset, there has been almost no call for the recuperation of that part of Indian tradition or history that recalls the vain pomp, circumstance, and exploitation of feudalism. However, this silence has been accompanied by a sense that tradition needs to be defined exclusively by those civilizational accomplishments that were untouched by India's compromised political past. Ray does not intend his ambivalence about the past to suggest that kingship (per se) should be reinserted in recuperations of tradition that critique the forms of Westernized, secularized modernity that seem to have gone so wrong and that constitute so problematic a part of the postcolonial predicament in India today. But he seems to be making the point that something important was lost with the death of kingship, that the political did constitute an important part of India's traditional inheritance, though for him what stands out in his reading of the past is the cultural aesthetic and patronage of the court.

However, Ray indulges in the ambivalence of nostalgia only ambivalently; he has no wish to return, and he condemns the past quite passionately. At the same time, even in a film that seems so complicit in colonial narratives, and so devoid of critical reference to colonialism, Ray displays some fragmentary sense of the role colonial rule played in the production of "traditional" politics. Remember how the ultimate breakdown of both the king and his court invokes Englishness through the zamindar's use of English. In that desperate dawn after the final jalsa, the zamindar unveils his full vanity and toasts his noble ancestors, through the translation of rakto into blood, of genealogy into a claim about privilege that rested ultimately on the recognition by a foreign ruler of his royal nature. Perhaps Ray is here reminding us that the decadent disjuncture between political accountability and cultural taste was, in the end, a product not of precolonial tradition but of the refashioning of this tradition under the peculiar conditions of the permanent settlement, in which a dynamic—if still deeply flawed—feudal system was translated into a simulacrum of the

English gentry, with all the distortions of colonial misrecognition and transformation.

If this reading seems to stretch Ray's intentions too far, I would turn briefly to *The Chess Players* (*Shatranj ke Khilari,* 1977), where Ray brings colonial rule directly into the picture, and sketches the terms of his own ambivalence about the histories of tradition in India rather more sharply than he does in *The Music Room.* Ray agonized a great deal over the final scripting of *The Chess Players,* in large part because he began with considerable disdain for the Nawabs of Oudh, whom he felt had simply fiddled while Rome burned, virtually inviting the British to conquer India through their own narcissistic hedonism and decadence. Indeed, Ray has been criticized in *The Chess Players* for doing precisely the opposite of what he did in *The Music Room.* While some have said he was too soft on the old regime in *The Music Room,* he was apparently too hard on it in *The Chess Players.* But Ray reported that after doing considerable research on the period, he came to take a different view; as he wrote in a letter to his collaborator Shama Zaidi, "The fact that he was a great patron of music— that was one redeeming feature about this king."[6] And so, at least in terms of the relationship between culture and production, we can see *The Chess Players* as a remaking, or at the very least a rethinking, of *The Music Room.*

Perhaps the most critical scene in *The Chess Players* comes in an exchange between General Outram and his aide de camp, Captain Weston. It is here that Outram elicits a kind of Orientalist reading of Wajid Ali through his interrogation of Weston about the king's interests and accomplishments. Not only do the king's extraordinarily subtle poems fail to translate powerfully into English, the life of the court is untranslatable as well or, rather, translates only into a full condemnation of the old regime in India. After hearing Weston's sympathetic view of the king, Outram expostulates that he would call Wajid far worse than eccentric; he would say he is a "bad king. A frivolous, effeminate, irresponsible, worthless king. . . . We've put up with this nonsense long enough. Eunuchs, fiddlers, nautch-girls and 'muta' wives and God knows what else. He can't rule, he has no wish to rule, and therefore he has no business to rule." Ray has no quarrel with part of Outram's judgment, and indeed he makes Outram into a partly sympathetic character in order to express his full ambivalence when contrasting the British with the Nawabs of Oudh. But in the end his evaluation of Dalhousie is harsher than his condemnation of the frivolity of the Lucknow court, for as much as Wajid brought his fate upon himself, the British clearly acted against the legal charter that justified their own high-minded rhetoric of rule.

In part, Ray wanted to use *Shatranj* as a story line that would provide the basis for an equal condemnation of feudalism and colonialism; his sense of the complexity of human actions and political affairs required a certain kind of symmetry to conduct his own special brand of filmmaking. As he said himself in 1978, "I wanted to make this condemnation interesting by bringing in certain plus points of both the sides. . . . I knew this might result in a certain ambivalence of attitude, but I didn't see *Shatranj* as a story where one would openly take sides and take a stand. I saw it more as a contemplative, though unsparing view of the clash of two cultures—one effete and ineffectual and the other vigorous and malignant. I also took into account the many half-shades that lie in between these two extremes of the spectrum. . . . You have to read this film between the lines."[7] And if I would then attempt to read it between the lines, I would take it slightly beyond Ray's sense of the need to portray both feudalism and colonialism negatively, for I read it in relation to other films, where Ray so critically probes the ambivalent problematic of modernity against the equally problematic hold of feudal or religious pasts. From one perspective, Ray shows us how the effeteness of Wajid was the product of a colonial lie, a history in which the obsessive concentration on poetry and chess could be cultivated only with colonial connivance, only to become the pretext for colonial conquest. In the final pathetic gesture of submission, Wajid hands his crown to Outram. But this very crown, which had already been sent to London for display in a colonial exhibition (for which, as Ray notes at the beginning of the film, Dalhousie lamented that he had not included his head along with the crown), had already been hollowed of all its former power, and it sat on Wajid's head as a prop for the theater state that was created and maintained by the British as a symbol of colonial enlightenment and tolerance.

If Ray condemns Indian feudalism, I would suggest that he at least allows us to see the relationship between what feudalism had become under the Raj and the nature of British colonial intervention. Such a framework disturbs Ray's own view that he wished only to remember the cultural accomplishment and patronage of the precolonial world; for by refusing to dismiss outright the kingly past, Ray does, I would argue, allow us to see, through his cinematic insistence on the complexity of moral choice and historical change, the hybrid nature of the categories that frame our evaluations of tradition and modernity, culture and politics, colonialism and postcolonialism. We sense the pathos of the zamindar's situation even when we see him swaying drunkenly in a scene that makes the uncultured Ganguli appear almost heroic; we feel the unbearable predicament of Wajid when he hands his crown to Outram rather than resist the annexation. Ray's uncanny evocation of loss never becomes the pretext for false nostalgia, as his critics have sometimes suggested, but instead sets the stage for his own relentless interrogation of the logics and conditions of the Indian postcolonial world in which he lived.

If Ray's depiction of the pathos of kingship is always softened by his fundamental sympathy with the modern, he does provide extraordinarily powerful ways to question the limits of modernity in colonial India. Ashis Nandy has recently argued that Ray's modern commitments do not prevent him—or at least his unconscious filmmaking self—from displaying the traditional femininity of characters such as Wajid in ways that convey a resistant strain to the choices available within modernity itself. As Nandy writes, "It is possible to argue that, unknown to Ray, Shatranj is an essay on the clash of two perspectives on womanhood, power and culture. These perspectives arise not from two irreconcilable sets of cultural categories represented by the East and the West; they provide an element of contradiction within each of the two confronting cultures too."[8] But in concentrating on these split complementarities to characterize the dilemmas engaged by the British conquest of India, the limits of Nandy's psychoanalytic interest become clear. Nandy shows how the repression of modern forms of hypermasculinity and the brutality of public politics recapitulate contradictions inherent to modernism, and he carefully probes the gendered pathologies of modern life. But in so doing he fails to critique adequately the construction of the categories of tradition and modernity under colonial rule. As Said has made clear, colonial subjects were coded feminine, and though Nandy has explored the extent to which this coding was the product of ambivalent anxieties on the part both of colonizer and colonized, he has also used a modern logic of the private and personal to seek refuge from the alienation of new forms of the public. Indeed, I would suggest that Nandy folds Wajid's dilemma into the split portrayed most powerfully by the conflict between

Outram and his ADC, in which the sympathy of the ADC is read sus-
piciously, if vicariously, by Outram as a sign of possible moral weakness and certain political failure. Nandy is correct to note the force of
this split for Wajid, but by collapsing the political story into a personal exchange, his recuperation of tradition is, in the end, far too heavily
shaded by a psychoanalytic interest in the personal and private relations of cultural and spiritual value, at the same time that it is unaffected by the active suppression of the political power of the court
that is the primary effect of annexation.

Nandy is also correct to stress the importance of the "woman's
question" for Ray, that is, the extraordinary ways Ray has probed the
experience of women's lives to explore the contradictions of modernity in many of his most effective films. But Nandy also separates the
problem of women, manifestly not part of the story either in *Jalsaghar*
or *Shatranj,* from the larger colonial problem of femininity, which is
fundamental to both films. Indeed, Nandy writes that "even in this
century, some men have subverted the ideology of masculinity more
successfully than most women have, and some women in turn have
been very imperfect carriers of the feminine qualities."[9] What Nandy
argues for is a return to a traditional position from which the values
of masculinity might be resisted, in which the androgynous possibilities both of self-fashioning and of public responsibility be addressed
and recuperated, even at the risk, as was the case with Gandhi's stress
on the feminine at the expense of the masculine, "of sounding mystical or romantic." Nandy has sketched out his insightful and compel-
ling argument before, characteristically including colonizing subjects
(Kipling, Outram, etc.) within the province of his general analysis.[10]
But his invocation of tradition as the authorizing referent for his
psychoanalytic reading is deeply problematic, not to mention part of
what Veena Das astutely recognizes as fundamentally a function of
"the nostalgia that one encounters in the midst of the new, the transitory and the fleeting, for an area of life that would remain untouched
by the newness of modernity" (see chapter 7). Granting his polemical
interests, I would nevertheless argue here that his concern about different kinds of selves rather than alternative forms of politics seems
particularly out of place, and is especially limiting in the context of
films about such historical figures as Wajid Ali. And it is here we can
discern the extraordinary complexity of Ray's films. Ray, as concerned
as Nandy about both the predicament of women and the gendered

confusion brought on for men and women in the modern age, and for all his apparent aversion to political analysis and solution, clearly depicts the colonial character of suppression and recognizes how other selves are constructed through cultural forms that are dependent upon the exteriority of the court. The pathos of both the zamindar and the Nawab is deeply implicated within the manifest relations of sovereignty and patronage that, however much they may too be part of a politics of impossibility, must be engaged with all their multiple contradictions if history is to provide any lessons at all.

Nandy's position is similar in some ways to that of Partha Chatterjee, who, as I mentioned above, argued that resistance to colonialism became signally inscribed within arenas of domesticity where women, and essential features of Indian civilization, reigned supreme. However, Chatterjee's interest is not psychoanalytic; he is much more interested in the politics of tradition (and its explicit rejection of the political) than Nandy. And Chatterjee's sense of history is complicated, his recognition that tradition is endlessly reconstructed in the dialectic movement of history subtle and nuanced. Chatterjee does see the feminine as a vestigial vehicle for those parts of tradition that, even as they became confined within new domestic forms under colonial rule, managed also to maintain some essential truths of an uncontaminated Indian civilization. Chatterjee is right when he demonstrates how in the nineteenth century tradition increasingly became defined by the home, the female, the spiritual, and the religious. But only in recent formulations, as in this volume (see chapter 2), does he stress sufficiently the extent to which this traditional formation is new, dependent largely upon colonial modernity, including both translations and inversions of European bourgeois domesticity. Indeed, it could be argued that women (and the domestic sphere itself) become the privileged site in which the contradictions of modernity, in particular of the development of the modern subject, are worked out.[11] Chatterjee's argument suggests the possibilities of an historical imaginary in which tradition might be recuperated as a strategy of resistance, but as his current writing makes clear, the arena in which these kinds of invocations of tradition are made today is imbued with the possibilities of political distortion and appropriation, which banish complexity from the moral denunciation of modernity and afford only one kind of reading of the past. When these appropriations take rightist political turns, as they so often do in these troubled times, they represent the apotheosis of modernity, neither its opposite nor its pre-colonial predecessor.

As an experiment in exploring an historical imaginary that might work to illustrate further the uses of tradition for critiques of modernity, as well as to recuperate not only the androgynous and domestic subversions but also the sovereign politics of the past, I turn in conclusion, if with some trepidation, to the writing of Georges Bataille. Here I return to my earlier concern that India's political past is dropped in most current considerations of tradition (whether by Ray, Chatterjee, Nandy, or other critics), in what seems at least in part an unfortunate internalization of the civilizational embarrassment produced in the first instance by colonial denunciations of India's political history. My point here is neither to argue for the return or justification of a feudal form of kingship, nor to limit myself to an historicist consideration of the politics of kingly rule. Rather, let us recall the pathos of both the zamindar and Nawab, two figures who have been overtaken by colonialism and modernity, by rationality and utility. Neither of our feudal heroes are much concerned with production; they are, rather, obsessively committed to consumption, to conspicuous stagings of poetry and music. Both figures become marked as signs of the decadence of India's political past, devoted as it was to extraction and expenditure, demonstrating its incompetence in the face of modern demands for fiscal accountability and managerial attention. The Indian colonial situation makes clear the extent to which these arguments about utility are linked to the higher utility of colonial accumulation; the measures of capitalist logic were used to disfranchise rulers of old but not to empower Indian capitalists, whose activities were severely limited and carefully linked to the expanding interests of British entrepreneurial capital in and colonial control over the Indian subcontinent. Capitalism in India was first and foremost a rhetoric of disparagement and denunciation, a logic demarcating decadence and progress, a language used to justify and celebrate the great gift of colonial modernity in Asia.

Aside from Marx, perhaps no Western theorist has argued more strenuously against the logic of capitalism than Georges Bataille. Bataille railed in particular against the naturalization of production as the foundational category of modern social and economic life. Developing Marcel Mauss's exposition of the gift, Bataille explored the possibility of what Mauss had simply used as an ideal category, the pure gift, the gift without obligation or expectation. Arguing passionately for the resacralization of society, Bataille writes about carnival, sacrifice, eroticism, even death, in order to loosen the bonds of utilitarian rationality on the concerns of philosophical and aesthetic discourse. For our purposes here, Bataille called upon the reader to appreciate "the quality of sovereignty" implied in the gift as "profitless expenditure." His favorite example was the potlatch, that blowout of generosity that could not easily be recuperated by utility logics applied to honor and prestige. In the potlatch, Bataille observed the overwhelming power of generosity, that form of excessive expenditure and giving that took on a logic, or illogic, of its own. As he wrote, "Ultimately it was the one who overdid who prevailed and whose sovereign character compelled respect."[12]

Bataille's writing is so provocative, so mischievous, and indeed so dangerous, that it is difficult to know how far to allow oneself to be seduced by his powerful critique. His call for a return to another world was taken by some as an apology for fascism, despite his strenuous criticisms of the fascist state and his careful contrast of fascist power with the state of sovereignty he used as the key metaphor for a logic of heterogeneity and *dépense* (expenditure). For Bataille, the king was significant precisely because his power (as sovereign rather than symbol) could not be harnessed to the apparatuses of state power, although his critique of liberal democracy seemed as ill timed in the France of the 1930s as Nandy's critique of secularism might seem in the India of the 1990s. But Bataille used the notion of sovereignty for his critique of the idea that production is naturally linked to need (i.e., that need produces the need for production) and to develop his extraordinary reading of consumption and transgression. And it is here that Bataille's polemic helps me to rethink the historical imaginary of kingship in precolonial India. He allows me to view the self-destructiveness of the Nawab and the zamindar neither as mere signs of feudal decay nor as vestigial remnants of precolonial glory but rather as transgressive rebellion against the colonial/capitalist regime. I can now view the precise commitments of these figures to expenditure and consumption not only as measures of a world in which prestige is more important than profit but also as windows through which to see certain forms of excess as direct challenges to the self-legitimating masquerades of colonial order (in the case of Outram) and capitalist economy (in the case of Ganguli). In condemning the effective domination of new forms of oppression in modern India, I need not attempt to celebrate the pre-colonial political as either exemplary or recuperable, even as I do not need to disparage the incapacity of this system to make accommodations with the new. Indeed, the potlatches of *Jalsaghar* and *Shatranj* are implicated precisely within colonial capitalism, the implosion of the old's impossibility within the new.

I thus use Bataille to attempt to understand the form of Nandy's reading of tradition against the grain of modernity. At the same time, Bataille allows me to keep the focus on kingship, sovereignty, and issues of politics more generally. The sovereignty depicted within these films need not be collapsed into authentic tradition but rather seen to point to the historicist transformations of the political realm that made politics as usual simultaneously transgressive and implosive. Nevertheless, my invocation of Bataille is still situated within the framework of my larger historicist argument that the forms of kingship cultivated by the British were designed precisely to showcase Indian tradition as the opposite of the new. Colonialism was complicit in the production of the charade of colonial kingship; the crowns of kings were rendered hollow simulacra of royal power.[13] The so-called impotence of the Nawab and narcissism of the zamindar would not have sustained their power in earlier days; the extravagance of their expenditure, the display of their consumption, was in fact a symptom of the destruction of the old by colonialism and capitalism. But the portrayal of these sovereign figures both referenced earlier forms of sovereignty and refused new forms of state and economy. And in the power of their dramatic demise, the new cannot be said to have triumphed completely.

Ray might not have sanctioned this reading of his films, modernist realist and rationalist that he was. But he too was aware of the need simultaneously to attempt historical accuracy and take some kind of position on the past in relation to the present. And in *Jalsaghar* and *Shatranj*, Ray took on the seductiveness of the past in terms of the contradictory relationship between irresponsible consumption and enlightened patronage. Ray's historical ambivalence here, I have argued, was centered on his despair at the capacity of the new to support the sublime, his fear that the market would drive the serious filmmaker into an embrace with the devil. Perhaps he did feel a vicarious nostalgia for the *dépense* of the Nawab's court and the tarnished music room of the zamindar's palace. And perhaps in the very impossibility of the past, Ray found the solace necessary to carry on, from low-budget film to film, from the fantasy of his cinematic dreams to the quotidian perfection of his aesthetic craft. His celebration of an older aesthetic was thus irrevocably linked to his deep suspicion of the modern "culture industry," in terms that conjure Adorno's critique of modern mass culture. Ray's reluctance to join the chorus of bellicose denunciation of India's feudal past and present thus might be seen as something altogether different from the usual dismissal of his politics as reactionary: a critique in other registers, politics by other means.

We might use Ray's abiding interest in the politics of history and in the history of politics to remind us of the vacuum created when the political is either ignored or seen as an altogether new phenomenon in South Asia. Partha Chatterjee's delineation of a domain of political society (chapter 2), problematizing the relationship between the state's construction of the people as population and the nation's commitment to democracy, provides a starting point for a theorization of the Indian modern that moves beyond the reactiveness of many contemporary critiques and their stubborn erasure of the political past. Given Chatterjee's recognition of the elite provenance of many earlier discussions of the problems of the Indian modern, circumscribed in large part by the colonially constituted spaces of civil society, it seems all the more necessary to reinvest the modern and its attendant genealogies of tradition with all the ambivalence of the political. For this purpose, these two films by Ray, with their consummate expression of the weight of colonial contradictions on the one hand and the fraught relationship between artistic production and political modernity on the other, seem especially critical places to begin. One lesson here is the need to write other political histories, positioned against and outside the colonial categories that produce both shame and embarrassment. As I have suggested elsewhere, we might then predicate an interrogation of modernity and tradition on histories that have the means to escape the colonial incarceration of political forms and imaginings, forms that, alas, resurface far too often even in the most promising arguments of contemporary postcolonial theory.

Notes

1. See Ranajit Guha, *A Rule of Property for Bengal: An Essay on the Idea of Permanent Settlement* (Durham: Duke University Press, 1996).
2. I use Clifford Geertz's phrase "theater state," from his *Negara: The Theater*

State in Nineteenth-Century Bali (Princeton: Princeton University Press, 1980), with a twist, as discussed in the final chapter of my *The Hollow Crown: Ethnohistory of an Indian Kingdom* (Cambridge: Cambridge University Press, 1987).

3. Partha Chatterjee, *The Nation and Its Fragments: Colonial and Postcolonial Histories* (Princeton: Princeton University Press, 1993).

4. See my "Home and the World: The Invention of Modernity in Colonial India," in *Revisioning History,* ed. Robert Rosenstone (Princeton: Princeton University Press, 1995).

5. I refer to films such as *Mahanagar* (1963) and *Company Limited* (1971).

6. Quoted in Andrew Robinson, *Satyajit Ray: The Inner Eye* (Berkeley: University of California Press, 1989), 243.

7. Quoted ibid., 251.

8. Ashis Nandy, *The Savage Freud: And Other Essays on Possible and Retrievable Selves* (Princeton: Princeton University Press, 1995), 212.

9. Ibid., 215.

10. See Ashis Nandy, *At the Edge of Psychology* (Delhi: Oxford University Press 1980), *The Intimate Enemy* (Delhi: Oxford University Press, 1983).

11. As has been argued, in different forms, by a number of powerful feminist analyses. See, for example, Kumkum Sangari and Sudesh Vaid, eds., *Recasting Indian Women: Essays in Colonial History* (Delhi: Kali for Women, 1989).

12. Georges Bataille, *The Accursed Share,* trans. Robert Hurley, vol. 3: *Sovereignty* (New York: Zone Books, 1988), 347.

13. See my introduction to the new edition of *The Hollow Crown: Ethnohistory of an Indian Kingdom* (Ann Arbor: The University of Michigan Press, 1994).

Seven

The Making of Modernity:
Gender and Time in Indian Cinema

Veena Das

In his essay on the painter of modern life, Charles Baudelaire stated that modernity is "the ephemeral, the fugitive, the contingent, the half of art whose other half is the eternal and the immutable."[1] This particular intuition about modernity, that it has to do with the fleeting, the transitory, the contingent, and that its privileged time is that of the eternal present, has led several scholars such as Charles Taylor and Alasdair McIntyre to look at the stable and the immutable as the characteristic of tradition.[2] Yet the past few decades, when the idea of multiple modernities was presented in the writings of scholars such as Eisenstadt, is also the period when the notion of stability of tradition was brought into question and the constructed character of tradition—the many ways in which it could be "invented"—was brought into sharp relief.[3] It may be pertinent to ask here whether so-called traditional societies have their own ways of constructing modernity. May we then speak of *alternative modernities* or *alternative histories of modernity* when we come to regard non-Western sites as equally the sites of modernity?[4] How does a tradition (or traditions) make itself knowable to the world and to itself in the medium of the modern?

As a way of addressing these questions I explore the imaginary institution of time and the construction of gender in Indian cinema,

166

through which I claim that the notion of modernity is addressed. Since time is not the overt object of cinematic construction, I address the question of modernity through the construction (and de-construction) of masculinity and femininity. Simultaneously, there is also the constant address to the question of what kind of past the cinema as a modern medium in India can acquire.

In one obvious sense one cannot speak about Indian cinema, any more than one can speak about Indian literature. An art form is, after all, not constrained or defined by politically defined territories. However, cinema in India makes the claim for itself as "Indian" through several cinematic devices. For instance, sometimes the device is used whereby the map of India appears onscreen and speaks to the people of India, as in *Mughal e Azam* (the Great Mughal), or the workers unite to form the outline of the map of India, as in the song sequence of *Sathi Haath Badhana* (Hold out Your Hand, Oh Friend) in *Naya Daur* (The New Dispensation). In an important sense, then, the cinema in India may claim that it has produced the disposition of an Indianness and not only represented it. But Indian cinema has not always been complicit with the aims of the state. Rather, in its enunciation of Indianness, we find such questions as the nature of the present, the production of the male subject, the desperate attempts by the female protagonist to make herself known, and a genealogy for cinema itself articulated.[5] As Robert Smith has remarked, perhaps we can think of the media as a form through which the nation produces its autobiography.[6]

In the analysis that follows I take certain encounters between tradition and modernity as providing the context within which the institution of time and the transformation of the subject take place in the cinema. I find it useful to think of these encounters in the following way: (1) tradition as the pretension of an inner space that fortifies Indian society against the wounds of modernity—the seduction of tradition; (2) tradition as it is claimed by the modern project of nation building and the claims of cinema as the monumental expression of that claim; (3) tradition as the "past present" that has become rotten, toward which the subject experiences a fierce nostalgia and a mountainous sense of loss, yet fidelity to the present requires its violent renunciation; and (4) tradition as the natural, and modernity as a journey of the self into an unknown future.

Tradition as Inner Space

In selecting the metropolis as the focal point for the analysis of modernity, the transitory character of the social relations struck Georg Simmel and the dominance of technological values (Simmel's objective culture) over personal values (his subjective culture) in the life of the metropolis.[7] But just as Baudelaire conceived of eternity as the other half of the fugitive, fleeting character of modern art, so Simmel thought of the interior of houses as the counterpart of the public spaces of the metropolis.[8] This interior, he said, was filled with furniture that had the character of fortification against the outside world and its transitory nature. This theme of the exterior, whose nature has become problematic, and an interior that is conceived almost as a protest against the passage of time may be found in both the social-science literature in India and various forms of representation, such as popular art and cinema.

In recent writings on nationalism, several social historians see the birth of the idea of the Indian nation as also the moment when the nature of modernity was problematized in Indian intellectual discourse. In a recent statement on the issue, Ashis Nandy has argued that an analysis of the distribution of male and female characters in the novels of Rabindranath Tagore would show that nationalism was an inauthentic response of the male subject attempting to overcome his loss of masculinity at the hands of colonial powers. The authentic recovery of the self, he says, required the male subject to get in touch with his feminine self again.[9] In this reading of that moment when colonialism and modernity came as twins into Indian society, Nandy argues that the authentic ways of being male were lost to the Indian man under the conditions of modernity. His tongue was penetrated by a foreign language; his dress codes altered to suit the new role of the *babu* (clerk, as opposed to *sahib*, the white officer); and his English education cut him off not only from his past but also from the more authentic ways of being Indian, by a sharp divide between the home and the world.

Against this penetration of the male subject by the colonialist discourses, many social scientists (especially those studying Bengal) argue that the sphere of the home was the feminine sphere, in which the continuities of tradition were maintained effortlessly by women. Thus Partha Chatterjee and Sudipta Kaviraj have both argued in different ways that the use of vernacular, the maintenance of traditions of female modesty, the code of dress, and the ritual encoding of tradition found their natural habitat in the home, which became the sphere in which Indian identity was protected from the colonial onslaught.[10] For Nandy, the pathologies of modernity were evident in an aggressive nationalism, which used the same framework of ideas and techniques that the colonial aggressor had used to defeat the Indian male.[11]

Commenting on the male protagonists of Tagore's three well-known novels, *Gora, Char Adhyaya,* and *Ghore Baire,* Nandy says:

> The apparent robustness of Sandip, Indranath, and the Hindu na-tionalist Gora, derives from the denial of aspects of their culture and self that are identified with effeminacy, especially maternity. The strongest resistance to them, too, finally turns out to come from women; they are the psychological barricade that the culture puts up to protect its *svadharma.*[12]

Thus, in Nandy's interpretation of Tagore, the *svadharma,* or the code of conduct that the culture confesses as its "own," is under assault from colonialism, which also stands for the *dharma,* the code of con-duct, of modernity. This code of conduct for Nandy is one that val-orizes hypermasculinity, devalues diversity, and worships homogene-ity. The Indian male's capitulation to this project of modernizing India by purifying it of its "caste-ridden, superstitious, idolatrous tradi-tions," as Nandy puts it, is essentially a project in which the male, cas-trated by colonial domination, tries to recover his masculinity. Thus, he comes to reject the feminine, both in the culture and in himself.

Nandy forms an equation between womanliness and the spirit of India and, on the reverse side, masculinity and the potent, cosmopoli-tan image of male authority that is found in the modern project of na-tionalism. The following example speaks in this vein.

> Gora senses that Anandmayi represents in her womanliness, the spirit of India, more fully than his pure, disinfected, masculine ver-sion of Indian nationalism and Hinduism.

One guesses that Anandmayi is the prototype of the character that in the later novels develops into the splintered personalities of Bimala and Ela. It is Anandmayi's authenticity that is being engineered, by Sandip in one instance and Indranath in another, in the cause of na-tionalism. This engineering breaks down the barrier between the pri-vate and the public by giving absolute priority to conjugality over ma-ternity, and it erects a new barrier between the home and the world, one that does not permit feminine values in the domestic space to invade or spill over into public life.[13] Nandy's analysis of the appropriation of the authenticity of the female characters by the male characters in the cause of nation building is a truly insightful reading of Tagore's novels. There are more threads in the weave, however, as far as the transfiguration of the woman in the projects of modernity is concerned. Nandy evokes the feminine as the value in which the "spirit" of India lives. In his understanding, it acts as a kind of natural barrier against the values of hypermasculinity. I take this as the nostalgia one encounters in the midst of the new, the transitory, and the fleeting, for an area of life that would remain untouched by the newness of modernity. Nandy invests this desire for stable frameworks of life in the spheres of femininity, a guarantee given to the male who is caught in the flow of the modern that continuity with the past is "naturally" assured in the way women live their lives. Thus modernity is experienced as a loss of authenticity and the male subject becomes devoid of an interiority due to this loss—the hidden presence of women in the interior is the only guarantee that the civilization has of an inner life of the spirit. But is the story of the woman to be told only through the male engineering of her self?

Finding Her Voice:
Male and Female Subjects in Popular Film

As a counterpoint to the view expressed by Nandy, let me evoke the production of the male and female subject under the conditions of modernity in one of the early films made after independence. *Mahal* (Palace) was an enormously successful Hindi-Urdu film produced in 1949 by Bombay Talkies, with which the director Kamal Amrohi made his debut in Hindi films. The famed Kathak dancer, Lacchu Maharaj, choreographed the film, and Dilip Kumar and Madhu Bala played the major roles. The story goes like this.

The Plot

Shankar (played by Ashok Kumar), the male protagonist, comes to an abandoned palace accompanied by a friend (a lawyer) because both have heard rumors that the palace is haunted by the spirit of a woman whose lover, the erstwhile young ruler of the palace, had died in an accident. The woman is said to have killed herself in grief over her lover's death.

Our first visual relation to Shankar happens on the screen as he looks at the portrait of the dead ruler and is immediately struck by its resemblance to himself. Was the story of the feudal prince his own story in an earlier existence? As Shankar gazes at the portrait, he is himself being watched by a woman, who later announces herself to be the wandering spirit of Kamini, the woman who had loved the man in the portrait. Shankar becomes infatuated by this spirit. His lawyer friend, who appears here as the rationalist, tries hard to break this infatuation with a dead past but does not succeed. How, then, can the lovers unite when one inhabits the world of the living and the other the world of the dead?

Shankar follows the spirit into the secrets of the palace, mesmerized by her presence, almost without possession of himself. Kamini suggests to him one day that while the distance between them must remain as long as she is a spirit, she could come into the world of the present if she could inhabit the body of a living woman. She implores him to kill Asha, the gardener's daughter, through a ruse. Then at the moment of her death she (Kamini) would enter Asha's body so that Shankar can be reunited with her, though in another body. Asha has always appeared veiled to Shankar: he does not even know what she looks like but is willing to kill her, as Kamini suggests. When he actually tries to strangle Asha, however, catching her unaware while she lays his tea on the table, he is interrupted by the unexpected arrival of his friend in the room. Disheartened, he returns with his friend to the city.

Back in the city, Shankar's friend relates the strange story to Shankar's father, who threatens to kill himself unless Shankar agrees to break out of his infatuation with Kamini. Desperate, Shankar agrees to marry Ranjana, with whom his marriage had been earlier arranged. He has every intention of consummating the marriage but fails because he hears the strains of a song, the leitmotif of the spirit, who calls him toward her. He decides to escape with his wife into the wilderness, but however far he goes, the song haunts him. His wife begins to suspect that he is betraying her with another woman. Heartbroken, she comes to the city and kills herself. To avenge herself, she leaves a letter for the police implicating Shankar in her murder.

The case against Shankar is tried in court. Did he kill his wife for the love of a spirit? Asha makes a surprise appearance in court. In the witness stand, as she lifts her veil, Shankar (and the spectators) receive a visual shock, for Asha and Kamini appear to be the same person. Asha reveals that it was she who had masqueraded as the spirit of

Kamini. As we hear her story, we learn that the daughter of the humble gardener had fallen in love with the portrait of the young ruler. Living her life of fantasy, she began to haunt the palace, imagining herself to be Kamini. But then she saw Shankar: was he the incarnation of the man she had imagined as her lover? But could she, a gardener's daughter, dare to love such a man? She thought her only hope of seducing Shankar into marrying her was to persuade him that she was the spirit of Kamini. As Shankar became bewitched by this haunting spirit she hoped that she would be able to reveal her true identity to him without jeopardizing their love.

The court finds Shankar guilty of the murder of his wife and sentences him to death by hanging. Shankar is now persuaded that Asha is indeed the reincarnation of the lost Kamini. He tells his friend that Kamini and he are fated to be separated. If one inhabits the world of the living, the other inhabits the world of the dead. The only way to bridge this distance between a past and the present is for Shankar to invite wounds on himself in this life: only through suffering would he be able to purify his soul and be reunited with Kamini in his future life. He begs his friend (the rationalist lawyer!) to marry Kamini so that Shankar can suffer these wounds on his soul.

In the final scenes we see wedding guests departing after the ceremony in which Shankar's friend and his beloved Kamini/Asha are married. In the prison, the noose is being prepared. But then a letter written by Shankar's wife to her friend (a confession that she is committing suicide) is found in the dead-letter post office. Two policemen roar away on motorbikes to retrieve it, and the letter reaches the judge just in time for a reprieve. Shankar makes his way back and finds his friend and his beloved in bridal clothes. He is again out of joint with time. His friend plans to kill himself so as to free his wife to marry her lover, but Shankar has already consumed poison. In the closing shots the screen is split, with Shankar's dead body, sprawled on a chair, occupying the middle. On either side are two doors. His friend departs from one and his beloved from another, both turning away from each other and from the audience. The last visual is of Shankar and the irresolution of his desire.

The Multiplicity of Registers
It is commonplace to say that cinema is experienced on a multiplicity of registers. There is not only the story but also the movement of im-

ages, the soundtrack, the multiplicity of visions, and in the case of Hindi cinema, the special place of the song sequences. In *Mahal*, the woman remains mute, struggling to find a narrative occasion on which she could find her voice, to reveal herself (that is, to reveal who she is). The inability of the male protagonist to see her except as he has fantasized her (always as Kamini, never as Asha) appears to me to be an allegory in cinematic language of the maleness of the dispersed public that makes up the viewing nation but is unable to see the woman for who she is. Let us dwell on some of the moments in which the complex visual encounters take place.

In the first encounter Shankar has with his portrait in this abandoned palace, he is being watched through the latticework of a window by Kamini. The portrait functions as a mirror, but in this whole transaction between the rational self and a forgotten self that inhabits the past, the visual field is defined by the gaze of Kamini. As she looks at this visitor who is both unknown and deeply known, the complicity between the spectators who are looking at the image on the cinematic screen and her eye through which the transaction is witnessed is established. Initially, it seems that her eye is the same as the eye of the camera. Her vision enables us to see the making of the male subject. Through this device the woman announces herself as a cinematic object. Her name, Kamini, refers to the desiring one. The complicity between her gaze, the gaze of the camera, the gaze of the spectator, as well as the not-too-hidden code of naming, makes the cinema a space on which desire of the spectator may be materialized. Unlike the rectangular frame of a painting, which is designed to keep the world out, the cinematic screen acts like a weaver's mold that weaves this desire into the images on the screen.

Already, there is a multiplicity of positions from which we may view this encounter. The male protagonist is looking at a portrait, which is a barely disguised mirror. Here is an analogy of the cinematic screen as a mirror for the spectator. The irony of knowing and not knowing is exquisitely portrayed. While initially it is the male protagonist who is in a state of non-knowledge about himself, as the story develops, it is the female protagonist whose attempts to make herself known are consistently foiled. She functions as a sign of a lost spirit, much as the woman functions in Nandy's narrative, but is always unable to tell her story truthfully.

Shankar is an educated man. Yet, he becomes fascinated by a ghost convinced that the call of this past must be answered. His friend devises a strategy to counter this fascination. He contracts two sisters, famous courtesans, to lure him away from the spirit that haunts him. The scene of seduction is completely the opposite of domestic sexuality. It is not a scene of monogamy, or even of fidelity to one woman. Gori-Sanwari (the fair and the dark), as the sisters are called in their self-description, are like the day and the night (again, a haunting analogy of the play of light and shadow on the screen), like two eyes but a single gaze. As they sing and dance in a moonlit courtyard to the strains of an invitation, *ye raat phir na ayegi* (this night will not come back again), Shankar hears the song of the wandering spirit calling him to her. He gets up as if in a trance and leaves.

The scene of marital sexuality fares no better. As Shankar is about to lift the veil on his bride's face he hears the clock strike twelve and the strains of the song. He walks toward the door but is hit by a hanging cage in which a parrot is imprisoned. He thanks the parrot for reminding him that, like the parrot, he is a prisoner of the demands of a rational social order.

Unable to consummate his marriage within the known spaces of a house, Shankar decides to take his wife into the wilderness. However, the sound of the clock striking midnight and the song of the spirit do not permit him to consummate his marriage. His wife, too, decides that she will not lift the veil from her face unless he decides to unveil her. Right to the end, Shankar is unable to lift this veil. The theme of the unknowability of the woman is repeated, it seems to me, in a minor register.

In one scene Shankar and his wife, Ranjana, witness a tribal ritual.[14] A man has accused his wife of infidelity. To prove her innocence she has to dance before the image of a tribal god, and the priest has to throw a knife four times in her direction. If she escapes the knife, she is innocent. Unfortunately for her, the fourth throw of the knife proves to be fatal, and the woman dies. Ranjana faints at this scene. The appearance of a tribal community, especially in a dance sequence, is an important icon in Hindi cinema. It is a device here for the permission to express a desire that is taboo. The respectable middle-class hero cannot be seen to wish his wife dead by cinema's own norms of censorship in this period.[15] Hence, the scene of the woman's death enacted on a "primitive" community allows the cinematic realization of this desire.

Finally, I will comment on the court scene. Shankar's criminal desire for the death of his wife and the reclaiming of his past love that had been enacted in the scene of the tribal ritual is now enacted in a diametrically opposed setting—a court of law. What appeared as mysterious, haunting, a tale of reincarnation, is shown to be part of a plot. But the moment that the veil is lifted from the face of the gardener's daughter, Shankar is certain of her identity, not as Asha, the gardener's daughter, but as Kamini, his lost love of past lives. The narration of the story in a modern rationalist mode by the gardener's daughter is played against a counterpoint, the psychic reality of Kamini's (and not Asha's) presence. The woman's story, when told in the iconic space for truth-telling in Hindi cinema, still remains unheard. Even the engagement with the audience is terminated in the final scene by the characters' turning their backs away from the spectators, retreating into lives not witnessed by the dispersed public, which has failed to hear the story of the woman.

The Subjunctive Mood

While the theme of reincarnation might appear at first reading as Hindi film's close alliance with mythology in an attempt to acquire a past, the frequent devices of using the portrait as a mirror; the veil as the cinematic screen on which desire may be materialized; the clock announcing not the passage of time but the return to the scene of the past; the choreography that makes the movement of both protagonists closer to movements in a dream than in life—all these point to the subjunctive mood in which the film is created.

The motif of reincarnation in the film is not so much about reincarnation as about cinema's capacity to materialize the desire for a life that the male could lead, as if in a different existence. The deep wounds of modernity are portrayed through the imprisoning metaphor. But the past does not offer a resolution either. The male is shown as incapable of mastering the past as part of the present. The wandering spirit through whose eyes we saw the movement of the film turns her face away from us. If the film is the realization of a wish, the wish of the modern Indian male to claim the past as his own, his wish is not resolved. In fact, the *mise-en-scène* in which an unconscious or dead male occupies the screen as the female protagonist is shown to disappear, away from the eyes of the spectator, is found in other films. The masculine self will awake to a different world from which the

feminine has been expelled. At an obvious level, the theme of the disappearance of the woman signals her inability to find a place for her
story in the making of the modern nation. However, if my reading that
the female appears here as a materialization of the male wish is correct, then her disappearance signals not only the loss of the woman's
voice but also that of the man's feminine voice. This interpretation
amplifies Nandy's formulation of the male subject under conditions of
modernity as one who has lost touch with his femininity but touches
on a different key of the imagination.

The women who inhabit the screen seem at first sight to be the desiring *subjects,* as in the case of Kamini. But I hope my interpretation
shows that they are much better understood as the materialization of
a male wish—the wish for an unfettered relation to the past, the wish
to encounter the woman never as a creature of flesh and blood but as
a haunting spirit. Women are marked by their disappearances: in
Mahal there is first the disappearance of the wife and then of the lover.

Acquiring a Past: *Mughal-e-Azam*

The nation as an imagined community may be itself historically shal-
low as a modern entity but there is a vast repertoire of images and stories from which it may acquire a deep past. One example is the famous historical melodrama *Mughal-e-Azam,* made in 1960, which
tells the story of the Emperor Akbar's son, Salim, and his love affair
with the courtesan Anarkali, in defiance of the emperor and the queen,
his mother.

The film opens with a map of India speaking to the spectators
about the legends of the past through which the history of this great
nation is created and which is about to be narrated.[16] Since the map
hangs like a screen, we can see that the impressions we are about
to receive are cinema's claim to taking up and molding the project of
nationhood. The film is famous not only for the stunning images of
Dilip Kumar and Madhubala, who act as Salim and Anarkali, but also
for Kamal Amrohi's dialogues, which are frontally shot and remind
one very much of the theatrical enactment of Prithvi theaters. Note
that the following scenes selected for my theme are not consecutive.

Scene one: The homecoming of Salim after a fierce battle that he has
won. A famous sculptor who has refused all royal patronage is persuaded to make a statue of a beautiful woman with whom the prince

would fall in love at first sight. He makes a living sculpture of the beautiful Nadira (again played by Madhubala). Salim witnesses this "statue" and is challenged to pierce the veil with his arrow. The statue does not flinch from the incoming arrow. As a reward for her beauty and her courage, Nadira receives from the emperor the honorific title of Anarkali (the bud of the pomegranate flower) and is given a special position as a royal courtesan. Salim falls in love with her.

Scene two: The emperor learns of Salim's love for Anarkali. Enraged, he goes to the prince's palace. Anarkali is with Salim. When she hears of the emperor's approach, she flees in absolute terror. In her blind flight she sees Akbar approach and, in a reflex action, runs back into Salim's arms. Salim holds on to her and faces Akbar defiantly. For anyone schooled in the Indian aesthetic tradition, the analogy of this voiceless, scared woman with a deer fleeing from the hunter is imme- diately evoked. The exchange of glances between Akbar and Salim that passes over the frightened woman also indicates a contest that is, to be sure, over her but that ironically excludes her voice completely.

Scene three: Under dire royal threats of imprisonment and death, Anarkali's mother promises that they will leave the palace. Salim hears of this and contemptuously insults Anarkali, saying that she does not know the meaning of fidelity. That very night Anarkali dances in the royal palace, the Sheesh Mahal. Defiantly she sings, *"jab pyar kiya to darna kya,"* when one has dared to love what is it then to fear? As Salim's eyes meet the angry gaze of Akbar, we see Anarkali reflected in the mirrorwork that forms the ceiling and the walls of the palace. Her image is refracted all around Akbar as he hears her sing defiantly. The contrast between the silent frightened girl in the earlier scene and this woman who has found her voice through song is explicit. I simply note here for later comment that it is in the transformation of speech into song that desire is articulated and finds a means for resisting the threats of power. This is true, though, only for the transfiguration of the woman. The place of song in relation to the making of the male self is a different story, one that I cannot tell here.

Scene four: A dialogue takes place between Jodha Devi, the queen, and her son, Salim.

JODHA DEVI: The map of India is not your heart on which a courtesan can rule.

SALIM: My heart is also not the map of India on which the command of the Emperor can rule.

Scene five: Salim declares his rebellion against his father, saying that his command infringed the customary right of all Mughal princes to choose their wives according to their hearts' desire. In the ensuing battle Salim is defeated and is sentenced to death. Anarkali bargains for his life with her own life. But she has one condition. Let us recreate the final dialogue between her and Akbar, a dialogue that the map later tells us is not part of recorded history.

ANARKALI: I will leave the prince forever but on one condition, that I be allowed to become the Queen of India for one night.

AKBAR: Even when you are facing death, the desire to become the queen of the country does not leave you.

ANARKALI: The prince had promised this slave that he would marry her and she would be his queen. I do not want the future Emperor of India to be ashamed for not having kept his word to a mere slave.

Akbar places the crown on her head.

AKBAR: You know the condition. At the end of the night you must give this drug to the prince and leave as he falls in a swoon.

ANARKALI: You will have no cause for disappointment. In return for your favors, this slave courtesan forgives you her murder. Now the corpse may be given permission to leave.

Scene six: This is toward the end of the film. It is a scene of celebration after the marriage of Salim and Anarkali. Women are singing auspicious songs. As dawn approaches, Anarkali puts the drug in Salim's wine and he falls in a swoon. The soldiers arrive to take away Anarkali. The farewell song is heard on the soundtrack: "We are leaving you, world. Arise and accept our greeting." The visual shows the prince slumped in slumber as the figure of the female disappears, completely disengaged from the spectator.

The folk legend of Anarkali says that she was buried alive but in the film she wins a reprieve, although the spectators know that she will never speak again. The final scene again shows the map of India, which tells us that it alone knows these hidden stories about India's history.

I have drawn attention to the map of India in this film as an explicit signifier for the cinematic screen. Thus, the narrative construction of a past for the nation is also cinema's reflections on itself. I am not suggesting that this act of declaring itself as cinema within the genre of popular cinema compares with the sophisticated self-reflexivity of the medium in the hands of such creative directors as Ritwik Ghatak or Kumar Shahani. But I nevertheless feel that in this particular case, the idea of the cinematic screen not only revealing a certain past but *burying* it, distinguishes it from the banal "special effects" or the appearance of a self-reflexive device such as the camera in a host of other Bombay films. In any case, one may surely regard this at least as a shadow of the (more aesthetically satisfying) ways in which cinema is able to make such declarations in what is popularly called "art cinema" in India.

Given this positioning of the map, what does the exchange between Salim and Jodha Bai on the analogy between the heart and the map signify? It is in his moment of defiance that Salim is able to declare his privacy against the dominance exercised by the state. There is an intriguing contrast here between the way in which Madhubala declares her defiance through the medium of the film, the magnification of her image in the hundreds of mirrors literally proclaiming her presence to the camera and to the spectator, and Dilip Kumar claiming that his heart is not the map of India, thus hiding himself from the gaze of the viewers. I call this contrast intriguing because one dominant way in which this question of the gaze has been posed with respect to cinema is to position the camera as the device that subjects the woman to the unreciprocated gaze of men. It is instructive for me, then, to look at how women may look back or even instruct the camera on how to look at them while men may need to hide their subjectivity, so that their stories also cannot be simply appropriated by the act of looking.

Anarkali's decisive transformation happens, as we saw, in the scene of her dance in the palace of glasses, when she responds to Akbar's threat not through dialogue but through song. The freedom of her body, the song, and her image refracted in the hundreds of mirrors seem to instruct the camera on how she may be seen at this moment. The sense of excess is created through the manifoldness of her presence in the song and the dance sequence. The glamorous courtesan is simultaneously registered in the eye of the spectator as a "star," a category that is the creation of modern cinema. Thus, the visual magnification displays her presence in a spectacular manner at the level of the image but ironically fails to let her find a voice that is ordinary or, say, her voice *in the ordinariness of life.*

In the case of *Mahal,* we saw the inability of the woman to tell her story so that the cinematic transformation of the woman into image (spirit?) was read as the materialization of the male fantasy of the woman as inhabiting a time that was different from his own time. In *Mughal-e-Azam,* the problem presents itself as a problem of naming.

Nadira is the "ordinary," "homely" name of the sign under which we first encounter Madhubala in this film. Her first appearance in the court is in the form of a veiled statue. She is rewarded for not uttering a sound when Salim directs an arrow toward her, which will pierce her veil. The price of her being elevated to the position of a court dancer (to a star?) is not only that she must be revealed but also that she must pawn her voice. The reward, in the form of an honorific name, is earned through her silence or, at any rate, through a disavowal of her voice.

It is when Salim falls in love with her that we see the beginning of a second transformation. Initially, she who had not flinched from the piercing arrow now runs like a frightened deer from the angry, menacing advance of the Emperor Akbar. Then another transformation begins to happen. Her love for Salim gives her the voice to defy the power of the emperor and to overcome her terror of him. The irony is that the first defiance takes place in the context of a spectacle. She can sing her defiance but she cannot, at this point, speak it.

When the second defiance happens she has taken the power to name herself. She is the queen of the young prince, even if for a day, and correctly names herself as a corpse. Only in the last scene, when her mother wins a reprieve for her so that she may not be buried alive, do we hear her name as Nadira again. The movement is from the ordinariness of her name to be spoken only among women, to the glamor of a star name bestowed by the emperor and used by men to name her either as a realization of their fantasies of power (Akbar), or love (Salim), to the moment when she can herself name herself as both queen and corpse. It appears that naming, misnaming, the right to claim a name (Queen) and to name it correctly (corpse) provide one of the codas through which the problem of how the woman is to be constructed in cinema is presented to the viewer. The map of India proclaims at the end that the generosity of the emperor in forgiving

Anarkali is completely unrecorded but that it (the map, the cinematic screen) alone knows these buried stories. Yet the voice-over cannot deafen us to the last spoken words of Anarkali, to the effect that she forgives the emperor her murder. The history of male connections is forged over the forgiveness of women as over their disappearance from the male world. Salim will wake to a world in which he will succeed his father as emperor but in which the woman as the courtesan, the one who brought him to his manhood, will have disappeared. The film places these questions within a story that is traditional or historical, but the cinematic devices signal the positioning of this tradition as an allegory for the construction of gender under the sign of modernity.

Tradition and Fierce Regret: Ritwik Ghatak

Tradition emerges as predatory, much as modernity appears as a site of violence, in the films of Ritwik Ghatak, who made films on Bengal, but from the subject position of an exile. Ritwik Ghatak was a product of the Indian People's Theatre Association, which was the cultural front of the Communist Movement in pre-independence India. In the description of Ghatak's project, Geeta Kapur writes, "he provided the impetus to see the Indian tradition turned inside out" and questioned the nurturing potential of perennial symbols by "confronting them with a historically framed subjectivity."[17] His last film, *Jukti Takko Aar Gappo,* made in 1974, is an autobiographical rendering of the simultaneous dissolution of the radical dream of India and Ghatak's own nightmarish descent into alcoholism. In the final scene of the film, Neelkantha, the protagonist, played by Ghatak himself, is caught in the midst of a crossfire and says, "One has to do something." This is a direct quote from a short story of Manik Bandopadhyay, in which a destitute weaver who is unable to get any thread for weaving continues to work on the loom, saying, "One has to do something." But before this wounding image of the suggested empty loom were Ghatak's films of the sixties, *Meghe Dhaka Tara* (Cloud-Capped Star) and *Subarnarekha* (literally, The Golden Line, the name of a river that flows along the border between India and Bangladesh).

Geeta Kapur considers *Meghe Dhaka Tara* to be the finest example of the "tradition turned inside out." The story portrays the life of a displaced family from East Bengal that has been made destitute and its transformation into "respectability" by the sacrifices it imposes on the eldest daughter, Neeta. Each member of the family (except the

father) exploits her labor for his or her ends. She cannot permit herself
to get married to the man she loves, as this would deprive her family
of her income. Neeta's younger sister, with the tacit compliance of her
mother, seduces her lover. She is now considered to be the more appropriate receptacle for the man's love. Exhausted by the constant demands being put on her by the family and the demands of her work,
Neeta sinks into devastating disease (tuberculosis) and unbearable
sorrow. Her brother becomes a famous singer; the man she had imagined as her lover marries her younger sister and the parents are saved
from the devastation of poverty. All this is built on the money she has
earned. Toward the end of the film, the family shrinks from this diseased daughter, fearing that she will contaminate them by her illness
and her sorrow. Her brother takes her to a sanatorium in the hills.

In the last few shots, the brother has come to visit her in the sanatorium. Brother and sister together occupy the center of the frame. As
the camera stands laterally to him, the brother describes the "normali-
ty" that the family has achieved—their two-storied house, her sister's
son who is learning to walk; then the camera foregrounds the face of
the sister as it pictures her top down, turned toward her brother, who
is outside the frame. Her voice takes over and she says, "Dada, I
wanted to live," and then she repeats, again and again, in a lament,
"Dada, I will live." In the last frame of their togetherness, her sorrow
has a support—she is leaning over the shoulder of her brother. Then
Ghatak's camera moves to take panoramic shots of the beauty and
splendor of the sky, the hills, and the majestic trees. The human faces
disappear from view. Only the cry "Dada, I will live" is heard, press-
ing its desperate demand on the viewer. The camera continues to move
away, capturing the beauty of nature and its complete indifference to
human suffering. At this point the soundtrack plays the refrain from
Ai go Uma Kole loi (Come, Uma, child, let me take you into my arms).
This song, in the voice of the mother of the mythic Menaka to her
daughter Uma, who had suffered the hardships of a terrible penance,
is used at several places in the film to announce Ghatak's presence in
the film. It seems to say that nature and society may be indifferent to
you, but I (Ghatak) hear you, I take you in my arms as if you were a
little girl though I know you have suffered the same hardship as the
mythical Uma.[18]

Ghatak's visuals are wounding in a way that I cannot compare
with the work of any other filmmaker in India. The suffocation of

Nita's voice is buried in the scenes of everyday life. It is not as if there are any dramatic moments of confrontation as in the popular films I analyzed earlier. It is simply that every time Neeta wishes to speak of her desire, she is suffocated by a small demand for money by the sister for a cosmetic, by the mother for buying vegetables to cook, or by the brother for an outing with his friends.[19] It is not even that there is no affection in these encounters but simply that the immediacy of their demands does not allow her voice to appear. In the case of *Mahal*, a flesh-and-blood woman moved around among the living in the guise of a spirit. In the case of Nita, her existence, her corporeality, her voice are unseen, unacknowledged. Only twice is she able to find her voice. The first time is when the rituals to prepare the bride (Nita's younger sister) for the wedding are taking place. Nita is urged by her brother to sing with her, and the two sing together marking their camaraderie but also, in that very moment, making it appear as already an event of the past. The second time is Nita's insistence that she wants to live, her voice rising in the wilderness to which neither nature nor society is able to respond. In *Jukti Takko Aar Gappo*, all that the filmmaker could say was "One has to do something," while in *Meghe Dhaka Tara* it seems to be cinema's statement about itself that it alone is able to hear the voice of the woman. Simultaneously, the cinema in this rendering is the eye that registers the horror of the predatory society. I conclude this section with the climax reached in the relation between a brother and a sister in *Subarnarekha* to illustrate this manner of showing what cannot be said.

The story of *Subarnarekha* also unfolds in the context of the partition of Bengal. A man who has lost his home in the eastern part of Bengal (Ghatak's own lost home) has escaped with his young sister and another young boy, an orphan, to West Bengal. As his sister and the young orphan grow into adulthood they fall in love with each other. But because the boy is of a lower caste, the brother does not consent to their marriage. They nevertheless get married and move to Calcutta. A few years later the sister's husband dies in an accident and she is left destitute with a young child of her own to support. I am not offering a detailed analysis of this film. I offer instead a vignette of the last shots.

The destitute sister has been broken into agreeing to receive a customer by a kindly neighbor, who is an elderly woman and perhaps knows that there is no easy way for the young woman to make her livelihood in the city. As she reluctantly awaits the man, her eye registers the face of the customer. It is her brother, who in a bizarre sequence of events has been persuaded by his friends after a drunken evening to visit a prostitute. The camera makes of the eye a surface on which terrifying images move as the girl in slow motion drives a dagger into her heart. The eye, enlarged to fill the screen, becomes the surface on which we can see the horror as it registers on the brother's face. In both these films, the woman's story becomes brutally abbreviated because the natal family refuses to acknowledge her desire. The scene of the everyday is itself then a scene of mourning for Ghatak, and cinema a text in which this mourning is buried. Unlike the idea of women as the natural barriers against the onslaught of modernity, it is they who become most vulnerabe to the violence of a modernity under which tradition is turned inside out.

The Continuous Unfolding of Tradition: Satyajit Ray

The theme of the present as having been born of the past and the corruption of the present as a temporary "forgetting" of origins is widespread in the representations of modernity. One of its best expressions is to be found in the oeuvre of Satyajit Ray. In his famous "Apu" trilogy, based on a two-part novel by Bhibuti Bhushan Bandopadhyay, Ray gives a subtle rendering of the movement from the rural, traditional setting to the anonymity of the urban setting, although the movement is not a once-for-all linear movement; it plays with a series of departures, returns, and re-entries. Geeta Kapur reads this trilogy as an ethnographic allegory, infused with a lyrical mood through which Ray claims both the Bengali literary and aesthetic tradition, and a place in a film lineage of the realist movement signaled by Jean Renoir and Vittorio de Sica, which influenced Indian filmmakers in a decisive manner.

Geeta Kapur picks up the motif of the journey in the Ray trilogy to argue that this motif is suggested in a way that the journeys of countless young men in independent India become allegorized as the national story—the rites of passage for the modernizing young men. Thus, she sees this journey prefigured in the way that Apu emerges from the shadows of his elder sister, Durga. For instance, in one of the early scenes of their childhood, she is combing his hair, holding on to his chin, turning his face this way and that. When she turns his face to make him look at the mirror, we realize that it is within her field of vision that he looks at himself. Durga is the spirit of the wilderness, epitomized not only in her name but also in her rain dance and in the movements of her body. That Apu is to grow out of these shadows is epitomized in the shot of a train cutting through the countryside as Apu runs in excitement to watch it. The train as the classic icon of modernity and of journey into modernity is transformed from its clichéd image by its reflections in Apu's eyes and the sense of mystery it holds for him.

Ray's treatment of tradition and its intimacy with nature is also portrayed with great tenderness through the figure of the old grandmother, as if she were the waif of tradition, and through the visuals of the childhood desires of Durga and her ecstatic monsoon dance. The death of the grandmother and of Durga are like the gentle leaving behind of the tradition and the rural childlike innocence from which Apu frees himself toward the path of freedom and sovereignty of the self. The movement of the family to the city, his father's death, his sudden and unexpected marriage to the daughter of a zamindar (landlord), and the subsequent death of his own wife in childbirth, mark his entry into adulthood through a series of separations.

More than in the narrative, it is in the image as presence that the journey of the self is portrayed. Let us look at the last episode in the third film of the trilogy, *Apur Sansar* (Apu's World). Apu had earlier refused to go to his wife's natal village, where she had died in childbirth. So wounded was he by her death that he had refused to even see his son. Now he has gone to the village and for the first time has encountered his son Kajal, who is now three years old. Kajal, not unexpectedly, completely rejects his overtures. So here is Apu, an adult, inhabiting the world in a kind of mourning. He had been almost compelled to marry a woman to save her from an arranged marriage in which the prospective groom had turned out to be a lunatic. Miraculously, they had been able to find love even in this hurriedly arranged marriage and then she had betrayed him by dying, or so it appears to his wounded self. Now when he is ready to go on with his world, his son rejects him. Dejected and beyond words, he walks away from the village.

As he walks away, Kajal is shown running after him. He turns round, is surprised, and then in one decisive movement hoists Kajal on his shoulders. The last scene depicts Apu walking with his son perched on his shoulders. The past of the village is behind him. The female presence in his life has been finally renounced. A male alliance toward a future is forged. In this last frame Apu and Kajal, made into a single vertical presence, occupy the extreme left of the frame, while the fading picture of pastoral serenity in the form of a pictorial composition of the green fields, the river, and the boat are on the right, almost touching Apu but claiming him no more. The dialogue between father and son constructs the future even as they walk facing the spectators, hence not withdrawing into a private world.

KAJAL: Do you know my father?
APU: Yes.
KAJAL: Will you take me to him?
APU: I shall try.

Geeta Kapur has critiqued Ray's position as characteristic of a subjectivity that is suffused with romantic nostalgia in which value is only in the past, while it resides in the present only as private sensibility. Hence, although Apu authenticates the modern and redeems himself by claiming his son, she feels there is an insufficient engagement with the present. In my interpretation I have tried to juxtapose the visuals with the dialogue that I feel change the meaning of the present. Even though Apu doubts that he can take his son to selfhood through the claiming of a paternal genealogy, he promises to try. For the Apu who had completely turned away from life, this gesture of forgiveness toward the woman whose death had devastated him so completely is an important promise of re-engagement with life and with the present, whatever the bruises it has given.

Concluding Comments

I have examined four different configurations of how cinema places the question of the gendered subject in the context of the advent of modernity in India. I am struck by the fact that the possibilities of cinema, especially that the woman may be simultaneously concealed and magnified, or that what is *seen* through the camera may be offset by a counterimage of what is *said* on the soundtrack, provide a different language with which to speak of the creation of the male and the female under conditions of modernity. Instead of a neat division between tradition and modernity as providing sure signs of where to place the woman in relation to the man, I have attempted to tell a complicated story about the making and remaking of men and women in the medium of the cinema. To the extent that this is a different story from the one told about similar questions in popular cinema in the West, I submit that there would have to be not one but several histories of modernity.

Notes

1. Charles Baudelaire, *The Painter of Modern Life and Other Essays,* trans. and ed. Jonathan Mayne (London: Phaidon, 1964), 13.

2. Charles Taylor, *Sources of the Self: The Making of the Modern Identity* (Cambridge: Harvard University Press, 1989); Alasdair MacIntyre, *After Virtue: A Study in Moral Theory* (Notre Dame: University of Notre Dame Press, 1981).

3. S. N. Eisenstadt, *Democracy and Modernity* (Leiden: E. J. Brill, 1992); Eric Hobsbawm and Terrence Ranger, ed., *The Invention of Tradition* (Cambridge: Cambridge University Press, 1983).

4. For the relation between locality and modernity, see Arjun Appadurai, *Modernity at Large: Cultural Dimensions of Globalization* (Minnesota: University of Minnesota Press, 1997).

5. For the purpose of this essay I am not making a distinction between "popular cinema" and "art cinema," nor am I defining a particular genre. My idea is to map the differences in the way that questions of tradition, modernity, creation of gender, and time are entangled in different configurations.

6. Smith writes, "Every day a nation's media, for example, will write the ongoing autobiographies of that nation. If the sense of 'autobiography' may be stretched in these ways, the nation represents itself to itself" (*Derrida and Autobiography* [Cambridge: Cambridge University Press 1995], 62). Useful as this analogy with the self is, it does not tell us whether the media is specially privileged to do this telling.

7. Georg Simmel, "Die Grosstadte und das Geistesleben," in *Die Grossstadt,* Vorträge und Aufsätz zur Städteausstellung, by K. Bücher, F. Ratzel, G. von Mayr, H. Waentig, G. Simmel, Th. Petermann, and D. Shäfer; *Jahrbuch der Gehe-Stiftung zu Dresden,* vol. 9 (Dresden: von Zahn and Jaensch, 1903), English trans., "The Metropolis and Mental Life," trans. H. H. Gerth with the assistance of C. Wright Mills, *The Sociology of Georg Simmel,* ed. Kurt H. Wolf (New York: Free Press, 1950), 409–24.

8. Georg Simmel, "Soziologie des Raumes," in Simmel, *Soziologie* (Berlin: Dunker and Humbolt, 1908), 460–526.

9. Ashis Nandy, *The Illegitimacy of Nationalism: Rabindranath Tagore and the Politics of Self* (Delhi: Oxford University Press, 1994).

10. Partha Chatterjee, *The Nation and Its Fragments: Colonial and Postcolonial Histories* (Princeton: Princeton University Press, 1993), and Sudipta Kaviraj, *The Unhappy Consciousness: Bankimchandra and the Making of a Nationalist Consciousness* (Delhi: Oxford University Press, 1995).

11. Nandy, *The Illegitimacy of Nationalism,* 80–90.

12. Ibid., 49.

13. Ibid., 41.

14. We are concerned here not with the political questions of indigenous groups but with the generic symbol of the tribal person that acts as an icon in literary and cinematic texts.

15. The anti-hero did not emerge in Indian cinema until the 1980s. The norms for

representing what was permissible sexuality of the hero and the heroine were very strict in this period. Criminal desire could only be portrayed in the villain or the vamp. The "tribal" dance was thus an important cinematic device for expressing forbidden desire in the protagonist.

16. This film has been seen as popular cinema's narration of the nation, especially in the account given by Sumita Chakravarty, who finds that images of landscapes, maps, charts, and particular forms of dress are used to evoke feelings of identification (see Sumita S. Chakravarty, *National Identity in Indian Popular Cinema, 1947–1987* [Austin: University of Texas Press, 1993]).

17. Geeta Kapur, "Cultural Creativity in the First Decade: The Example of Satyajit Ray," *Journal of Arts and Ideas* 4 (1993): 28–47.

18. There is still a further layer of interpretation that could be offered. Nita is being identified in song as Uma; her brother's name is Shankar, the mythic husband of Uma. The sibling pair signals the incestuous desire that cannot be transformed into domesticity in both of Ghatak's films, yet there is the longing for the suffering daughter or sister to be magically returned to childhood.

19. Ashish Rajadhyaksha and Paul Willeman suggest that the film language here opens the story to a mythic dimension and the evocation of a parallel narrative in the Bengali legends of the goddess Durga (Ashish Rajadhyaksha and Paul Willeman, *Encyclopedia of Indian Cinema* [Delhi: Oxford University Press, 1994]).

Eight

Body Politic in Colonial India

Gyan Prakash

January 10, 1836, was a special day in Calcutta. As Pandit Madhusudan Gupta, a student at the newly established Medical College, plunged his knife into a human body, a taboo was broken. Indians, it was said, had finally risen "superior to the prejudices of their earlier education and thus boldly flung open the gates of modern medical science to their countrymen." Fort William celebrated modern medicine's assault on the body and its onward march by firing a gun salute. A century later, Mahatma Gandhi referred to another kind of assault on the body by writing frankly about his unsuccessful efforts to conquer desire. Describing his condition in 1936 in Bombay, where he was convalescing, he wrote that whereas all "my discharges so far had occurred in dreams. . . . The experience in Bombay occurred while I was fully awake and had a sudden desire for intercourse."[1] For Gandhi, the conquest of sexual desire was an important part of his philosophy of self-control directed at the body. He believed that *brahmacharya,* or the practice of celibacy, was crucial for the maintenance of healthy bodies.[2]

Between Fort William's gun salute to modern medicine and Gandhi's failed effort to control the body through the suppression of desire, we can identify the emergence of what Michel Foucault called "biopower." By biopower, Foucault means a political technology whose ultimate concern was with the body of human beings as a species, over which the exercise of mastery had to be secured at the level of the processes of life itself.[3] But whereas Foucault identifies the formulation of biopower in modern medical knowledge and tactics, Gandhi saw modern medicine as evil. Yet, the two discourses were also connected; they shared a concern with the disciplines of the body, with its materialization in knowledges and tactics. If the combination of the knife, the dissected human body, the broken taboo, and the gun salute brings to mind Foucault's analysis of modern disciplines of the body as a form of war, Gandhi too saw himself engaged in a war; his was a battle against desire, a struggle to produce an Indian self located in a body organized and ordered by sexual discipline. Between the two discourses, then, there lies the history of the subjection of Indians to a new form of surveillance and control, their constitution as modern subjects.

If this appears to confirm Foucault's analysis, it also calls for bringing to light what remains hidden in his description of biopower, namely the functioning of the new political technology through colonial distortions and displacements. For what the colonial location of biopower brings into view are effects produced by the need to formulate and apply the species knowledge of the *colonized* body, a body perched precipitously between colonialist and nationalist projects of hegemony. What emerges in practices ranging from the colonial management of the health of the population to nationalist claims over the Indian self is a form of biopower formed in an embattled field of tactics, practices, and institutions of dominance. Colonial modernity was never simply a "tropicalization" of the Western form but its fundamental displacement, its essential violation. Utilitarian theorists from Jeremy Bentham to Fitjames Stephen, including James and John Stuart Mill, had maintained that British rule in India must necessarily violate the metropolitan norm: only despotic rule could institute good government in India; only a Leviathan unhindered by a Demos could introduce and sustain the rule of law in the colony. Produced at the point of such an estrangement of Western rule in despotism, colonial rule represented a peculiar construct, radically discontinuous with the metropolitan norm whose violation had given rise to it.

Foucault's concept of biopower, however, as Ann Laura Stoler points out, remains resolutely blind to its imperial frame, disconcertingly silent about the articulation of European sexuality in the management of colonial bodies.[4] His historical account acquires an unmistakable whiggish drift as he defines modern biopower as the resolution of the centuries-old confrontation between biology and history. According to him, the French Revolution marked the beginning of the end of "thousands of years" of the pressure exerted by the biological on the historical: "Western man was gradually learning what it meant to be a living species in a living world, to have a body, conditions of existence, probabilities of life, an individual and collective welfare, forces that could be modified, and a space in which they could be distributed in an optimal manner."[5] Signifying society's threshold of modernity, biopower established its full presence in the West, while the non-Western world remained vulnerable to famine and biological risks to the species. In this perspective, the colonies, marked by their failure to achieve the "threshold of modernity," can only appear as pale copies of their metropolitan original. Given Foucault's Eurocentric view that biopower was constituted fully within the borders of the modern West, its career in the colonies can only be seen as a dim reflection of its full-blooded form in the metropole. But this was not the case. If anything, colonies witnessed an unrivaled application of the political technology of the body. According to David Arnold, colonial India demonstrates, "in a manner unparalleled in Western societies, the exceptional importance of medicine in the cultural and political constitution of its subjects."[6] With an extraordinary involvement of state medicine, the body was colonized, that is, it was inserted in a new field of tactics and institutions aimed at achieving mastery over life.

The "colonization of the body," however, requires another specification if we are to fully explore the colonial workings of biopower. Arnold is right to stress the extraordinary importance of state medicine in British India in the production and subordination of subjects, but to understand the nature and the field of knowledges and practices opened by Western therapeutics, we must ask: What was colonial about the colonization of the body? How was the materialization of the body in institutions and tactics affected by conditions of alien rule, by the dislocations with which colonialism was compelled to operate?[7] These questions point to the disjunctive articulation of modernity in the colonies, to its obligation to occupy two positions at once, Western and Indian; they bring into view the body's embattled history as it emerges between the war to regulate the life processes of the aggregate population through modern medicine and the battle to discipline the sexual life of the Indian self through rules of continence.

The disjunctive history of modern biopower in British India must be sought in its functioning as an aspect of the governmentalization of the colonial state, that is, as a part of the development of that state rationality which located the exercise of power in the application of strategies to secure the welfare of the colonized population. Such an understanding of the rationality of the colonial state draws on Foucault, who distinguishes governmentality from sovereignity—which is concerned with territory, legitimacy, and obedience to law—and from disciplines—which are elaborated in such institutions as prisons, schools, armies, manufactories, and hospitals. Locating modern power in a sovereignty-discipline-government triangle, he defines governmentality as a mode of "pastoral power" aimed at the welfare of each and all; which functions by applying economy, by setting up "economy at the level of the entire state, which means exercising towards its inhabitants, and the wealth and behavior of each and all, a form of surveillance and control as attentive as that of a head of a family over his household and his goods."[8] The application of economy at the level of the state was rendered possible by the appearance of population as a category. Population, with "its own regularities, its own rates of deaths and diseases, its cycles of scarcity, etc.,"[9] was irreducible to family and became the object of schemes to promote its health and wealth. There emerged "a sort of complex composed of men and things . . . men in their relations, their links, their imbrication with those other things which are wealth, resources, means of subsistence, the territory with its specific qualities, climate, irrigation, fertility . . . in their relation to that other kind of things, customs, habits, ways of acting and thinking . . . in their relation to that other kind of things, accidents and misfortunes such as famine, epidemics, death, etc."[10]

Governmentality in British India also developed in response to the outbreak of epidemics, death, and famines, and represented an effort to act on the population, to nurture its health and cultivate its resources. But British India was marked by the absence of the elegant sovereignty–discipline–government triangle that Foucault identifies in Europe. Fundamentally irreconcilable with the development of a civil society, the colonial state was structurally denied the opportunity to mobilize the capillary forms of power. Thus, colonial governmentality developed in violation of the liberal conception that the government was part of a complex domain of dense, opaque, and autonomous interests that it only harmonized and secured with law and liberty.[11]

This violation, however, should be regarded as a productive breach, not a restrictive liability; it initiated a generative dislocation, not a paralyzing limitation. For what it set into motion was a powerful process of bureaucratic expansion and rationalization under which the population's economic, demographic, and epidemiological properties were surveyed, enumerated, measured, and reconstituted so as to bring into existence a *colonial* "complex of men and things," that is, a population constituted as subordinated subjects, whose health, resources, productivity, and regularities were the objects of governance. Emerging as a part of the colonial complex of "men and things," the body, then, was a materialization of institutions and practices with which colonial power was resituated and exercised as colonial governmentality.

The appearance of the body as an aspect and effect of governmentality represented the rise of a new field of power, a new zone of contention and constitution of subjects. Colonial institutions and knowledges dominated and defined this field, but it was an arena of contention. For, although colonial knowledge and colonial regulation could never function as self-knowledge and self-regulation, this was precisely what governmentality required and attempted to accomplish. The British enacted sanitary measures and regulations, established Western medical therapeutics and institutions, and inaugurated campaigns against epidemics. If these materialized the body in a grid of knowledge and tactics, this grid was always haunted by the stereotypical images of Indians as diseased, unhealthy, unhygienic, superstitious, and unscientific. Because such stereotypes justified colonial power, they could never be eliminated. The body rendered knowable by physiology, pathology, and surgery, and visible in diseases, epidemics, and deaths, therefore, could never be fully instituted in the ghostly, precolonial body of colonial representations. Coercion, failure, partial and fragmentary success always punctuated the operation of tactics and effects in which medicalized bodies appeared.

It was at the site of this predicament that British India witnessed other contending strategies that restaged colonial medicine and colonial governmentality. These projects struggled to define an Indian subject by acting upon the body materialized by the colonial network of power, by restaging indigenous knowledges, customs, habits, living patterns, and cultural values as disciplines for the production of modern, self-subjecting individuals. It was in this struggle to develop ascetics or tactics of self-governance for a body brought into existence by colonial governance that the nationalists developed the notion of the uncolonized, "inner" domain of culture and tradition.[12] But the "inner" and "spiritual" domain of the nation, its cultural "essence," were, in fact, produced by the application of disciplines, by subjecting them to the pressure and procedures of the "outer" domain of colonial science. The nationalist resistance, its construction of an uncolonized domain of self-constitution, represented negotiations of the terms of governance. It resituated the knowledges and tactics of governance to include indigenous principles, recoded and redesignated the materialized body as Hindu and male, thereby marshaling a strategy of self-subjection that colonial governmentality could never deploy effectively. The nationalist discourse arose squarely within historical power relations, not outside the field of colonial modernity, and it intervened in the same arena to deflect governmentality along different lines.

Colonial Institutions and the Emergence of the Body

While medicine and colonial power were linked together soon after the establishment of British rule, it was not until the late nineteenth century that this relationship produced the native body as an object and effect of medical attention.[13] It was then that the effort to control and contain the alien environment of India, to regulate and reform the "tropics," where the unhealthy climate combined with the fevered irrationality of the people to unleash virulent outbreaks of sickness and death, gave rise to a new network of knowledge and tactics. This emergent regime of knowledge produced the image of an anterior and spectral body composed of unhygienic habits and superstitious beliefs upon which modern knowledge and tactics were to be applied in order to reform it, to restore its health and well-being. Similarly, indigenous knowledge and materia medica, previously incorporated as inferior but useful supplements to Western therapeutics,[14] appeared as a collection of unscientific and inaccurate beliefs under whose misrepresentations there lurked a real body. The reading of indigenous therapeutics as mistaken and imprecise signs of the existence of the body as a real object justified the application of strategies that materialized the body in a different set of institutions and effects; it posited the body as an a priori object, as an entity whose existence preceded the discourse within which it appeared as a matter of medical scrutiny and regulation.

Predictably, it was the anxiety about the security of the empire that aroused interest in the health of the population. Initially, this in-

terest focused on the army, whose indispensability for the maintenance of the colonial order had been driven home by the 1857 revolt.
Shaken to its foundation by the upheavals of 1857, the British government became concerned about the well-being of its army. The British
troops in India had experienced a death rate of 69 per 1,000 (three
times the rate in Britain), and epidemics had severely affected the conduct of military operations during the Mutiny.[15] With sanitation and
hygiene in the military placed under the spotlight by the Crimean
War, the bleak record of sickness and death in the British army in
India caused alarm. Under the pressure of Florence Nightingale's resolute campaign, the British Parliament appointed a royal commission
in 1859 to inquire into the sanitary state of the British army in India.[16]
The commission issued its report in 1863, stating that fevers, dysen-
teries, diseases of the liver, and epidemic cholera were the most injurious diseases in India for British soldiers and that science could offer
no relief because it had been unable to determine their cause. But a
"rational mode of inquiry" had discovered, the commission declared,
that improved drainage and sanitary conditions could counteract the
intensity of the transmission of diseases. A meticulous attention to hygiene, habitation, and habits could protect Europeans from the risk of
epidemics in a place like India, where the unhealthy effects of heat and
moisture had to be assumed and where malaria was an ever-present
danger.[17]

The magnified attention to sanitation represented a shift in the
colonial medical discourse that occurred as part of the victory of the
"anglicists" over the "orientalists" in the 1830s. The triumph of the liberal imperialist vision had opened the floodgates of contempt for
Indian beliefs and knowledges, and had led to the replacement of the
Native Medical Institution with the Calcutta Medical College in
1835. The emergent discourse broke with the Anglo-Indian medical
tradition of the late eighteenth and early nineteenth centuries that had
shared much with the humoral pathology of ayurvedic and yunani
medical systems and had found them useful, if not altogether correct.
By the mid-nineteenth century, however, while the belief in India's
distinct disease environment was not abandoned, the possibility of in-
corporating indigenous practices into Western therapeutics and accli-
matizing European constitutions to Indian medico-topographical conditions were ruled out.[18] Both the Indian environment and Indian
knowledges appeared so utterly alien and unremittingly perilous to

health that only their containment and suppression could preserve the well-being of the colonial order. The discourse of sanitation both contributed to and reflected this change insofar as it, unlike climatological determinism, brought into existence objects over which control could be exercised.

Sanitation represented a new order of knowledge and power. Florence Nightingale articulated its specificity when she enthusiastically described the sanitary inspectors' reports as "bringing to light what is the real social state of the mass of Indian peoples." These reports had removed "the veil of romance woven by poets over Hindostan," she added, and revealed "peoples to be numbered by tens of millions living under social and domestic conditions quite other than paradisiacal." They lived "amidst their own filth, infecting the air with it, poisoning the ground with it, and polluting the water they drink with it," and "some even think it a holy thing to drink filth."[19] This description was consistent with the prevalent theory of climatological determinism, according to which soil and air produced miasmas that caused and communicated diseases, but it also marked a departure insofar as it rendered human habits and habitation into objects of medical attention and regulation. Filthy cities, open drains, decomposing animal carcasses, rotting vegetable matter, irrational beliefs, and unscientific therapeutics appeared as errors that signified the truth of the Indian body. The "real social state of the mass of Indian peoples," after all, was revealed by the disclosure that Indians, "numbered by tens of millions," "lived amidst their own filth," trapped by their unhygienic habits and beliefs. Muck and misunderstanding were read as signs that pointed to the existence of the body as an object prior to the dirt, disease, and dogma in which it was buried and independent of the discourse that brought it into view. Such a positioning of the truth of the Indian body, as a specter of filth and error, set the stage for the sanitary policing and regulation of the population. The British appointed sanitary commissioners in Bengal, Bombay, and Madras Presidencies, and in the provinces of Punjab, Burma, United Provinces, and Central Provinces, and charged them with the responsibility of preparing monthly and annual returns on diseases and of drawing up plans for the sanitary regulation of the population.[20] The establishment and expansion of municipalities followed, the state apparatus grew, and the sanitary policing of the population became regularized.

Sanitary policing in India followed a design different from the metropolitan pattern. Considering the model of the English municipal institution "unsuitable and inefficient" for India, the British stressed centralized control rather than local self-government. Inspector-generals were to preside over local sanitary inspections which, unlike in Britain, were to be carried out by low-level "lay" inspectors, not well-paid medical officers of health, and they were "to see to the abatement of nuisances and to the bringing of cases of nuisance before the magistrates."[21] Administering a system designed and controlled by the center, local sanitary officers in India, again unlike in Britain, did not work in just an advisory capacity; instead, they operated as executive officers with vast powers and responsibilities. They supervised the conservancy work, controlled a large subordinate staff and laborers, administered the registration of births and deaths, investigated the causes of deaths and epidemics, addressed public complaints, and advised on sanitary requirements of buildings.[22] A bureaucratic machine was found necessary for sanitary work because the state considered the colonized to be incapable of self-governance. As Nightingale put it, the state in India had to accomplish single-handedly what was achieved in Britain in conjunction with the "habits of self-government."[23] When Lord Ripon, the Viceroy of India, did introduce local self-government in 1882, his Gladstonian liberalism made sure that it was extended only to Europeans and a small group of wealthy Indians.[24] The limits of local self-government in India meant not only an enlarged role but also an altogether different positioning of the state as it sought to make up for the effacement of the colonized. In this regard, Nightingale's bold declaration that "Government is everything in India" neatly captured the ineluctably colonial nature of the governmentalization of the state in India.[25]

Sanitation in colonial India functioned as the knowledge and regulation of the Other; it was deployed as a Western discipline for the governance of indigenous habits and habitation. In the first instance, this produced a discriminatory sanitary order that constituted Indians and the Indian environment as sources of diseases from which Europeans had to be protected. Descriptions of filth figured prominently in colonial investigations of "fevers" in Indian cities.[26] The focus on unsanitary conditions itself was understandable in view of Sir Edwin Chadwick's *Report on the Sanitary Condition of the Labouring Population of Great Britain* (1842), which had placed cities under the spotlight as centers of squalor and disease in Britain.[27] But whereas Chadwick's work had highlighted unsanitary conditions in relation to the Industrial Revolution and the conditions of the working class, colonial reports projected dirt and disease as signs of India's otherness. Thus, when the sanitary commissioner described Calcutta in 1864 as a "scandal and disgrace" to the "civilized Government," he blamed the native population as a whole, not just the "poorer classes."[28] Colonial officials returned repeatedly to remark on the open and clogged drains, on the stench of the night soil and its ugly sight that greeted the unfortunate visitor to the "black towns," on the gut-churning piles of garbage heaped in bazaars, on the crowded, ill-ventilated, haphazardly designed native houses. Not just colonial prejudice was at work in these denunciations but a language of governance, a knowledge and discipline of the other. These representations justified the creation of European enclaves of hygienic havens located in military cantonments, "civil lines," and "hill stations," separated from swampy, "malarial" grounds and the native population, and governed by sanitary standards prevalent in Britain.[29] Such hygienic enclaves were expected to reduce the threat to European health posed by Indians, but the British also recognized that their sanitary protection could not be fully secure unless Indian habitations were also regulated.[30] So, as municipal authorities favored the civil lines and cantonments inhabited by Europeans, they also realized the necessity of extending sanitary regulations to "black towns," which had acquired a menacing meaning since the Mutiny.[31]

As colonial officials set out to control the recurrent outbreak of epidemics during the second half of the nineteenth century, statistics came to occupy a prominent position in the developing medical profile of the indigenous population. The use of statistics was not peculiar to India. By the mid-nineteenth century, as Ian Hacking has shown, Europe had already witnessed statistics acquiring an important role in understanding reality, in making the world apprehendable in terms of statistical laws.[32] Statistical data and laws rendered chance appear less capricious; they discerned order and regularities in such indeterminate events as epidemics, thereby offering a mode of understanding and controlling natural and social processes. Such a conception of statistics had become widespread and was endorsed by Edmund Parkes's *A Manual of Practical Hygiene* (1864), the standard medical text for British officials in India. Writing of the government's duty to maintain "watchful care over the health of the people, and a due regulation of matters which concern their health," he had recommended the use of "figures which admit no denial."[33] In British India, however, colonialism shaped such figures because they were produced in the exercise of alien power. Not surprisingly, the government's "watchful care" in India produced a colonial knowledge of the population. The data on the outbreak of epidemics was organized to show their differential effects on Europeans and Indians. These revealed a disturbingly high rate of mortality of European soldiers in India compared to Indian sepoys, leading to the appointment of a royal commission that never visited India but pored over the statistical data to understand the condition of army sanitation and to make its recommendations.[34] The reliance on statistics grew and became more complex and sophisticated in the late nineteenth century as the British were called upon to cope with the ravages of cholera, smallpox, plague, and enteric fevers vastly aggravated by urban crowding, rapid and increased communication facilitated by railroads, and the malarial environment bred by irrigation works.[35] Colonial officials collected detailed numerical information on sickness and fatalities; they investigated the relation between the outbreak of cholera and plague with race, region, climate, and habitation; they measured the success of vaccination versus inoculation in resisting smallpox; they assessed the rate of mortality of Europeans and Indians in hospitals and clinics; and they hungered for more accurate data in order to enhance the "taming of chance" in the alien and hostile environment of India.[36]

The desire to bring diseases and deaths under the statistical gaze represented an effort to relocate the indigenous population, to bring it under the colonial "complex of men and things," where its regularities in relation to the climate, topography, habits, and habitation could be observed and acted upon. Government officials searched for agencies that reached down to the village in order to collect vital information on births and deaths, and complained that inaccurate diagnoses and medical treatments provided by indigenous practitioners enabled sickness and mortality to escape the net of statistics.[37] The volume and complexity of statistical information grew with the regularization of the collection of mortality figures of the civil population and the institutionalization of the decennial census in the 1870s. These, together with systematic metereological records kept by the government, extended the reach of the colonial establishment and enabled the formulation of a discursive formation that represented the body in different combinations and correlations of diverse statistical series. The body was firmly located in India and yet scientifically observable only through the knowledges and practices of colonial medicine, which developed different and conflicting ideas about diseases and their treatment. Thus, as cholera raged, so did debates between the proponents of climatological determinism and the contagion theory, both of whom drew on statistical information to build their respective arguments. The theory that miasmas caused and communicated cholera received powerful support from J. M. Cunningham, the sanitary commissioner of India from 1868 to 1884, and was elaborated in a number of monographs that used and generated data that situated bodies and diseases in relation to climate and topography.[38] The opposing contagion theory, expressed originally in John Snow's *On Continuous Molecular Changes, More Particularly in their Relation to Epidemic Disease* (1853), found less support in India, but it was also elaborated with the help of statistical data.[39] Disagreeing over the understanding of the etiology of cholera and methods of prevention, both theories used statistics to dislodge the body from indigenous beliefs and practices and materialize it in a new set of knowledges and tactics.

Statistics constituted an element of the wider discourse concerned with the medical specification of India's difference. This concern generated debates and theories, but the state's "watchful care" remained focused on formulating knowledges and identifying objects of governance. Thus, when the colonial government finally accepted the contagion theory in the mid-1890s—a decade after Robert Koch, the German bacteriologist, had discovered the cholera bacillus in a Calcutta tank in 1884—the Indian environment did not drop out of focus. "In their insistence upon the physical or climatic idiosyncrasies of India," Arnold remarks, "the environmentalist school was in curious accord with its contagionist opponents with their eyes firmly fixed not on the heavens or the soil, but on pilgrim hordes."[40] The International Sanitary Conference at Constantinople in 1866 had placed its sharp attention on Hindu pilgrims as sources of cholera epidemics, causing great embarrassment to the British. But the government itself feared the large collection of Indians at religious fairs and pilgrim sites. An official report attributed the cholera epidemic in northern India in 1867 to the Kumbh fair in Hardwar, attended by three million people, a number swelled by the recent introduction of railways. The administration made sanitary arrangements, including the disastrous one to bury the night soil from the latrines in the banks of the Ganges River. As pilgrims bathed in the river, they transmitted cholera to others, killing more than a hundred thousand.[41] To combat the epidemic, the government prohibited fairs, sanitary cordons of police were formed, cholera hospitals and camps were established, the bodies of the dead were cremated or buried as soon as possible, and the clothing of victims was destroyed. The returning pilgrims were diverted from large towns and detained in quarantine camps for as long as five days, and they were obliged to wash and have their clothes fumigated before being allowed to re-enter their villages and towns.[42] Cholera broke out again during the fair in 1892, in spite of elaborate sanitary arrangements made by the administration, leading the government to disperse the pilgrims, empty the lodging houses, and prevent dips in the holy waters of the Ganges. These measures helped prevent the spread of the disease and positioned the colonial state as a form of "pastoral power" under whose "watchful care" indigenous religious observances were regulated in "secular," medical terms.[43]

Even more so than cholera, the outbreak of smallpox and plague epidemics sparked the development of knowledges and practices to seize the body from its indigenous cultural location. Unlike cholera, smallpox brought the British face to face with a traditional method of treatment, that is, variolation, which entailed inoculation with live smallpox matter in order to induce a more manageable presence of the disease in the body.[44] Reports demonstrated to the government that while areas "notorious for their crowded, filthy, ill-ventilated and ill-condition were the chief receptacles and hotbeds of this contagion and disease," variolation was as destructive and prolific as the natural occurrence of smallpox.[45] The government's investigation disclosed that the Hindus practiced variolation as a religious duty, prompting the circulation of questionnaires to Hindu pundits to determine its textual status. The replies by pundits were equivocal, suggesting that law books did not enjoin variolation specifically but included it as part of religious ceremonies recommended for those struck by smallpox.[46] In British eyes, however, variolation was not a harmless religious ceremony but a "murderous trade"; it was not prescribed by "Hindoo Law and Theology" but perpetrated because there was no shortage of "bigots to mislead the ignorant Hindoos, and to prejudice their credulous and simple minds, against whatever may be falsely represented to them as an innovation, or an interference with their religious privileges."[47] As Arnold shows, a battle ensued to suppress variolation and replace it with vaccination. Co-opting the inoculators (the *tikadars*) as vaccinators, the government steadily increased the number of vaccinations in British India from 350,000 annually in 1850 to 8 million by the end of the century.[48] This did not happen without resistance. The opposition was provoked by the arm-to-arm method, which remained the predominant form of vaccination in British India until World War I, when it was replaced by the cowpox vaccine. Unlike inoculation, this method involved the transferral of body fluids from one individual to another, causing higher castes to fear that they would be ritually polluted by the bodily matter of lower castes. Undeterred by this resistance, and following the recommendation of the smallpox commission, the British outlawed variolation and enacted laws for compulsory vaccination.

The process of removing the body from areas "notorious for their filthy, ill-ventilated and ill-condition," and freeing it from "ignorant and simple minds" achieved an exceptional dimension during the bubonic plague epidemics of the late nineteenth century. As Arnold points out, plague brought to the fore an unparalleled state intervention because the disease "was specifically identified with the human body and thus occasioned an unprecedented assault upon the body of the colonized."[49] The list of instructions that Waldemar Haffkine, the Russian bacteriologist, prepared for the use of municipal authorities to identify the disease required the examination of the body for fever, trembling limbs, pain and swelling of glands, delirium, constipation, and diarrhea. To diagnose whether or not these were plague symptoms, the skin over the gland was to be washed with carbolic lotion and pricked with a needle to reach the gland. The gland was then to be pressed to squeeze out a whitish substance, which was then to be placed under the microscope.[50] Because only the physical examination of the body could identify the disease, the interdiction of the body became necessary for understanding and controlling the disease. Thus, the outbreak of the 1896–97 epidemic in Bombay prompted the municipal commissioner to issue a notification claiming the right to enter any building to disinfect it and remove any item, to remove any person suffering from the disease to a hospital, and to isolate any house in which the disease existed.[51] The British authorities examined passengers at railway stations to detect if the fleeing residents of the plague-stricken areas were carrying the disease, segregated and hospitalized plague victims, and carried out extensive cleaning and disinfection of drains. Such interventions sparked widespread opposition, particularly in Pune, where the military carried out much of the house-to-house inspection to detect if plague victims had been shielded from hospitalization.[52] B. G. Tilak, the Maratha nationalist leader, portrayed the plague operations as an unacceptable interference in Indian life, and the fervent hostility to the government's policies led to the assassination of W. C. Rand, the chairman of the plague committee, in 1897. Elsewhere, the government's "assault on the body," as Arnold puts it, did not provoke assassinations, but the practice of seizing plague victims from their relatives and hospitalizing them met with violent opposition.[53] Faced with sustained opposition, the British had to moderate their draconian policies, and eventually they were able to win the support of educated Indians.

Inspection, segregation, vaccination, and hospitalization dramatized both the general process of the elaboration of the state's concern with the governance of Indians and its colonial nature. On the one hand, the urgent need to combat epidemics mobilized and brought into play a range of knowledges and techniques—sanitary laws and tactics, studies of diseases and strategies of control based on statistics, vaccination, quarantine, hospitalization, municipal government—that had been developing in a variety of locations over several decades. The epidemic victims in hospitals and clinics furnished details on the pathology of diseases, their symptoms and treatment, and these were combined with sanitary and statistical facts and laws to render the body as an organism, as a constellation of functions, designations, symptoms, ailments, immunities, vulnerabilities, and therapies. On the other hand, epidemics also brought to a flashpoint the confrontation entailed in tearing colonized bodies away from the specter of native habits and habitation and materializing them in disciplines and technologies of colonial governance. The development of governmentality as the knowledge of the Other could not but position the application of disciplines as a battle. P. C. H. Snow, the municipal commissioner of Bombay, wrote: "The people would not believe that the hopeless condition of their own dark, damp, filthy, overcrowded houses was their real danger, they raved about the sewers and became phrenzied if a scavenger was remiss . . . every form of obstruction was resorted to when the Municipality attempted to deal with their dwellings." The municipal employees had to carry out their work "in the face of hostile, and sometimes violent crowds, and almost invariably in the teeth of sullen, if passive opposition."[54] Colonial officials attributed such hostility and indifference to ignorance, misinformation, and the "hopeless inability" of Indians to appreciate the value of sanitation and scientific therapeutics. The British officials told each other that Indians were driven to opposition by the rumor that hospitals killed the patients, took out their hearts, and sent them to Queen Victoria to appease the wrath aroused by the disfigurement of her statue in Bombay; that they distrusted hospitals because a large number of patients, having been brought at a moribund stage, died soon after being admitted; that they misconstrued the subcutaneous injection used to resuscitate patients as an attempt to kill them to prevent the spread of the disease.[55] If such retellings of rumors underscored the unavailability of capillary forms of power to the colonial state, they also reinforced the British resolve to continue with the impossible task of re-forming Indians as self-governing subjects in spite of their will. The irreducible difference of Indians both limited and empowered the development of colonial governmentality; if "rumors" and "misconceptions" bedeviled the application of disciplines, they also justified the effort to place Indian bodies in the colonial grid of knowledges and practices.

Body and Therapeutics

The British were fully aware that they ruled as an alien power and that their therapeutics functioned as an alien discipline. But they also exercised power and applied disciplines as if these could bridge the unbridgeable gap between the colonizer and the colonized, as if the absolute otherness of Indians was also knowable. This effort to achieve what was structurally impossible produced an embattled zone of governance, a space of practices created but not contained by the state. This sphere of governance was a peculiarly colonial space of political practice created by sanitary regulations, measures to control epidemics, the statistical representation and organization of the population, and medical knowledge and tactics. Here, it is pertinent to refer to Partha Chatterjee's essay in this volume and his concept of the "political society," which he defines as a mediating space between the people and the state. This mediating space is created by governmentality and is founded on the idea of a population that, unlike civil society, is an empirical and descriptive, not a normative, category. In British India, the concept of population permitted the application of modern technologies on inhabitants who were otherwise seen as unfit for and incapable of reason and progress, thereby creating a space for practices connecting the state and the people.[56]

The Western-educated Indian elite was quick to recognize this new space of mediation and sought to intervene by placing itself as an agent of modern transformation. This was true even of those who largely shared colonial representations of Indians such as Dr. S. G. Chuckerbutty (Chakrabarty), a professor at the Calcutta Medical College, and a respected figure in the *bhadralok* milieu. Speaking at the Bethune Society in 1852 on the issue of sanitation in Calcutta, he placed the entire mode of Indian living under scrutiny. Food, drink, cooking, clothing, housing, drainage, sports, leisure activities, and intellectual pursuits—all were examined from a sanitary point of view. From this examination, he concluded that unlike Europeans, "East Indians" were living examples of "the passive exercise of bodily and mental powers." He illustrated these "passive" East Indians and their "diseased habits" with pictures of the idle, "fat Zemindar," philosophers so given to mental culture that they neglected even the most elementary bodily exercise, the half-clad Brahmin without gloves or stockings, the dirty and damp dwellings, the open gutters and sewers.[57] Such representations were directed at providing more reliable and authentic information to facilitate the state's planning and implementation of sanitary policing of the population. They did not differ in content from colonial disciplines, but insofar as they were descriptions of "our countrymen" by Indians, they posited that the Western-educated man would act as a mediating force between the state and the people, that the elite would diffuse knowledges and practices with which Indians would constitute themselves as modern subjects. Distancing itself from the "fat zemindar" and the ill-clad Brahmin, the elite represented itself as an agent of modern transformation, as a force that would assist the state and educate the people in the regulation and improvement of the health of the population. When smallpox, cholera, and plague epidemics raged between the 1870s and the 1890s in United Provinces and in Bombay and Madras Presidencies, the elite swung into action to offer advice and relief.[58] The focus of its effort centered on the body brought to light by colonial knowledge, that is, a body manifested in filth, statistics, unhygienic habits, and superstitious beliefs.[59] The elite incessantly highlighted and criticized the

Indians' allegedly characteristic neglect of their bodies and their supposed fatalism in order to diffuse "a knowledge of the laws of health"
without which municipal laws and sanitary reforms could not combat
epidemics.[60]

The attempt to educate the "public" in health and hygiene, to dis-
seminate colonial disciplines as self-disciplines, however, could not
avoid the question of difference. Indeed, colonial governmentality was
founded on the notion that the body in India was a peculiarly complex
effect of the environment, habits, beliefs, and knowledges. The discipline of "tropical hygiene" had arisen on the basis of this recognition;
British medicine in India, as Arnold suggests, was not simply the practice of Western therapeutics in a non-Western location but a peculiarly
colonial discursive formation.[61] The attempt to address Indian difference opened Western medicine to revision and reformulation, and a
debate broke out on the status of Western medicine in India. Dr. U. N.
Mukerji, a Bengali doctor, published a pamphlet in 1907, calling for
the establishment of a system of national medicine. Offering a tren-
chant critique of the practice of medicine in Bengal, Dr. Mukerji stated
that he was tempted to put an advertisement in the daily papers asking: "Wanted urgently a treatise on medicine, for treatment of Indians,
written by an Indian." Why was an Indian treatise needed? He acknowledged that the "question may be asked if it is really necessary to
have medical books written by Indian doctors, seeing specially . . .
that a disease is a disease all over the world and remedy is a remedy
everywhere, just as a man is physically at least a man wherever he
is found." Declaring that "the truth lies exactly the other way,"
Dr. Mukerji went on to outline a number of differences between an
Englishman and a Bengali. Whereas the average pulse beat of an
English adult is 72 per minute, it is 80 for a Bengali; whereas the liver
of an Englishman commences two inches below the right nipple, the
Bengali's liver lies three and a half inches below. If such a Bengali were
to be examined in Britain, the diagnosis would be that he was suffering from the contraction of the organ.[62] Diseases differed, as did the
functions of organs in India. But colonial medicine, according to Dr.
Mukerji, failed to take this difference into account. Medical colleges
and English books in India produced an "endless regurgitation about
eastern apathy, dirty habits, and oriental custom and oriental prejudice."[63] These did not teach Indians medicine but trained them to
function as a class of medical subordinates to the British. Expressing

similar sentiments, Jadu Nath Ganguli's *A National System of Medicine in India* (1911) described the Indian practitioner of Western medicine as a "foreigner in his own land." He was aware of the limitations of Western medicine, but he had no knowledge of either the medicinal properties of plants in India or of ayurveda, which for centuries had cured millions.[64] This is why India needed its own medical system, which, unlike colonial therapeutics, could take into account the particular conditions and resources of the country.

The concept of "national medicine," however, emerged under the shadow of colonial medicine's authority, and it sought to act upon a body brought to the surface by the knowledges and practices of colonial governmentality. For these reasons, it operated as a strategy of reinscription, not rejection, of colonial therapeutics. Thus, Jadu Nath Ganguli, in specifying a "system of medicine on national lines," did not rule out allopathy but proposed its combination with homeopathy, ayurveda, and yunani. While the call to include ayurveda and yunani was an attempt to invoke Indian cultural resources, the enthusiasm for homeopathy challenged the supremacy of colonial medicine. Both Western-trained doctors and non-medical men in cities took to homeopathy, and pitted it against allopathic medicine. Its initial stronghold was in Calcutta, where its endorsement by Mahendralal Sircar in the 1860s engulfed medical practioners in a bruising debate. The controversy was all the more fierce because Sircar had been trained in Western medicine and was a well-known doctor and public figure in Calcutta. Sircar did not reject Western medicine but held that because the body was subject to different laws and conditions, the mode of treatment must also be multiple.[65] But this did not satisfy his critics in the colonial medical establishment, who saw his defense of homeopathy as a betrayal and bitterly attacked him and his new cause. Homeopathy overcame this bitter attack and struck roots among the educated elite, profiting from the fact that its practice did not require institutional apprenticeship and certification. Thus, educated middle-class men, with varying degrees of training and expertise, took up the practice of homeopathy either as full-time practioners or as part-time charitable work. When epidemics broke out, they combined homeopathy with ayurveda and Western medicine to formulate a system that reinscribed colonial therapeutics.[66] Journals and newspapers published health columns offering advice on topics ranging from epidemics to pregnancy and childcare.

The reform of households, particularly women, received a prominent place in the reinscription of colonial governmentality. In this arena, the Arya Samaj was the most conspicuous in north India. From its very inception, this religious and social reform movement had focused on women, setting them up as symbols of Vedic virtues and the Hindu nation and establishing a regulatory ideal of conduct for them. In addition to promoting female education, it published journals aimed at women and directed at applying medicalized disciplines. One such important journal aimed at women was *Panchal Pandita,* which started in 1897 as a bilingual English and Hindi periodical but became an exclusively Hindi publication in 1901. It focused on diffusing modern knowledge authorized by the invocation of the Vedas and regularly published articles on healthy diet, cleanliness and hygiene, the care of children, the follies of astrology, and other such topics.[67]

This project to assemble a code of action for women extended beyond the Arya Samaj. Middle-class women themselves participated actively in this project. An example was Yashoda Devi of Allahabad, who ran an ayurvedic clinic along with her husband and was a prolific writer and publisher. She started a journal for women in 1908, followed it up with two more in 1910, and started yet another in 1930.[68] She published a book in 1924 that gives an ample sense of the nature of governance aimed at women.[69] It concerned food and offered directions on cooking based on rules of health and hygiene, not taste. She established the justification for the rules of health and hygiene by narrating a fictional tale of a man who comes very close to death because he took his meal at an improper time. The man's near-death provides the basis for a dialogue between two women who, drawing lessons from this incident, discuss the nutritional qualities of different kinds of food and the rules to follow in cooking and managing the household. This dialogue on ill health caused by ignorance becomes the grounds for outlining what constitutes proper Indian womanhood. The boundaries between health, hygiene, morals, and social institutions blur as instructions on preparing healthy food lead to the injunction that women must take full responsibility for maintaining the health of the household. A responsible Indian woman, the text suggests, rises early and takes charge of the household, prepares food according to the laws of nature and season. She must not depend on the servant who has no knowledge of the rules to be followed. In fact, the servant's services should be dispensed with because these encourage indolence and distract women from their responsibility. Disciplined living requires total devotion of women to their responsibilities. No sleeping late, no lazing about, no gossiping with neighbors after the husband leaves for work and children have gone to school; make the bed, bathe, cook the food appropriate for the season, look over the household accounts, and perform other household chores. The evening routine is more of the same—cook, manage, and facilitate the running of the household.[70]

Yashoda Devi produced this extraordinary prescription for women by seizing on the near-death of a Hindu male caused by the neglect of the rules for nutrition by his wife. Curing the body, however, served as the ruse for the formulation of rules and routines calculated to render the body useful, healthy, and productive. It was in this network of rules and tactics directed at the body that there emerged a project to reform the Hindu wife, to reproduce the gender hierarchy. As the scrutiny and subjection of the body redeployed and renewed the family, the medical gaze became inseparable from gender. The boundaries between the two were crossed, and transgression became the site for transforming both body and gender relations. There appeared a blueprint for a modern middle-class Hindu family, imprinted on a body anchored in gender hierarchy and disciplined by an economy authorized by science.

What shaped the language and provided an arena for the reconstitution of gender relation was the attention to governance, the concern with the health of the population that developed during the second half of the nineteenth century. The middle class debated the status and relevance of Western medicine, homeopathy, ayurveda, and yunani in its search to define what was appropriate for India. In this search, a range of therapeutics—some new and some old and of different provenance—found eager enthusiasts concerned to produce disciplined bodies. These included chromopathy (a system of therapeutics based on colors), mesmerism, hypnotism, and mechanotherapy, and were circulated widely among the middle class through the nineteenth-century print culture.[71] Books, pamphlets, and newspapers frequently advertised and discussed these systems, and the efficacy of different patent medicines were items of urban middle-class conversations. Such discussions were not always systematic and learned, and they did not seriously threaten the dominance of Western medicine. But they point to the importance the elite attached to defining an appropriate therapeutics for India. For at issue in this definition was the body materialized by state institutions. Insofar as the body was produced as an effect of knowledges and tactics, attempts to reinscribe colonial therapeutics were efforts to intervene in the relationship between the state and the population. Nothing succeeded like excess as the elite produced a surfeit of therapies that exceeded and estranged colonial science to delineate its own intervention on the body. These excesses and transgressions did not negate colonial domination but sought to renegotiate its terms to administer a nationalist remedy.

Sexuality and Ascetics

The strategy of recoding colonial therapeutics could not stop at the level of national medicine. To the extent that therapeutics formed part of a set of practices concerned with specifying and regulating "India," the strategy of reinscription had to bring under its purview the entire process of subject-formation. This meant not only interventions in the field of medicine to outline medical knowledge and hygiene along "national lines" but also the assimilation of indigenous forms of self-subjection into the field of governmentality. Since the object was to produce a national subject that was different at once from both the "superstitious" and "ignorant" masses and "the foreigner in his own land," the elite sought to identify an "Indian" rationality of governance. It was in this context that elite nationalism produced what Milind Wakankar calls a "Hindu nationalist ascetics." At the center of this effort to outline an "Indian" modality of governmentality was a claim that one possessed a self, defined oneself in a body placed to serve the nation.[72] The possibility for this strategic combination of the "body-as-self" and "nation-as-ascesis" was produced by colonial governmentality, but what elite nationalism attempted to identify was a "national" mode of the governmental relationship between the body and the body social. In this process, there emerged the idea of the Hindu origin of the nation, expressed by men ranging from such prominent nationalist writers as Bankim Chandra Chattopadhyaya in Bengal to such powerful religious reformers like Swami Dayanand in north India.

A sense of the "lack" of fullness in the nation's present animated the notion of the origin. This lack was all too evident in colonial subjugation, in the enfeebled state of the body, in its diseased condition and unhygienic surroundings. An acute awareness of this deep chasm drove the nationalists to search for a past when the nation was fully present, when disciplines of self-subjection trained the body in the service of the nation. But the "origin" erupted; it did not evolve into the present. This structure of the origin as a "before" of the nation's present permitted the assimilation of archaic Hindu disciplines of self-subjection into the logic of modern governmentality; it enabled the translation of the "inner," uncolonized space of tradition in the "outer" language of colonial modernity. For the same reason, however, the representation of the contemporary national self in the differential sign of return and repetition of another time introduced a profound uncertainty in the language of the mythic past and the organic Hindu nation. The Hindu ascetics were always under pressure from "corruption" and error, always embattled and struggling to "restore" the body to its "original" Hindu-national condition. It was through such a pulsating, mobile, displacing deployment of Hindu signs that elite nationalism acted on the medicalized, "corrupt," and enfeebled body to render it healthy and Hindu-national.

The preoccupation with sexuality developed in the attempt to explain the weak state of the national body. The Western-educated elite internalized the colonial representation of Indians as effete weaklings. It was to transform this weak, disease-prone body that Gandhi had secretly experimented with eating meat during his youth.[73] A body culture developed that was aimed at sculpting strong, vigorous physiques and brought within its ambit traditional arenas of wrestling, gymnastics, and sports.[74] Attention also turned to sexuality as several Indian intellectuals argued India had fallen to foreign rulers because Indians had been rendered weak and passive by their self-indulgence and by their vulnerability to the seductions of sensual and materialist enjoyment. Sharing these views, prominent late-nineteenth-century religious reformers like Swami Vivekanand and Swami Dayanand advocated the practice of sexual discipline as a means of national regeneration.[75] Relocating the texts and practices of Hindu traditions to act upon the body, to sketch the disciplines of its self-constitution as a national subject, such prescriptions were widely disseminated in the middle-class culture.

Consider, for example, the Hindi pamphlet, *Ārogya Vidhān: Vidyārthi Jivan* (1929), a book of advice focusing on sexual discipline. Its author was Yashoda Devi, the woman we have met before as the author of journals and books directed at women. Aside from being an author, she also ran a flourishing ayurvedic practice in Allahabad that included a small hospital, with branches in Banaras, Patna, Muzaffarpur, and Gaya. While the practice specialized in the treatment of infertility, her books and journals dealt with bodies gone awry because of the neglect and loss of principles that she presented as scientific and Hindu, and the purpose of these texts was to promote a nationalist discipline of the body in order to restore its health. Like her middle-class contemporaries, she was also troubled by the physical weakness of Indians, by their self-indulgence and vulnerability to the seductions of modern life. The text on sexual discipline was addressed to students and offered advice on how to maintain healthy bodies and dispositions. It began with a depiction of the physical weakness and sexual diseases that she enountered commonly in her patients. Her female patients complained of their husbands' weakness, of the lack of their sexual desire and prowess.[76] The cause was masturbation, a practice the men picked up as students when they read "dirty literature" and fell into bad company. Such men not only produced weak offspring but also infected their wives with venereal diseases. In addition to hearing accounts of such men and treating them, she also encountered the debilitating effects of this habit among young men. A twenty-year-old son of a wealthy man wrote her that he had become forgetful, suffered from dizziness, body ache, backache, and constipation. When she began treating him, she learned that he had been masturbating since the age of ten, not missing a single day. In addition, he often had wet dreams, rendering him so weak that he dare not go near a woman. This was a widespread condition among the youth, she argued. Many young men had become so diseased by the habit that they no longer had the capacity to be even near a woman, let alone have intercourse with her. She combined the denunciation of masturbation with a blistering condemnation of homosexuality, noting with regret that even women had become victims to the habits of masturbation and homosexuality.[77] Lost in sexual pleasure, Indians had destroyed themselves, she declared.

This tirade against masturbation, homosexuality, and sensuality was followed by the recommendation that young men follow *bramhacharya*. By bramhacharya she did not mean prohibition of sexual intercourse but the preservation of sperm; men could have intercourse for procreation, but they should not destroy their strength in masturbation. The text proposed a set of rules to guide young men: Do not think of women; do not listen to accounts of their beauty; do not try to meet women, certainly not alone; do not read books that describe women or recount love stories; do not consume garlic, onions, and spices excessively, or smoke cigarettes because they contaminate the sperm. The function of these rules of sociability and dietetics was to teach young men to conserve their semen, to develop a celibate disposition.[78] The production of such a disposition was not a matter of just the corporeal; it involved thoughts, reading, speech, and social relationships. Only when the relationship between men and women was governed by bramhacharya, only when the strength of the corporeal body was controlled and redeployed by the will of the spirit, could the nation cease to destroy itself.

It is tempting to read the recommendation on brahmacharya as the resurgence of tradition, and indeed Yashoda Devi extols it as a practice authorized by traditions. Unlike classical texts, however, the regimen of brahmacharya she proposed did not concern the religious status or the life-cycle of the celibate, or his relations with the ritual world of the community; rather, she posed brahmacharya in terms of health.[79] Brahmacharya was dislocated from its classical context and "repeated." In this process, tradition was made to speak the language of health and treat the body as a constellation of not just ritual and religious signs but also medical facts.

This was also the case with Gandhi, who posited brahmacharya as a matter of health: "Many are the keys to health, and they are all quite essential; but one thing needful, above all others, is *Brahmacharya*."[80] This is not to say that he was unaware of the religious significance of brahmacharya. On the contrary, he considered it a practice necessary for spiritual self-control and self-realization that restored human beings to their god-given natural state. But he also regarded sexual intercourse that did not have procreation as its aim as deeply injurious to health. Sexual pleasure itself was evil. The difference of opinion among doctors over whether or not "young men and women need ever let their vital fluid escape," according to him, could not be used to justify sensual enjoyment. "I can affirm, without the slightest hesitation, from my own experience as well as that of others, that sexual enjoyment is not only not necessary for the preservation of health, but is positively detrimental to it."[81] Brahmacharya signified the purity of thought, a spiritual cleanliness that was just as essential for the maintenance of health as clean air and water. This conception of health did not endorse modern Western medicine. Gandhi was a well-known and outspoken opponent of modern Western therapeutics, including vaccination and inoculation, and he advocated "natural" forms of treatment. But the regimen of sexual and dietary behavior he proposed assumed the existence of the body as a site of medical facts and tactics. Within this body, sexuality existed as an instinct. Bhikhu Parekh notes perceptively that Gandhi viewed sexuality as an impulse, not as a relationship, and had no conception of love that included passion and sensuality.[82] Desire appeared as a physical instinct, and brahmacharya represented the triumph of spiritual discipline, of soul over "animal passion."[83]

The suppression of sexual desire as a strategy for the recuperation of enfeebled bodies applied to both men and women, but it was profoundly masculinist. While women were also asked to restrain their sexuality, the ideology of brahmacharya identified energy and strength in the semen alone, and its discipline of restraints was designed to conserve the vitality that the male body contained. Men were to husband their semen with rigid self-discipline and transmit it into energy and power.[84] Such a perspective had no conception of sexual desire, let alone of women's sexuality. Despite Gandhi's wish to overcome the male/female distinction and his self-representation as "half a woman," he could not recognize female sexuality. He represented women in the desexualized image; they appeared only as mothers, sisters, and wives whose pure conduct was to serve as a model for men who possessed the "animal passion" for sex.[85] The feminine virtues of chastity and purity were to be used in controlling the virile male bodies, in conserving semen and transforming it into a source of power and energy, and in achieving the self-control that Gandhi associated with freedom. This set up a normative and regulatory bodily discipline that excluded all but procreative sex as ideal.

This discourse represented the body in a "traditional" frame of cultural intelligibility. Its attribution of power to semen and the recommendation of sexual restraints as a means of spiritual control and energy reiterated ideas and norms contained in such ancient and authoritative sources as Manu. These ideas on semen and the practice of brahmacharya were formulated originally in a Brahminical context and referred specifically to the lifecycle of Brahmin students. The modern discourse of brahmacharya departed from this specific concern with Brahmin students and generalized the practice of chastity as a strategy for all Indians. Projecting Brahminical ideals as normative principles for all Indians, it implied a deeply hierarchical vision of sexuality, society, and religions. Importantly, this projection operated as a strategy of recoding the body, of reconfiguring governmentality along national lines. We have to view this discourse in the same field as sanitation, hygiene, statistics, and therapeutics because, like them, it also functioned as a tactic for forcing together the body-as-self and body social. Like them, this discourse also fastened on the body as the locus of the Indian self, found it weak, vulnerable, oversexed, and decaying, and advanced the conservation of semen as the strategic national goal.

Body and Colonial/National Governmentality

To identify a certain intimacy between the plunge of Madhusudan Gupta's knife and Gandhi's confessions of the flesh is to push Foucault's concept of biopower beyond its Eurocentric frame and to recognize that the formation of modern subjects in the colonies was necessarily embattled. Distortion and displacement, revision and reinscription were central to the political technology of the body because it was obliged to operate in and rearticulate the colonial divide.

Thus, the operation of biopower in British India from the very beginning was based on a strong sense of Indian difference and on a deep awareness of the unbridgeable gap between the state and the people. It was to bridge this unbridgeable gulf, to appropriate the otherness of Indians that the British were driven to erect an elaborate grid of knowledges and practices that sought to produce a colonial complex of "men and things." Through sanitary regulations, statistical enumeration and representation, measures to control epidemics, and colonial therapeutics, the state opened a vast new field of practices connecting it to the population. This field treated the body as a complex configuration of effects of habits, habitation, race, climate, topography, religious beliefs and cultural dispositions. Western medicine, established in British India through such a combination of knowledges and practices, achieved power and exercised influence on the lives of the people, but there remained always an uncloseable gap between state medicine and the colonized population. The necessary failure of the British to achieve the object of producing self-subjecting individuals incited Indian elites to intervene in this field. Mediating between the people and the state, the elite sought to develop an "Indian" modality of governance. This was never a matter of simple negation of colonial governmentality, but its reinscription. Although the nationalists represented their efforts as resistance to colonial domination, these are better understood as strategies of survival and hegemony that operated on the very body that colonial governmentality made available. Through subtle practices of displacement, dislocation, and repetition, through a contradictory combination of transgression and subordination, not demotic resistance, nationalism subverted colonial governmentality and pursued its own program of the "welfare of the population." Acting squarely within historical power relations, in the field of colonial modernity, the nationalist discourse intervened in the same arena to deflect governmentality along different lines. Such deflections took a range of forms, rendering the category "India" uncertain and unstable. This was inevitable, for the elites attempted to render India in terms that were alien; the "inner" sphere of the nation was constituted in the shadow of the "outer." As the nationalists advocated ayurveda, yunani, and brahmacharya as "Indian" disciplines, they brought these into the field of operation created by colonial governmentality. There, the nationalists, like the colonialists, were confronted with objects that always threatened to slip out of control, forever vulnerable to filth, "dirty literature," lust, and ignorance. Its disciplines of self-subjectification, therefore, were always deeply hierarchical; they were poised constantly to identify and eliminate the enemies of the nation. Formed on the borderlines of such political, social, and cultural differences, "India" emerged as a nation fabricated at the site of its fissures, at once embattled and expansive. Produced in the establishment of a governmental relationship between the state and the people, a process in which nationalism shared a proximity with colonialism, its modernity was disjunctive; it was obliged to emerge both in the firing of the gun salute at Fort William in 1835 and in Gandhi's century-later confession that he had failed to conquer sexual desire. Between the two incommensurable framing events, then, there arose a mode of governmentality that located the modern Indian subject in the body and that formulated its norms by normalizing alterity.

Notes

I am grateful to the participants at the conference on "Questions of Modernity" at New York University, where this paper was first presented. In particular, I am thankful to Uday Mehta, Timothy Mitchell, Lila Abu-Lughod, and Veena Das. I have also benefited from criticisms and suggestions received at its subsequent presentation at Harvard University, where Pratap Mehta, as usual, offered incisive and imaginative comments. Milind Wakankar generously offered unusually detailed and thoughtful suggestions. My colleague Gerald Geison's expert and vast knowledge of the history of medicine has been invaluable. This is a slightly revised version of chapter 5, "Body and Governmentality" in my book *Another Reason: Science and the Imagination of Modern India* (Princeton: Princeton University Press, 1999).

1. M. K. Gandhi, *Collected Works of Mahatma Gandhi* (Ahmedabad: Navajivan, 1958), vol. 62, 428 ff. Cited in David Arnold, *Colonizing the Body: State Medicine and Epidemic Disease in Nineteenth-Century India* (Delhi: Oxford University Press, 1993), 6.

2. Mahatma Gandhi, *A Guide to Health*, trans. A. Rama Iyer (Madras: S. Ganesan, 1930), 64–65.

3. Michel Foucault, *The History of Sexuality*, vol. 1: *An Introduction,* trans. Robert Hurley (New York: Vintage, 1980), 139–43.

4. Ann Laura Stoler, *Race and the Education of Desire: Foucault's* History of Sexuality *and the Colonial Order of Things* (Durham: Duke University Press, 1995).

5. Foucault, *The History of Sexuality,* 142.

6. Arnold, *Colonizing the Body,* 9.

7. In specifying the history of Western medicine in British India, Arnold goes on to suggest, correctly, that the colonial construction of the body entailed negotiation with appropriated knowledges and subjects; the body as a site of power witnessed a range of Indian responses—resistance, accommodation, participation, and appropriation (*Colonizing the Body,* 10). But negotiations can hardly be said to have been restricted to colonial locations; contestation and accommodation also characterized the history of medicine in Western societies.

8. Michel Foucault, "Governmentality," in *The Foucault Effect: Studies in Governmentality,* ed. Graham Burchell, Colin Gordon, and Peter Miller (Chicago: University of Chicago Press, 1991), 92.

9. Ibid., 99.

10. Ibid., 93.

11. Partha Chatterjee has called this displacement of liberal principles "the rule of colonial difference." See his *The Nation and Its Fragments: Colonial and Postcolonial Histories* (Princeton: Princeton University Press, 1993), 18. David Scott's otherwise fine essay, "Colonial Governmentality," *Social Text,* 43 (1995) ignores this peculiarity of colonial governmentality, viewing it merely as the mode of the universalization of modernity.

12. Chatterjee, *The Nation and Its Fragments,* 6–13.

13. During the early part of the nineteenth century, the British treated Indians as part of the landscape, as creatures of its soil, drainage, water, climate, and diseases, which they surveyed and distributed into distinct medico-topographical regions. Animated by the idea that India represented a unique environment, the colonial medical establishment concentrated its focus on identifying distinct health and disease regimes. For further details, see Arnold, *Colonizing the Body,* 24–43.

14. Beginning with the late eighteenth-century Orientalist researches, the British studied and translated classical texts, and investigated indigenous medical practices in an effort to incorporate both indigenous medical knowledge and materia medica into Western medicine. Although these were never considered equal to Western medicine, the British believed that the examination of indigenous medical ideas, practices, and drugs, conducted under their superior eyes, could yield elements useful for the development of a therapeutic system suitable for India (see Arnold, *Colonizing the Body,* 43–50).

15. Mark Harrison, *Public Health in British India: Anglo-Indian Preventive Medicine, 1859–1914* (Cambridge: Cambridge University Press, 1994), 61.

16. Great Britain, Parliamentary Papers, vol. 19, pt. 1, sess. 1863, *Report of the Commissioners Appointed to Inquire into the Sanitary State of the Army in India.* On the appointment and the work of this royal commission, see Arnold, *Colonizing the Body,* 67–98, and Harrison, *Public Health in British India,* 60–66.

17. *Report of the Commissioners Appointed to Inquire into the Sanitary State of the Army in India,* xxx, xxxii.

18. Typical in this respect was James Ranald Martin, a surgeon who became the president of the East India Company's Medical Board and served as a member of the Royal Commission on army sanitation. A proponent of climatological determinism, he wrote bitingly about the sanitary habits of Indians and poured scorn on their medical practices. See his *Notes on the Medical Topography of Calcutta* (Calcutta: Huttman, 1837), 24–28, 60, and *The Influence of Tropical Climates on European Constitutions, Including Practical Observations on the Nature and Treatment of the Diseases of Europeans on their Return from Tropical Climates* (London: Churchill, 1856).

19. Cited in Great Britain, *Report on Measures Adopted for Sanitary Improvements in India, from June 1869 to June 1870; Together with Abstracts of Sanitary Reports for 1868 Forwarded from Bengal, Madras, and Bombay* (London: HMSO, 1870), 40.

20. Initially, sanitary commissioners were responsible for the army and the civilian population, but they were relieved of the charge for military hygiene after 1867. For further details, see Harrison, *Public Health in India,* 9, 23–29, 76–82; Radhika Ramasubban, "Imperial Health in British India, 1857–1900," in *Disease, Medicine, and Empire: Perspectives on Western Medicine and the Experience of European Expansion,* ed. Roy Macleod and Milton Lewis (New York: Routledge, 1988), 38–60.

21. "Abstract of Report of Sanitary Commissioner for 1864," in Great Britain, *Memorandum on Measures Adopted for Sanitary Improvements in India up to the end of 1867,* 42.

22. J. A. Turner and B. K. Goldsmith, *Sanitation in India,* 2nd ed. (Bombay: Times of India, 1917), 985–87.

23. Quoted in *Report of the Commissioners Appointed to Inquire into the Sanitary State of the Army in India,* 370.

24. H. R. Tinker, *The Foundations of Local Self-Government in India, Pakistan and Burma* (London, 1954), 74–75.

25. Cited in Edmund A. Parkes, *A Manual of Practical Hygiene* (London: Churchill, 1864), 563.

26. The Calcutta Fever Hospital and Municipal Enquiry Committee (1836–47), for example, had drawn a grim picture of the sanitary state of Calcutta. The disposal of night soil, for instance, involved its collection from private privies by *mehtars,* who were responsible for conveying it to depots, from where it was taken to boats and carried downstream and thrown into the river. An educated Bengali complained to the committee that the *mehtars* "walk through the streets and high roads with baskets full of stink on their heads" and that "when it happens to the lot of a person, who has just made a hearty meal, to face before any one of these mehtars, it is needless to say how it is felt by him" (cited in S. W. Goode, *Municipal Calcutta: Its Institutions in their Origin and Growth* [Edinburgh: T. and A. Constable, 1916], 169). In fact, only a small proportion of the city's night soil was ever transported to boats; 90 per cent was thrown into public drains.

27. See W. F. Bynum, *Science and the Practice of Medicine in the Nineteenth Century* (Cambridge: Cambridge University Press, 1994), 72–77.

28. "Abstract of the Report of Sanitary Commissioner for 1864," in Great Britain, *Memorandum on Measures Adopted for Sanitary Improvements in India up to the end of 1867*, 41.

29. Following the commission's recommendation and the prevailing medical opinion, nearly a sixth of British troops were relocated to the "hill stations" by the 1870s, and barracks were reconstructed to protect them from the effects of India's weather (Arnold, *Colonizing the Body*, 78–79). The government followed these steps to isolate and protect the troops from the supposedly diseased environment with others, such as rationing the consumption of alcohol and enacting the Contagious Diseases Act in 1868 to permit the medical inspection, detention, and treatment of prostitutes (see Harrison, *Public Health in India*, 72–76, and K. Ballhatchet, *Race, Sex, and Class under the Raj: Imperial Attitudes and Policies and Their Critics* [London: Weidenfield and Nicolson, 1980], chs. 2 and 3).

30. *Report of the Commissioners Appointed to Inquire into the Sanitary State of the Army in India*, 371; Great Britain, *Memorandum on Measures Adopted for Sanitary Improvements in India up to the end of 1867; together with Abstracts of the Sanitary Reports hitherto forwarded from Bengal, Madras, and Bombay* (London: HMSO, 1868), 2.

31. Veena Oldenberg's *The Making of Colonial Lucknow* (Princeton: Princeton University Press, 1984), ch. 4, contains a persuasive account of the application of sanitary measures as an instrument of colonial control. She argues that unlike Britain, where pauperism and squalor were viewed as the root cause of disease, the municipal authorities in India paid scant attention to poverty; afflicted by a "curious myopia," the British were never able to develop "a comprehensive long-range plan to drain and cleanse the city" (142–43). Cf. J. B. Harrison, "Allahabad: A Sanitary History," in *The City in South Asia: Pre-Modern and Modern*, ed. Kenneth Ballhatchet and John Harrison (London: Curzon Press, 1980), 167–95.

32. Ian Hacking, *The Taming of Chance* (Cambridge: Cambridge University Press, 1990).

33. Parkes, *A Manual of Practical Hygiene*, xviii.

34. Notable in this respect was Joseph Ewart's *A Digest of Vital Statistics of the European and Native Armies in India* (London: Smith, Elder and Co., 1859). For an analysis of Ewart's figures, see Arnold, *Colonizing the Body*, 67–68.

35. Cf. Ira Klein, "Death in India," *Journal of Asian Studies* 32 (1973), 632–59, and "Urban Development and Death: Bombay City, 1870–1914," *Modern Asian Studies*, 20 (1986): 725–54.

36. The use of statistics is too widely present in colonial records to be singled out. But, for some examples, see Government of India, *Report of the Commissioners appointed to Inquire into the Cholera Epidemic of 1861 in North India* (Calcutta, 1862); "Abstract of Bengal Sanitary Report for 1865," in *Memorandum of Measures Adopted for the Sanitary Improvements in India up to 1867*; the series Government of Bengal, *Report on the Calcutta Medical Institutions for the year 1871* . . . ; and Government of Bengal, *Report of the Commisioners Appointed under Section 28 of Act IV (B.C.) of 1876 to Enquire into Certain Matters connected with the Sanitation of the Town of Calcutta* (Calcutta: Bengal Secretariat Press, 1885).

37. Government of India, *Proceedings of the First All-India Sanitary Conference* (Calcutta: Government Printing, 1912), Apps. 11, 12, and 13.

38. For example, see James L. Bryden's *Epidemic Cholera in the Bengal Presidency: A Report on the Cholera of 1866–68, and Its Relation to the Cholera of Previous Epidemics* (Calcutta: Superintendent of Government Printing, 1869). Bryden, a surgeon

in the army, served in the office of the sanitary commissioner. See also T. R. Lewis and D. D. Cunningham, *Cholera in Relation to Certain Physical Phenomena* (Calcutta: Superintendent of Government Printing, 1878).

39. The *Report of the Commisioners appointed to Inquire into the Cholera Epidemic of 1861 in North India* used figures on meteorology, topography, and cholera epidemics to argue that while there was an undeniable relationship between the disease and the season of the year, cholera was neither caused nor communicated by the atmosphere; rather, human intercourse, it suggested, was responsible for the transmission of the disease (199–205). For details on the struggle between miasma and contagion theories, see Harrison, *Public Health in British India,* 52–62, 99–116, and Arnold, *Colonizing the Body,* 189–98.

40. Arnold, *Colonizing the Body,* 195. Thus, Sir Leonard Rogers wrote two monographs that traced the connection between climate and epidemics, using the accumulated records on meteorology and diseases to formulate a system for predicting the outbreak of diseases. See his *Small-Pox and Climate in India* (London: HMSO, 1926), and *The Incidence and Spread of Cholera in India; Forecasting and Control of Epidemics* (Calcutta: Thacker, Spink and Co., 1928).

41. Katherine Prior, "The Angry *Pandas*: Hindu Priests and the Colonial Government in the Dispersal of the Hardwar Mela in 1892," *South Asia* 16, no. 1 (1993): 40.

42. "Abstract of the Fourth Annual Report of the Sanitary Commissioner with the Government of India, 1867," in *Report on Measures Adopted for Sanitary Improvements in India during the year 1868, and up to the month of June 1869; together with Abstracts of Sanitary Reports for 1867 forwarded from Bengal, Madras, and Bombay* (London: HMSO, 1869), 11–30.

43. Katherine Prior, "The Angry *Pandas*," 40–42. Prior argues that this intervention was part of a larger transformation of religious fairs that occurred as a result of the British conquest. The British disarmed the warrior ascetics, took over the policing duties of the fair, and assumed its civil government, so that by the 1830s and the 1840s the fair was "a shadow of its eighteenth-century self." Ironically, such measures eliminated the cultural and political aspects of the Hardwar fair and rendered it into a purely religious event (26–32).

44. For more on the British confrontation with indigenous treatments of smallpox, see Arnold, *Colonizing the Body,* ch. 3.

45. Government of Bengal, *Report of the Smallpox Commissioners* (Calcutta: Military Orphan Press, 1850), 5, 18, 31.

46. Ibid., 28–30, appendix, xxii.

47. Ibid., 54–55.

48. Arnold, *Colonizing the Body,* 141.

49. Arnold, *Colonizing the Body,* 202–03.

50. M. E. Couchman, *Account of Plague Administration in the Bombay Presidency from September 1896 until May 1897* (Bombay: Government Central Press, 1897), 15–16.

51. Ibid., 5.

52. Government of Bombay, *Supplement to the Account of Plague Administration in the Bombay Presidency from September 1896 till May 1897,* 5–9.

53. Aside from the famous Arthur Road Hospital incident in 1896, when nearly a thousand mill workers attacked the hospital, "street tumults" were frequent because Indians viewed quarantine and hospitalization with suspicion (P. C. H. Snow, *Report on the Outbreak of Bubonic Plague in Bombay, 1896–97* [Bombay: Times of India, 1897], 18). See also Arnold, *Colonizing the Body,* ch. 5, and I. J. Catanach, "Plague and the

Tensions of Empire: India, 1896–1918," in *Imperial Medicine and Indigenous Societies,* ed. David Arnold (Delhi: Oxford University Press, 1989), 149–71.

54. Snow, *Report on the Outbreak of Bubonic Plague,* 18–19.

55. Ibid., 213.

56. Partha Chatterjee, "Two Poets and Death: On Civil and Political Society in the Non-Christian World," this volume, ch. 2.

57. "A Discourse on the Sanitary Improvement of Calcutta, By Dr. Chuckerbutty," in *Selections from the Bethune Society's Papers* (Calcutta: P. S. O'Rozario and Co., 1854), 52–53. Kanny Loll Dey (Kanai Lal Dey), also a doctor and a teacher at the Calcutta Medical College, struck a similar theme in describing the Hindu body housed in dwellings that were not far from being "little black holes," crowded, unclean, and full of noxious air. See his *Hindu Social Laws and Habits Viewed in Relation to Health* (Calcutta: R. C. Lepage and Co., 1866).

58. Gobind Chunder Dhur, *The Plague: Being a Reprint of Letters Published in the Indian Mirror for Allaying Popular Alarm and Conciliating the People to the Action of the Authorities* (Calcutta: Sanyal and Co., 1898), for example, advised the government to practice moderation in its policies of segregating and hospitalizing plague victims while asking "my own countrymen" to follow the advice of the health officer (2).

59. Thus, M. A. Mulraj's *A Sanitary Primer: Being an Elementary Treatise on Personal Hygiene, For the Use of Indian Schools and General Public* (Allahabad: Victoria Press, 1879), one of several pamphlets of its kind, extolled the virtues of sanitary science based on accurate facts on the population derived from the registration of births and deaths (2).

60. M. L. Dhingra, *The Science of Health for the Public in India showing how health may be preserved, disease prevented, and life prolonged* (Allahabad: Pioneer Press, 1900), ii.

61. Arnold, *Colonizing the Body,* 9. On tropical hygiene, see Harrison, *Public Health in India,* ch. 2. Harish Naraindas' "Poisons, Putrescence and the Weather: A Genealogy of the Advent of Tropical Medicine," *Contributions to Indian Sociology* (n.s.), 30, no. 1 (1996): 1–35, is a particularly sharp study of tropical medicine, which makes the important point that its colonial genealogy has to be understood in relation to its rise after the acceptance of the germ theory.

62. U. N. Mukerji, *Medical Practice in Bengal* (Calcutta: S. Lahiri and Co., 1907), 2–7.

63. Ibid., 38.

64. Jadu Nath Ganguli, *A National System of Medicine for India* (Calcutta: Beni Madhav Ganguli, 1911), 2–3.

65. Mahendralal Sircar, *A Sketch of the Treatment of Cholera* (Calcutta: Anglo-Sanskrit Press, 1870), iv. On Sircar's account of his conversion to homeopathy and the controversy it generated, see *Reminiscences and Anecdotes of Great Men of India,* ed. Ramgopal Sanyal (1894; rpr. Calcutta: Riddhi-India, 1984), 55–56.

66. For example, Prem Bihari Mathur's *Plague-Panacea or a Pamphlet on Plague and its Remedies* (Agra: Damodar Printing Works, 1907) recounts how the author established a dispensary to treat plague victims, using "Greek, Indian, and Homeopathic systems of treatment" (46–56). Unlike state-sponsored sanitary primers, such as J. M. Cunningham's *A Sanitary Primer for Indian Schools* (Lahore: Arya Press, 1882), Indians commonly invoked homeopathy, ayurveda, and yunani. See B. B. Biswas, *Half-Hour with Plague* (Calcutta: n.p., 1907), and Rai Bahadur Lala Baijnath, *The Plague in India: Its Causes, Prevention and Cure* (Meerut: Vaishya Hitkari Office, 1905).

67. See, for examples, *Panchal Pandita* 4, no. 1 (November 15, 1900): 4; no. 3

(January 15, 1901): 4; no. 4 (February 15, 1901): 4; no. 6 (April 15, 1901): 4; no. 7 (May 15, 1901).

68. These are noted in Shaligram Srivastava, *Prayāg Pradeep* (in Hindi) (Allahabad: Hindustani Academy, 1937), 161.

69. Yashoda Devi, *Grihini Kartayvashāstra, Ārogyashāstra arthāt Pākshastra* (in Hindi), 3rd ed. (Allahabad: Hitaishi Yantr laya, 1924).

70. Ibid., 47–66, passim.

71. Pandit Jwala Prasad Jha, *Chromopathy or the Science of Healing Diseases by Colours* (Madras: Theosophical Book-Depot, 1912).

72. Milind Wakankar, "Body, Crowd, Identity: Genealogy of a Hindu Nationalist Ascetics," *Social Text 45* (Winter 1995): 46.

73. M. K. Gandhi, *Autobiography: The Story of My Experiments with Truth*, trans. Mahadev Desai (New York: Dover, 1983), 16–20.

74. John Roseselli, "The Self-Image of Effeteness: Physical Education and Nationalism in Nineteenth-Century Bengal," *Past and Present 86* (February 1980): 121–48.

75. Dayanand Sarawati, *Satyārth Prakāsh*, 44–45, 58–68.

76. Yashoda Devi, *Arogya Vidhān: Vidyārthi Jivan* (Allahabad: Stree Aushadhālaya Press), 2–4.

77. Yashoda Devi, *Ārogya Vidhān*, 17–18, 21–23.

78. Ibid., 43–47.

79. On the medicalization of *brahmacharya*, cf. Joseph S. Alter, "Celibacy, Sexuality, and the Transformation of Gender into Nationalism in North India," *Journal of Asian Studies 53*, no. 1 (February 1994): 45–66.

80. Mahatma Gandhi, *A Guide to Health*, 64.

81. Ibid., 70.

82. Bhikhu Parekh, *Colonialism, Tradition and Reform: An Analysis of Gandhi's Political Discourse* (New Delhi: Sage, 1989), 183.

83. M. K. Gandhi, *Self-Restraint v. Self-Indulgence* (Navjivan: Ahmedabad, 1947), 63. This quotation comes from Gandhi's article in Gujarati published originally in 1924 and translated and republished in this collection.

84. Mahatma Gandhi, *A Guide to Health*, 65.

85. Cf. Bhikhu Parekh, *Colonialism, Tradition and Reform*, 179–80, 182.

Contributors

Lila Abu-Lughod is professor of anthropology and gender studies at Columbia University. She is the author of *Remaking Women: Feminism and Modernity in the Middle East* and *Writing Women's Worlds: Bedouin Stories.*

Dipesh Chakrabarty is professor of history and South Asian languages and civilizations and a member of the Committee for the History of Culture at the University of Chicago. He is the author of *Rethinking Working-Class History: Bengal, 1890–1940* and *Provincializing Europe: Postcolonial Thought and Historical Difference.*

Partha Chatterjee is the director of the Centre for Studies in Social Sciences, Calcutta. He is the author of, among other books, *Nationalist Thought and the Colonial World: A Derivative Discourse* (Minnesota, 1986) and *The Nation and Its Fragments: Colonial and Postcolonial Histories,* and the editor of *Texts of Power: Emerging Disciplines in Colonial Bengal* and *Wages of Freedom: Fifty Years of the Indian Nation-State.*

Veena Das is professor of sociology at the University of Delhi. She is the author of *Critical Events: An Anthropological Perspective on*

Contemporary India and *Structure and Cognition: Aspects of Hindu Caste and Ritual.*

Nicholas B. Dirks is professor of anthropology and history and chair of the anthropology department at Columbia University. He is the author of *The Hollow Crown: Ethnohistory of an Indian Kingdom* and the forthcoming *Castes of Mind: Colonialism and the Making of Modern India* and editor of *Colonialism and Culture* and *In Near Ruins: Cultural Theory at the End of the Century* (Minnesota, 1998).

Timothy Mitchell is associate professor of politics and director of the Hagop Kevorkian Center at New York University. He is the author of *Democracy and the State in the Arab World, Egypt in American Discourse,* and *Colonising Egypt.*

Stefania Pandolfo is associate professor of anthropology at the University of California, Berkeley. She is the author of *Impasse of the Angels: Scenes from a Moroccan Space of Memory.*

Gyan Prakash is professor of history at Princeton University. He is the author of *Bonded Histories: Genealogies of Labor Servitude in Colonial India* and *Another Reason: Science and the Imagination of Modern India.*